Testing Regimes, Accountabilities and Education Policy

Around the globe, various kinds of testing, including high stakes national census testing, have become meta-policies, steering educational systems in particular directions, and having great effects on schools and on teacher practices, as well as upon student learning and curricula. There has also been a complementary global aspect to this with the OECD's PISA and IEA's TIMSS and PIRLS, which have had impacts on national education systems and their policy frameworks. While there has been a globalized educational policy discourse that suggests that high stakes standardised testing will drive up standards and enhance the quality of a nation's human capital and thus their international economic competitiveness, this discourse still manifests itself in specific, vernacular, path dependent ways in different nations. High stakes testing and its effects can also be seen as part of the phenomenon of the 'datafication' of the world and 'policy as numbers', linked to other reforms of the state, including new public management, network governance, and top-down and test-based modes of accountability. This edited collection provides theoretically and empirically informed analyses of these developments. This book was originally published as a special issue of the *Journal of Education Policy*.

Bob Lingard is a Professor in the School of Education at The University of Queensland, Brisbane, Australia. His research areas are the sociology of education and policy sociology in education. He is the co-editor of the journal *Discourse: Studies in the Cultural Politics of Education*, and is the author and/or editor of more than 20 books, the most recent of which is *Globalizing educational accountabilities*, (Routledge, 2015).

Wayne Martino is Professor of Equity and Social Justice Education in the Faculty of Education and also an affiliate faculty member of the Department of Women's Studies and Feminist Research at The University of Western Ontario, London, Canada. He is one of the editors for the book series *Routledge Critical Studies in Gender and Sexuality in Education*, and is author/editor of 14 books, most recently *Gender, Race and the Politics of Role Modeling* (with Goli Rezai-Rashti, 2012). His forthcoming book is entitled *Queer Studies and Education: Critical Concepts for the Twenty-First Century* (with Ed Brockenbrough, Jennifer Ingrey and Nelson Rodriguez).

Goli Rezai-Rashti is Professor of Critical Policy, Equity and Leadership Studies in the Faculty of Education at the University of Western Ontario, London, Canada. Her research and teaching focus is broadly located in the field of sociology of education. She is the author of *Gender, Race and the Politics of Role Modeling* (2012, with Wayne Martino), and series editor of the book series *Routledge Critical Studies in Gender and Sexuality in Education*.

Testing Regimes, Accountabilities and Education Policy

Edited by
**Bob Lingard, Wayne Martino and
Goli Rezai-Rashti**

Routledge
Taylor & Francis Group

LONDON AND NEW YORK

First published 2016
by Routledge
2 Park Square, Milton Park, Abingdon, Oxon, OX14 4RN, UK

and by Routledge
711 Third Avenue, New York, NY 10017, USA

First issued in papperback 2017

Routledge is an imprint of the Taylor & Francis Group, an informa business

© 2016 Taylor & Francis

British Library Cataloguing in Publication Data
A catalogue record for this book is available from the British Library

ISBN 13: 978-1-138-24073-5 (pbk)
ISBN 13: 978-1-138-95580-6 (hbk)

Typeset in Times New Roman
by RefineCatch Limited, Bungay, Suffolk

Publisher's Note
The publisher accepts responsibility for any inconsistencies that may have
arisen during the conversion of this book from journal articles to book chapters,
namely the possible inclusion of journal terminology.

Disclaimer
Every effort has been made to contact copyright holders for their permission to
reprint material in this book. The publishers would be grateful to hear from any
copyright holder who is not here acknowledged and will undertake to rectify
any errors or omissions in future editions of this book.

Contents

Citation Information

The chapters in this book were originally published in the *Journal of Education Policy*, volume 28, issue 5 (September 2013). When citing this material, please use the original page numbering for each article, as follows:

Chapter 6

Untangling the global-distant-local knot: the politics of national academic achievement testing in Japan
Keita Takayama
Journal of Education Policy, volume 28, issue 5 (September 2013) pp. 657–675

Chapter 7

Coloniality and a global testing regime in higher education: unpacking the OECD's AHELO initiative
Riyad A. Shahjahan
Journal of Education Policy, volume 28, issue 5 (September 2013) pp. 676–694

Chapter 8

Expert moves: international comparative testing and the rise of expertocracy
Sotiria Grek
Journal of Education Policy, volume 28, issue 5 (September 2013) pp. 695–709

Chapter 9

The OECD and global governance in education
Sam Sellar and Bob Lingard
Journal of Education Policy, volume 28, issue 5 (September 2013) pp. 710–725

For any permission-related enquiries please visit:
http://www.tandfonline.com/page/help/permissions

Notes on Contributors

Sotiria Grek is a lecturer in social policy at the School of Social and Political Science, University of Edinburgh, UK. She works in the area of Europeanisation of education policy and governance, and is currently funded by the Economic and Social Research Council (ESRC) to do research in the areas of transnational policy learning, and governing by inspection. She has recently co-authored (with Martin Lawn) *Europeanising Education: Governing a New Policy Space* (2012).

David Hursh is a Professor in the Warner School of Education at the University of Rochester, NY, USA. His research has both critiqued the rise of high-stakes testing within neoliberal regimes and proposed alternative conceptions of education that promote interdisciplinary thinking and acting. Examples of the former include his book *High-Stakes Testing and the Decline of Teaching and Learning: The Real Crisis in Education*. Examples of the latter include his recent book (co-authored with Camille Martina) *Teaching Environmental Health to Children: An Interdisciplinary Approach*, as well as his research and teaching on education for environmental sustainability in sub-Saharan Africa.

Jaakko Kauko is a postdoctoral researcher working in the Research Unit on New Politics, Governance and Interaction in Education, at the University of Helsinki, Finland. His current research interests are in applying the ideas of political dynamics in the fields of comparative, higher and compulsory education. He is working on a three-year postdoctoral project, 'Expanding the theoretical frontiers – contrasting the dynamics in education politics in England and Finland' funded by the Academy of Finland.

Bob Lingard is a Professor in the School of Education at The University of Queensland, Brisbane, Australia. His research areas are the sociology of education and policy sociology in education. He is the co-editor of the journal *Discourse: Studies in the Cultural Politics of Education*, and is the author and/or editor of more than 20 books, the most recent of which is *Globalizing educational accountabilities*, (Routledge, 2015).

Pauline Lipman is a Professor of Educational Policy Studies at the University of Illinois at Chicago, USA. Her research focuses on race and class inequality in schools, globalization, and the political economy and racial politics of urban education. Her latest book is *The new political economy of urban education: Neoliberalism, race, and the right to the city*. She is a Director of the Collaborative for Equity and Justice in Education, which does community collaborative research, and is active in coalitions of teachers and community organizations challenging neoliberal education policies in Chicago.

Wayne Martino is Professor of Equity and Social Justice Education in the Faculty of Education and also an affiliate faculty member of the Department of Women's Studies and Feminist Research at The University of Western Ontario, London, Canada. He is one of the editors for the book series *Routledge Critical Studies in Gender and Sexuality in Education*, and is author/editor of 14 books, most recently *Gender, Race and the Politics of Role Modeling* (with Goli Rezai-Rashti, 2012). His forthcoming book is entitled *Queer Studies and Education: Critical Concepts for the Twenty-First Century* (with Ed Brockenbrough, Jennifer Ingrey and Nelson Rodriguez).

Goli Rezai-Rashti is Professor of Critical Policy, Equity and Leadership Studies in the Faculty of Education at the University of Western Ontario, London, Canada. Her research and teaching focus is broadly located in the field of sociology of education. She is the author of *Gender, Race and the Politics of Role Modeling* (2012, with Wayne Martino), and series editor of the book series *Routledge Critical Studies in Gender and Sexuality in Education.*

Risto Rinne is Professor of Education and the Director of the Centre for Research on Lifelong Learning and Education at the University of Turku, Finland. He is also the director of the national Finnish Graduate School in Education and Learning, and a member of the Finnish Academy of Science and Letters. He has published over 400 scientific publications and led many research projects. His main interests and publications include sociology of education, international comparative education, educational policy and history of education.

Sam Sellar is a postdoctoral research fellow in the School of Education at The University of Queensland, Brisbane, Australia. His research focuses on schooling and higher education policy. He has recent sole and co-authored publications in *Discourse: Studies in the Cultural Politics of Education*, the *Cambridge Journal of Education,* and *Critical Studies in Education.*

Riyad A. Shahjahan is an Assistant Professor of the Higher, Adult, and Lifelong Education program at Michigan State University, East Lansing, MI, USA. His areas of research include the globalization of higher education policy, teaching and learning in higher education, equity and social justice, and the role of anti-/postcolonial theory in higher education.

Hannu Simola is Professor of Sociology of Education, and the Head of the Research Unit on New Politics, Governance and Interaction in Education, at the University of Helsinki, Finland. He is an internationally recognised researcher of sociology and politics of education. Recently, his intellectual interest has been focused on developing and applying a new theoretical approach, Comparative Analytics of Dynamics in Education Politics (CADEP), for international educational studies.

Keita Takayama is a senior lecturer in the School of Education at the University of New England, Armidale, Australia, where he teaches sociology of education and antiracist pedagogy. His current research focuses on globalization in education, more specifically, the role of OECD's PISA in education policy, transnational networks of education policy discourse in Asia, and postcolonial rethinking of comparative education.

Janne Varjo is a postdoctoral researcher working in the Research Unit on New Politics, Governance and Interaction in Education, at the University of Helsinki, Finland. His current research interests are in applying the ideas of governance of compulsory education at sub-national level and the political economy of education. He is currently working on a three-year postdoctoral project, 'Travelling policies and embedded politics – an analysis of dynamics of local education politics' funded by the University of Helsinki.

INTRODUCTORY ESSAY

Testing regimes, accountabilities and education policy: commensurate global and national developments

Bob Lingard[a], Wayne Martino[b] and Goli Rezai-Rashti[b]

[a]The University of Queensland, Brisbane, Australia; [b]The University of Western Ontario, London, Canada

This paper focuses on outlining, contextualising and theorising the rise of global and complementary national modes of test-based, top-down accountability in schooling systems. The effects of these infrastructures of accountability on schools, teachers' pedagogical work, on the width of curriculum and on the goals of schooling are also alluded to. These developments are theorised in terms of rescaling of the policy cycle globally, as a well as the topological turn that sees the globe reconstituted as a single space of comparative and commensurate measurement of the performance of school systems, as part of the move to new global forms of networked governance. We argue that we are seeing a new *global panopticism,* with national school systems variously positioned within the global market place and global educational policy field with important effects within national policy-making. The analysis and theorising provided serves as a contextual backdrop and introduction to the papers included in the special issue of the *Journal of Education Policy* on the theme of Testing Regimes, Accountabilities and Education Policy. We argue, and the papers demonstrate, the significance for policy sociology today of recognising testing as a, perhaps the, major policy steering systems and the work of schools today.

Introduction

In this introductory essay, we first outline the contexts of the rise of testing regimes globally and nationally for schooling and attempt to theorise their emergence and effects. We show quite clearly that these effects are of multiple kinds and function at multiple levels. These are the contexts to the papers included in this special issue of the *Journal of Education Policy*. We also document the reductive impact of top-down, test-based accountability associated with current testing regimes and suggest the need for alternative, more educative and socially just forms. After contextualising and attempting to theorise this changed situation in education policy, we move to consider the significance today of testing as a major policy steering schooling systems and its global manifestations. Specifically, we comment on the implications of considering testing as policy and its interactions with the other elements of what Bernstein (1971) called the 'message systems' of schooling, namely, curriculum and pedagogy. We then briefly outline the foci and arguments of the papers included in this special issue, showing the centrality of education policy to contemporary politics, before moving to a concluding statement about testing regimes, accountabilities and education policy.

Contexts

Around the globe, and particularly in Anglo-American and Asian nations, testing of various kinds, including high-stakes national census testing, has become a meta-policy, steering educational systems in particular directions with great effects in schools and on teacher practices, on curricula, as well as upon student learning and experiences of school. There has also been a global aspect to this with the OECD's Programme for International Student Assessment (PISA) and the International Association for the Evaluation of Educational Achievement's (IEA's) Trends in International Maths and Science Study (TIMSS) and Progress in International Reading and Literacy Study (PIRLS), which also have had considerable impact on national education systems throughout the globe, having policy effects. The responses in England, the USA and Australia to Shanghai-China's performance on PISA 2009 are an exemplary case in point (Sellar and Lingard 2013a). There is a complementarity to global and national testing regimes as part of the rescaling of educational politics and policy-making. As Novoa and Yariv-Mashal (2003) put it, in terms of educational governance, today the 'global eye' complements the 'national eye', as policy as numbers constitutes the globe as a commensurate space of measurement (Lingard 2011). These developments have been partnered by the rise of what has been called the 'infrastructure of accountability' (Anagnostopoulos, Rutledge, and Jacobsen 2013) and have come to constitute what we identify as a form of *global panopticism*, with the global eye functioning in a regulatory capacity across and within national states.

We argue that the OECD has played an important role in the new global governance in education (Woodward 2009), as also noted by Sam Sellar and Bob Lingard in their review essay that concludes this special issue, and that new forms of national educational governance are also at work through national testing. International testing is part of the infrastructure that Sassen (2007) argues is a central feature of globalisation and assists, we would argue, in constructing the globe as a commensurate space of measurement, in effect globalising comparison in schooling policy as a mode of governance (Novoa and Yariv-Mashal 2003). This has seen a globalisation of educational standards. As part of the globalising of education policy, there has also been a globalised educational policy discourse that suggests that high-stakes standardised testing will drive up standards, and enhance the quality of a nation's human capital and thus their international economic competitiveness (Stobart 2008). However, while we note the homogenising effects of such discourses, they still manifest in specific ways in different nations, what we might see as 'vernacular globalization' in education policy (Appadurai 1996; Lingard 2006).

These matters are also part of a broader change of state structures and policy frames associated with neoliberal globalisation, with effects on the education policy cycle. Here Ball (2013a) provides an account of the new technologies of governance through market, management and performance that affect agenda setting, policy text production and enactment in schooling systems around the globe. Testing at various scales is part of this new assemblage or ensemble of policy technologies, or perhaps 'policy dispositif' (Bailey 2013). Furthermore, as Ball (1998, 128) has presciently noted elsewhere, 'this ensemble changes the way that education is organised and delivered, but also changes the meaning of education and what it means to be educated and what it means to learn'. We see here a significant restructuring of the loosely coupled relationships hitherto the norm between central offices and schools and classroom practices. As Rutledge, Anagnostopoulos, and Jacobsen (2013, 215) observe in respect of the new infrastructures of accountability, and they are writing about the USA, but we believe their observation has broader relevance, 'State and federal policy makers direct student, teacher, and school performance from afar by controlling the collection, processing, and dissemination of data and attaching sanctions to them'. Despite enhanced global 'policyscapes' in schooling (Ball 1998), reflecting a new post-Westphalian reconstruction of the nation state and rescaling (Brenner 2004; Dale 2005), schooling policy, though, is still rearticulated through national concerns about history, culture, language, citizenship, social cohesion and national economic competitiveness. As noted, what we see in practice are vernacular versions of a global policy discourse, hybrid manifestations that are a melange of local histories, cultures and politics, and are mediated by political structures (e.g. unitary or federal forms of government). In this rescaling of the polity, the nation state remains important, but now works in different ways, with education policy within the nation central to national economic policy formation. With the globalisation of the economy, human capital formation has become a central economic focus of national policy, resulting in the economisation of education policy. The human capital framing of meta-policy in education is associated with new state structures, and steering at a distance through data and performance measures. The significant role that numbers play within this context, with its increasing emphasis on *evidence-based policy-making*, cannot be denied. As this special issue illustrates, policy as numbers continues to be manifested particularly in terms of the 'statistics/state relationship' (Lingard 2011, 357) with regard to what is to count as evidence and equity (Luke, Green, and Kelly 2010), and is inextricably tied to the constitution and proliferation of an audit culture of neoliberal governance and performativity (Power 1997). Given the national significance of schooling, it is important to recognise how numbers as a technology of distance (Porter 1995) help constitute the globe as a commensurate space of measurement in relation to national schooling systems. The space has become a space of comparison of national performance in schooling as tests such as PISA, TIMSS and PIRLS make the globe legible for governing.

High-stakes testing and its effects can also be seen as part of the phenomenon of 'policy as numbers' (Ozga and Lingard 2007; Ozga 2009; Lingard 2011), linked to other reforms of the state, including new public management and new forms of accountability, all set in the context of neoliberal globalisation and the emergence of a related audit culture (Power 1997). Data and numbers are central to the new mode of governance, as is comparison, and are now central to governmentalities. It is worth quoting Rose at some length here on numbers, grids, league tables, data banks as central to these mundane technologies of governance:

> Democratic mentalities of government prioritise and seek to produce a relationship between numerate citizens, numericised civic discourse and numerate evaluations of government. Democracy can operate as technology of government to the extent that such a network of numbers can be composed and stabilised. In analyses of democracy, a focus on numbers is instructive, for it helps us turn our eyes from grand texts of philosophy to the mundane practices of pedagogy, of accounting, of information and polling, and to the mundane knowledges and 'grey sciences' that support them. (Rose 1999, 232)

And, of course, computer capacities have grown exponentially with the increasing availability of data and data-sets *inter alia* as technologies of governance, associated with new infrastructures and linked to market, management and performance technologies documented by Ball (2013a). There is now a complex infrastructure underpinning contemporary policy as numbers. Some have also spoken of the 'infrastructure of accountability' framed around testing regimes (Anagnostopoulos, Rutledge, and Jacobsen 2013). We have entered the era of 'big data' where computer capacity and the 'datafication' of the world have seen an emergent epistemological shift from concerns with causality and understanding to concerns of correlation and predictability (Mayer-Schonberger and Cukier 2013). As the contributors to this special issue illustrate, this scalar dimension of 'datafication' also has particular policy effects in terms of mobilising biopower and driving neoliberal forms of governance.

Miller and Rose (2008), for example, point out that rationalities and technologies of markets are tied to a form of biopower mobilised through numbers as *inscription devices* in both constituting and targeting specific populations as the basis for identifying certain policy concerns. Rose (1988) also speaks specifically about the role of numbers as a function of biopolitics in establishing 'a regime of visibility' and 'a grid of codeability' for creating a navigable space of commensurability, equivalence and comparative performance, thereby rendering the population amenable to administration, statistical mapping and governance (187). It is in this sense that a *global panopticism* of a kind emerges with the OECD's PISA functioning as a regulatory mechanism for nations in terms of the scaling and rescaling of educational accountabilities within nations. We see the disciplining effects that these codes and grids of visibility have, and their capacity for ranking and pitting education systems against one another. Measurement, and the systems of accountability that they enable, is thus an integral feature of the political technologies of governance with 'their techniques for achieving subjugations of bodies' and the management or 'control of populations' under a global panopticonic gaze of other nations (Foucault 1998, 140), as is illustrated in the various papers in this special issue of the *Journal of Education Policy*. These panopticonic and regulatory effects are manifested in terms of the ranking and positioning of nations, and their education systems within the global policy field and global market place.

Big data as motivated by biopolitical concerns, thus have significance for both businesses and governments, and are concerned with predictability, surveillance, control and keeping the system functioning; there are related issues to do with a potential democratic deficit here, as rescaling occurs and as businesses are more involved in the global and national fields of schooling and policy production and enactment. On this point, Ball and Junemann (2012) have written about the rise of network governance in education as a development within new public management that acknowledges both rescaling and the involvement of edu-businesses in the policy cycle in education. It is interesting that all OECD data, including in respect of PISA, are publicly available in an open and democratic fashion. The paradox here, though, is that this means publicly funded data (nations pay the OECD to participate in PISA) are readily available for private business interests, 'edu-businesses'; such data are also available to policy entrepreneurs. This is another case of the rejigging of education policy in respect of the neoliberal and rescaling of education accountabilities; there is more private sector involvement in policy production and delivery, and these new public/private relationships central to neoliberal restructuring are now imbricated across the global scale.

We can see this in the recent 50-page *Learning Curve* report produced by global conglomerate Pearson (see Ball 2012, 124–128) and *The Economist's* Intelligence Unit, also owned by Pearson. This report provides a meta-analysis of the comparative educational performance of many nations across the globe, utilising *inter alia* PISA, TIMSS and PIRLS data, with available national data. The *Learning Curve* notes, '… we have assembled in one place a wide range of data sets which will enable researchers and policymakers to correlate education outcomes with wider social and economic outcomes more easily than ever before' (3). The political and economic function of classificatory systems and how the use of numbers is tied to managing and rendering populations amenable to governance emerge as important considerations in terms of attending to 'the complex technical work' and normative judgements that drive measurement and the global rescaling of educational accountabilities (Rose 1988, 208). We note that the *Learning Curve* is accompanied by the *Learning Curve Data Bank* that provides accessible databases. At the same time as such big data developments and meta-analyses, we acknowledge the trialing in 2012 of PISA for schools.

Both phenomena are manifestations of the rescaling of contemporary governance associated with globalisation, a form of deterritorialisation (Brenner 2004). What we see here is meta-data, international comparative data of national systems' performance, complementary national data, along with new school-based measures such as PISA for schools – all indicative of rescaling and deterritorialisation endemic in the contemporary policy moment. As well as rescaling, we also see the globe here as a single surface of comparison (Amin 2002). It is this phenomenon of *global panopticism* and how it is effected through these systems of accountability, therefore, that we are concerned to highlight – this idea of the global eye and how it is functioning in a regulatory capacity within nation states – with the national eye – to facilitate a form of neoliberal governance in terms of the ranking and marketing of education systems, both internally and internationally (Novoa and Yariv-Mashal 2003). Further, such testing at multiple levels, when set against the privatisations associated with neoliberal globalisation (Ball 2007), opens up spaces for private edu-businesses (Ball 2012) in the development of tests, in test data analysis and indeed in respect of related services (text books, professional development, etc.). Education has become a new focus for business interests and perhaps we can see Pearson's involvement in the *Learning Curve* as an attempt at rebranding their educational work globally, as a global edu-business.

At one level, these matters, policy as numbers writ global, can be seen to reflect what some have seen as cultural turn that has been described as topological (Lury, Parisi, and Terranova 2012; Ruppert 2012). This cultural change is analogous with the distinctions between Euclidian and topological spaces, where the former sees space as fixed between points, topology in contrast sees space as constantly in formation and deformation, continuous and discontinuous. Movement, mobility, change and flows are the cultural norm now, rather than stability and fixity. In this new cultural context, statistics, grids, tables, numbers, data, correlations between variables and so on can be seen to offer some continuity in an ever changing, discontinuous, culture and world. Here big data can be seen to proffer a form of structure in a globalising culture expressed in continuous change, allowing the conception of new correlations, continuities, commonalities and connivances between disparate things, producing new forms of continuity in liquid times. For Ball (2013b, 124), this topological approach results in 'the fitting together of disparate techniques, processes, practices and relationships within a regime of truth to form a grid of power which operates in many different ways from many different points'. Technological and computational capacities are increasing exponentially, as are data bases, and both are central to topological culture; this topological culture is heavily mediatised, in one sense virtual and central to constituting the globe as a single space and the emergent cosmopolitan habitus of senior policy-makers at national and international organisation (e.g. OECD, IEA) levels.

We have pointed out above how testing has been important in relation to the new technologies of governance in schooling systems and how these systems are inextricably embedded in a biopolitical project for managing populations through techniques of measurement that enable nation states to position themselves and their education systems within the global market place. Testing and related technologies have also been very important in the reconstitution of new neoliberal versions of educational accountability with real implications for teachers' work in classrooms (Ranson 2003). Comparative performance measures have been constructed as central to a vertical, one-way, top-down, one-dimensional form of accountability with restrictive and reductive effects on the work of principals and teachers, and on the school experiences of students and their parents. Test results have been central to this vertical accountability. It is accurate to observe in many schooling systems around the globe that test-based accountabilities have crowded out other potentially more educative accountabilities (Henig 2013, xi). Regarding this dominance of test-based accountability, Henig rightly observes (2013, xi), 'Mistrust of "so-called" experts [here teachers] has led us to build systems based on algorithms attached to automatic sanctions'; he then asks 'in the process, have we swung too far in separating accountability for education from informed judgment by professionals?' Our resounding answer would be 'yes'!

With this dominant test-based form of accountability, there is no horizontal accountability of schools to their communities or communities to their schools and research one of us is currently conducting suggests that the strength of the vertical top-down gaze delimits the possibilities of these more horizontal gazes linked to the broader purposes of schooling (see Sellar 2013). Yet, we do acknowledge that there are contestations and challenges to this form of accountability. There is also no talk of 'opportunity to learn standards' (Darling-Hammond 2010), a form of bottom-up vertical accountability, which facilitates the expression of demands by schools and their communities to be made on schooling systems, articulating demands about what resources of various kinds are necessary to the achievement of the goals set by the system, and often by governments and politicians. On the latter, the Australian Prime Minister, Julia Gillard, has set a target of Australia again being in the top five of performers on the OECD's PISA by 2025. We know the distorting impacts when targets drive practices. The steering at a distance associated with this new mode of governance – accountability at a distance (Sellar 2013) – and through policy as numbers, almost deflects accountability and policy responsibility concerns away from governments, and onto schools and teachers. As Henig notes:

> Suspicion that attention to non-school factors – concentrated poverty, social services, housing, and public health – will be used to excuse poor teaching has led to an accountability system narrowly focused on what happens within school buildings; in

the process, we are missing opportunities to build more comprehensive data bases that situate accountability for learning within broader social and economic contexts. (xi–xii)

Henig is talking here about US systems of accountability, but we would suggest this observation applies in other national systems as well and that the reductionism he refers to focuses simply on the decontextualised performance of teachers. Our mention here of both opportunity to learn standards and horizontal accountabilities is to speak back to such reductionism and also to imply that other modes of accountability – giving an account – ought to be utilised, such as narratives, for example, and be linked to the wide plethora of a school's social and academic goals.

To summarise what we have argued to this point: policy as numbers and test-based accountability reflect two layers of significant change to both the content and processes of policy-making in education. The first is a rescaling which includes new scalar relations from the local through provincial to national and global in what emerges as a *global panopticism*, which we have referred to above. The enhanced significance of the OECD's data work, including PISA, is significant here, as are the meta and deterritorialised modes of rescaling referred to above in respect of the *Learning Curve* and PISA for schools, and the complementarity between international and national testing regimes. As well as rescaling, the topological refers to the emergence of a conception of the globe as single space.

The other significant element in education policy is the involvement (both actual and potential) now of private interests, edu-businesses and philanthropic organisations both nationally and globally (Ball 2012), which are central to what Ball and Junemann (2012) refer to as 'network governance', creating 'heterarchies' that mix together bureaucracy, markets and networks in new ways. Pearson's *Learning Curve* is a good case in point, as is their heavy involvement in the testing industry globally and nationally. Pearson Philanthropy is also involved in work with the OECD. Ball (2012, 93) argues that to analyse education policy today, including in respect of testing, that we need to consider the complex interweavings and involvements of the global and the national, the role of international organisations in the former, but at the same time we need to recognise the enhanced involvement of edu-business at all scalar levels in policy and policy production in education. The take-up of testing at all levels across education systems across the globe has opened up a fertile space for edu-businesses and philanthropic organisations. The potential effects of such involvement go beyond providing services. As Rutledge, Anagnostopoulos, and Jacobsen suggest (2013), private sector involvement in the creation of accountability infrastructures can potentially establish 'competing centres of calculation', that is, state vs. corporation. They note as well that the decisions built into data systems created by edu-businesses imply particular visions regarding the purposes of schooling. Herein, we see a potential 'democratic deficit'.

As noted above, Ball and Junemann (2012) argue that this structural change in policy production has also seen the move beyond the new public management to new network forms of governance as a further part of the move from government to governance. Policy networks now reflect both rescaling of global/national relationships and public/private partnerships involved in education policy at all levels of this rescaling. These are important considerations in any emergent sociology of testing regimes within a policy sociology framework, which must recognise the potential privatisation of policy production in education in the developments adumbrated here. Such a sociology would also look beyond the decisions about what data to collect in test-based accountability systems, how they are analysed and how they are used in policy terms, as well their effects on schools, teachers, students and the education that is provided.

Rose (1999) has written most instructively about the politics of single numbers in contemporary governance and how the single number hides the technical work that has gone into category creation, measurement, the creation of metrics, data collection and analysis. In writing about the infrastructure of accountability, including computational capacities, Anagnostopoulos, Rutledge, and Jacobsen (2013) note that:

> The data that fuel test-based accountability are, thus, the products of complex assemblages of technology, people, and policies that stretch across and beyond the boundaries of our formal educational systems. (2013, 2)

This assemblage then might be seen in Foucault's terms as dispositif (see Bailey 2013; Ball 2013b, 124), consisting of both material and discursive aspects and needs to be understood in terms of a biolpolitical project of neoliberal governance – the effects of such systems are not just 'disciplinary'; they also have a regulatory function in *managing* education systems within nation states under a panopticonic system of global competitiveness. As Kelly (2004), drawing on Foucault (2003), argues, 'Where discipline is the technology deployed to make individuals behave, to be efficient and productive workers, biopolitics is deployed to manage population' (59). It is this political assemblage and these practices or *technologies of governance* that might be the focus of a sociology of testing regimes, a sociology that would regard testing as policy, a matter we consider in the next section.

These then are the contexts and some of the issues that the papers in this special issue of the *Journal of Education Policy* on 'Testing regimes, accountabilities and education policy' address. While most of the papers are concerned with schooling, high-stakes testing and 'hyper-accountability' (Barker, 2010), Riyad A. Shahjahan contributes a paper that looks at such matters in relation to higher education, specifically the development of the OECD's AHELO that seeks to measure the 'value-addedness' of higher education across the duration of an undergraduate degree, focusing in the first instance on the disciplines of Economics and Engineering. There is a way in which the reworking of the nation-state in the global context and the restructured state and new modes of governance have reframed all sectors of education on a global scale. We point out that subsequent to Shahjahan writing his paper on AHELO that the OECD, at its March, 2013 meeting of the Education Policy Committee, has noted a number of concerns about AHELO. Specifically for Australia there is the issue of whether the unit for comparative analysis ought to be the nation or individual institutions, particularly given that it is the Australian government that is paying for Australia's participation in the programme. This indicates that national politics still count within the global field.

To this point in this introduction to this *Journal of Education Policy* special issue, we have attempted to contextualise the specific accounts provided in each of the papers. We do this as a central element of policy analysis, but also because much contemporary education policy decontextualises schools, denying the impact of structural inequality (both within and between nations) and lays all responsibility for performance at the feet of teachers and individual schools (see here Condron 2011), as reflected in the reductionism of test-based accountability. Hattie's (2008)

Visible Learning, which provides a meta-account or meta-literature review of what teacher classroom practices have the most effect on student learning (feedback, for example), notes in the preface that societal factors such as socio-economic background and poverty might have more effects, yet the book is utilised by systems and schools as suggesting that it is only teachers that count. A recent Queensland government policy, *Great teachers = Great results*, for example, actually asserts this assumption quite strongly and combines the observation with an assertion that increased expenditure on schooling does not necessarily lead to improved student learning outcomes; rather the policy observes that it is more targeted funding that will make the difference – a stance made for times of austerity in public sector expenditure.

Testing as policy

These papers on testing in education are appearing in the *Journal of Education Policy*. We think in the contemporary educational policy context as alluded to already (see also Rizvi and Lingard 2010; Ball 2012, 2013a), that we must now begin to see testing in education systems as policy. Thus a significant point of departure here is our thinking about high stakes testing (central to new accountabilities in education) as policy. This is an argument proffered by Rizvi and Lingard (2010):

> Education policy studies have tended to focus on almost all aspects of educational processes except those relating to curriculum, pedagogy and evaluation. Policy studies have thus, for example, addressed issues of funding and equity, but have not usually linked them to their effects on practices of curriculum, pedagogy and evaluation. The fields of curriculum and education policy have thus been considered as separate, located in different academic and organisational spaces. (93)

On the basis of the restructurings of the state alluded to above, new public management and the subsequent emergence of network governance, that affect the production rules for education policy, including global framing affected by globalised education policy discourses, Rizvi and Lingard argue that curriculum, pedagogy and evaluation should now be seen as policies and become an important focus of policy sociology in education. That is the stance of these papers, part of the *raison d'etre* of this special issue, and also implicitly at least of a recent paper in this journal by Gerrard and Farrell (2013) that sought to develop an approach to understanding policy development in respect of the new, emergent Australian national curriculum. This is not to say that there is no place for curriculum studies (and here see McGregor forthcoming; Yates, Collins, and Connor 2011; Yates and Grumet 2011; Priestley and Biesta 2013), but to argue that the message systems should also be the focus of policy sociology in education, given their central roles now in 'steering' schooling systems. Regarding the testing message system as policy requires a different approach to it and also a different approach to curriculum from that of curriculum studies.

Bernstein (1971) wrote within the sociology of education about the three message systems of schooling, namely, curriculum, pedagogy and evaluation. His argument was that the three message systems sat in symbiotic relationships with each other, with changes in one affecting the others. He was also interested in how these message systems linked to the broader society and culture. This is reflected in the opening observation in his influential essay, 'On the Classification and Framing of

Educational Knowledge' in Michael Young's ground-breaking collection *Knowledge and Control* (1971). Bernstein stated: 'How a society selects, classifies, distributes, transmits and evaluates the educational knowledge it considers to be public reflects both the distribution of power and principles of social control' (1971, 47). While he was acknowledging the 'selective tradition' in curriculum construction here, also the focus of much of Michael Apple's influential work on curriculum, his major focus was the internal workings and 'recontextualisations' of schooling systems and schooling, yet he did acknowledge that pedagogy was a cultural relay ensuring social and cultural production and reproduction (Bernstein 2004, 196). Thus, while he was concerned with recontextualisations of the 'pedagogic device' through systems to school and classroom practices, we might see these message systems as framing educational system policies as well, with pedagogy most often implicit in systemic systems of evaluation and in curriculum. In a recent paper, using Bernsteinian theory to understand the policy cycle in education published in this journal, Singh, Thomas, and Harris (2013, 3) suggest that, 'The pedagogic device is the ensemble of rules or procedure by which policy knowledge is selectively translated into what is taught to whom, when, where, why, and how it is evaluated or deemed as acquired'.

We can also see pedagogy as the way these two message systems (curriculum and evaluation) are enacted in schools and classrooms – pedagogy as policy implementation in one sense, if we regard curriculum and evaluation systems (including testing) as policies. Though policy on pedagogy is usually implicit in most schooling systems, we acknowledge that some systems have moved to policy about pedagogy as the policy focus has narrowed to a reductive, decontextualised emphasis on quality teachers and quality teaching. The quality pedagogy framework in New South Wales is one case in point here. The Blair government's literacy hour in England might also be regarded as an implicit policy about pedagogy. Research on productive pedagogies in the Queensland schooling system also had policy effects (see Hayes et al. 2006). As an aside, it might very well be the case that the most likely impact of systemic education policy is through teachers' classroom pedagogies. Think of social justice policy, inclusion policies, gender equity policies and the like.

Researchers undertaking policy studies in education have tended to leave curriculum to curriculum studies researchers and the other elements of Bernstein's message systems to other sub-specialisms in education, but this is changing too as governments seek more control over curriculum. This traditional policy studies/curriculum studies binary distinction could be seen in Bourdieusian terms as reflecting the fact that both are academic fields with their own logics of practice, hierarchies, valorised capitals and so on. So an underpinning assumption here is that today Bernstein's message systems might also be seen as policies in their own right and thus as important topics for work in policy sociology on education. Think of Thatcher's Education Reform Act of 1989 as a good case in point of curriculum change as policy change; think of current Secretary of State for Education, Michael Gove's attempts to change the national curriculum in contemporary England, to change the GCSE; think of the *Curriculum for Excellence* Reform in Scotland (Priestley and Biesta 2013); think of the current moves towards a national curriculum in Australia, where schooling remains, in Constitutional terms at least, the responsibility of the States and Territories (Lingard 2010). We could also think of the move in the USA to produce national standards in Maths and English in a polity where the federal government has less presence in schooling policy than is the situation in Australia, where the extensive degree of vertical fiscal imbalance allows the federal government to practise funding/compliance trade-offs in respect of schooling, which is a Constitutional responsibility of the States and Territories, and one which they jealously seek to protect. In this context, policy scholars are beginning to focus on curriculum as systemic policy (e.g. Gerrard and Farrell 2013; Menter and Hulme 2013; Singh, Thomas, and Harris 2013), implemented or enacted in schools and classrooms through pedagogy and framed by systemic evaluation, assessment and testing policies.

As Bernstein noted some time ago: 'differences within and change in the organisation, transmission and evaluation of educational knowledge should be a major area of sociological interest' (1971, 47). In terms of sociological analyses of such changes, we can see the broader context of such moves as manifesting the way globalisation has affected the nation-state and the way the nation-state has responded in the context of an emergent global education policy field (Lingard and Rawolle 2011), and situated within a rescaled contemporary politics (Dale 2005; Robertson, Bonal, and Dale 2006).

In the complex assemblage of policy changes in education, globally and nationally, that we have documented in the previous section, we see the evaluation message system, manifested most often as high-stakes testing linked to a narrow form of educational accountability, as a new meta-policy in school systems framing practices in schools, including its impacts on curriculum in use and pedagogies. This is the focus of most of the papers in this special issue of the *Journal of Education Policy*, namely, the policy reality that the evaluation systems of school systems has become a major policy driving the work of schools and teachers.

As already alluded to, we note that in the context of globalisation and its effects, there is a global as well as national element to these policy changes as part of the rescaling of contemporary politics, with the nation-state remaining important, but functioning in different and complex ways. We see this functioning as an exemplary case of what we consider to be a regime of *global panopticism*. In a research project, one of us is currently conducting, a senior policy-maker at the OECD noted that with the economisation of education policy (our term) that nations today need both international and national testing for accountability purposes, but also for instantiating agendas of improvement. His argument was that national data might indicate improvement, but international comparative data might at the same time demonstrate decline in comparison with the performance of other national systems of schooling (Sellar and Lingard 2013b).

With the focus of education policy now the production of the requisite human capital for ensuring an internationally competitive global economy, international comparisons of the performance of national schooling systems have become important to nations. Taken together, all of these tests, including category alignment across nations, are helping to constitute the globe as a commensurate space of measurement linked to the rescaling of politics, the topological turn and creation of global educational policy field (Lingard and Rawolle 2011). A central feature here is the constitution of global epistemic communities of policy-makers (Kallo 2009) with aligned habitus and dispositions, who do the 'commensurative work' (Espland 2000) necessary to the creation of a global field of education policy, constituting the globe topologically as a single space of measurement and comparison, with effects into national fields.

Anglo-American schooling systems, beholden in public policy terms, to variations of neoliberalism, have constituted school reform strategies that function around what Sahlberg (2011) has felicitously called the Global Education Reform Movement (GERM) with a stress on literacy and numeracy, high-stakes testing linked to accountability, competition between schools, market mechanisms such as parental school choice discourses and the like (tests and comparison help constitute quasi-markets in schooling), a policy assemblage (see Rizvi and Lingard 2011) or dispositif (Bailey 2013) that is implicitly, if not explicitly, mistrustful of teachers and restrictive of their professionalism. Sahlberg contrasts GERM with the Finnish school reform agenda, which functions around deep trust of teacher professionalism, much autonomy for schools, a strong commitment to intervening and remediating early, a universal system of government schools that collaborate rather than compete, no high stakes testing, political consensus about schooling policy across left/right divides, situated in an equal society with a low Gini coefficient of inequality.

The Anglo-American nations now use both international data and national performance data to 'steer' – or perhaps 'drive' might be a more appropriate verb here – schooling systems and the work of schools and teachers. This is the rationale for most of the papers in this special issue of the *Journal of Education Policy*. Shahjahan's paper indicates that a similar logic is now at work in respect of higher education policy, globally.

The papers

This special issue begins with three papers from North America (Lipman, Hursh, and Martino and Rezai-Rashti). Pauline Lipman's paper deals with an assemblage of schooling policies in Chicago that develops an argument beyond that articulated in her recent books (2004, 2011), and which demonstrates the broader, devastating social effects of particular educational accountability policies in Chicago and shows how important educational policies are today in urban politics. This is a searing analysis of the effects of a vernacular expression of neoliberal globalisation in Chicago. It also demonstrates how education policy is now at the centre of contemporary politics and linked to the global restructuring of capitalism, which has differentiated classed and raced effects. David Hursh, in his paper, brings us up to date regarding developments in respect to high-stakes testing and accountability in New York, also narrating an update of his book, *High-Stakes Testing and the Decline of Teaching and Learning* (2008). We note how reforms in the New York school system have been an important reference for national school reform in Australia and also note how their policy architect now works for the edu-business arm of Rupert Murdoch's global enterprise. Both papers, Lipman's and Hursh's, also indicate the centrality of a global disposition to a progressive politics today, a politics of resistance.

Wayne Martino and Goli Rezai-Rashti deal with the province of Ontario, Canada and look at the globalisation of educational accountability as it is played out in that province, which has become a 'poster system' for the OECD in relation to PISA performance. In their paper, they articulate a policy critique of the gender achievement gap and show how this 'gap talk' and the 'failing boy' discourse are connected to the neoliberal system of accountability that eschews and actually misrecognises fundamental equity concerns in the Ontario schooling system, related specifically to minority and economically disadvantaged school populations in urban centres such as Toronto. Their paper also indicates how there is a limited national federal presence in Canadian schooling, unlike Australian federalism that in the context of globalisation has seen an ever-strengthening federal presence in schooling. There is a national body in education in Canada, consisting of the ministers of education from the provinces, but no national policies in schooling as such.

International comparative tests such as PISA, and TIMSS and PIRLS are interesting in terms of how they are used and work in the particular federal or other political contexts. We note how while the UK is the unit of analysis for PISA, that Scotland pays for participation and data analysis in PISA as an almost separate and independent nation, another manifestation of rescaling and deterritorialisation. State participation in PISA in Australia also demands oversampling, so that State systems (sub-national political units) can trace and document changes in performance over time in their systems. At the same time, these data are now of central importance to national governments; witness the impact of Shanghai's outstanding performance on PISA 2009 in the US with President Obama describing this as a wake-up call for US comparable to Sputnik in 1957.

Following the focus on three North American papers, dealing with urban schooling systems and a provincial system, the focus then turns to national schooling systems. Hannu Simola and his colleagues deal with the idiosyncrasies of the Finnish system in the context of globalisation. Their interesting paper shows how Finland has taken its own path of school reform, a stance strongly articulated in Sahlberg's (2011) book, *Finnish Lessons*. The Finnish system remains of great interest around the globe because of its continuing excellent performance on PISA. Lingard and Sellar deal with what they call 'catalyst data' and its effects in Australian schooling. They show how data on the performance of state systems of schooling on national literacy and numeracy testing are being used to hold state systems to account by the federal government with perverse effects. There has been much research documenting the perverse effects of high-stakes testing on schools and teachers' work (Nicholas and Berliner 2007; Stobart 2008), but not much that looks at systemic effects. Lingard and Sellar focus on the effects when testing results become high stakes for systems. Keita Takayama writes of the politics of changing approaches to accountability and testing in Japan. It is worth remembering that Japanese schooling was an important 'reference society' (Schriewer 1990) for the USA during the 1980s and the era of *A Nation at Risk*. Takayama demonstrates the ways in which national political concerns remain important in national policy developments in respect of testing regimes, as of course do international measures of comparative performance.

As mentioned earlier, Riyad Shajahan looks at the OECD's AHELO, a new accountability measure that the Organisation for Economic Cooperation and Development is developing for universities. This test is currently being trialed and seeks to measure the value-added effects of university teaching and education on students. The focus in this development stage has been on Engineering and Economics. This paper is important in that it reminds us that new forms of testing and accountability have not only been prevalent in school systems, but are also starting to influence other education sectors. Ball (2013b) makes this point really clearly in his new book on Foucault, where he notes that neoliberalism is not only out there – something we research and analyse – but also in here, affecting us and our work in universities, thus demanding an ongoing critical reflexivity in our work.

Furthermore, Shajahan's paper demonstrates how the success of PISA has encouraged a focus in the Education Directorate at the OECD on other possible international comparative tests. The OECD's Education Directorate has found a new policy niche for itself in a post-Cold War world (Sellar and Lingard 2013b). We would also note here the Programme for the International Assessment of Adult Competencies, a measure of the skills of the 16–64-year-old workforce of nations, which has also recently been developed by the OECD. Sotiria Grek, who has researched PISA (Grek 2009) and the OECD (Grek 2013), deals in her paper with how supranational spaces are made commensurate for testing purposes through meetings, and, we would add, through an alignment between the policy habitus of national and international organisations' policy-makers. Grek also proffers some very interesting observations about data for policy and knowledge in education today. She implies that the policy as numbers turn carries significance for the construction of educational research today. This reminds us of Luke and Hogan's (2006) observation, in the context of the rise of so-called evidence-based policy-making (Head 2008; Wiseman 2010) and the centrality of data and numbers to contemporary modes of governance of the restructured state (Lingard 2011; Ozga 2009), that: 'current debates over what counts as evidence in state policy formation are indeed debates over what counts as educational research and what should count as curriculum and pedagogy' (Luke and Hogan 2006, 170).

A review essay by Sam Sellar and Bob Lingard deals with four books, two documenting the history and functioning of the OECD in global governance and two dealing with the global impact of the OECD's PISA in schooling systems around the globe. They utilise the work of Woodward (2009) to talk of the role of the OECD and PISA in relation to the emergent global policy field in education and the role of the OECD in global governance. They suggest that Woodward's normative and cognitive modes of global governance can be seen as part of what they call 'epistemological governance' (cf. Kallo 2009). They also argue that the creation of a global infrastructure of measurement facilitates what Woodward refers to as 'palliative governance'.

Concluding comment

We have contextualised the papers included in this special issue and shown how the policy cycle has been rescaled and now includes the involvement of edu-businesses, along with international organisations in the setting and delivery of the global testing and accountability agenda. These developments have been accompanied by new and complementary moves around educational accountability inside nations. This has tended to be top-down, test-based accountability that has reductive effects on the provision and experiences of schooling, particularly on the experiences of disadvantaged young people, as curriculum width is reduced to ensure the enhancement of test scores, set against growing social inequality, and in the process closing down opportunity and reinforcing the centrality of appropriate parental capitals to the school performance of children; thus reproducing inequality in a Bourdieusian sense.

The infrastructures of accountability also have helped constitute a global policy field, one element of the topological turn within culture, as the globe is created as a single commensurate space or surface of measurement. We have drawn attention to how these infrastructures of 'datafication' function as a form of *global panopticism*, and are tied to neoliberal forms of governance as a central component of the rescaling of educational accountability, both within and across nation states. There are two global elements here: the topological, constituting the globe as a single space and rescaling, constituting new relations between policy agencies within and across nations and the globe. The new accountabilities have opened up market and investment possibilities for edu-business, globally and nationally. There are also potential impacts on the purposes of schooling.

Given these changes, we see a strengthening of technologies of governance in education as a result and a weakening of political debates about what imagined and better future, schools ought to be helping to produce and how we might think about accountability in education in more productive and educative ways, including opportunity to learn standards and horizontal accountabilities. These matters appear to have been closed down to a considerable extent, as testing, both international and national, has become perhaps the major top-down, policy steering contemporary education systems. Here we agree with Rutledge, Anagnostopoulos, and Jacobsen (Rutledge et al. 2013, 227–228) that we need to think about the important broader purposes and goals of schooling beyond a concern to simply raise test results for individual schools and nationally and globally, so as to ensure the competitiveness of the national economy. We would suggest our days are numbered, if we forget what really counts.

Acknowledgements
The authors thank Dr Sam Sellar for his comments on various versions of this essay and for pointing out the significance of the distinction between Foucault's 'disciplinary power' and Deleuze's 'control society' to our argument. We would also like to acknowledge Aspa Baroutsis for her assistance with the editing of this paper.

References

Amin, A. 2002. "Spatialities of Globalization." *Environment and Planning* 34 (3): 385–399.
Anagnostopoulos, D., S. Rutledge, and R. Jacobsen, eds. 2013. *The Infrastructure of Accountability: Data Use and the Transformation of American Education*. Cambridge, MA: Harvard Education Press.

Appadurai, A. 1996. *Modernity at Large: Cultural Dimensions of Globalization.* Minneapolis, MN: The University of Minnesota Press.

Bailey, P. 2013. "The Policy Dispositif: Historical Formation and Method." *Journal of Education Policy.* doi:10.1080/02680939.2013.782512.

Ball, S. J. 1998. "Big Policies/Small World: An Introduction to International Perspectives in Education Policy." *Comparative Education* 34 (2): 119–130.

Ball, S. J. 2007. *Education Plc: Understanding Private Sector Participation in Public Sector Education.* London: Routledge.

Ball, S. J. 2012. *Global Education Inc: New Policy Networks and the Neo-Liberal Imaginary.* London: Routledge.

Ball, S. J. 2013a. *The Education Debate.* 2nd ed. Bristol: The Policy Press.

Ball, S. J. 2013b. *Foucault, Power and Education.* New York: Routledege.

Ball, S. J., and C. Junemann. 2012. *Networks, New Governance and Education.* Bristol: The Policy Press.

Barker, B. 2010. *The Pendulum Swings: Transforming School Reform.* London: Trentham Books.

Bernstein, B. 1971. "On the Classification and Framing of Educational Knowledge." In *Knowledge and Control,* edited by M. F. D. Young, 47–69. London: Collier-MacMillan.

Bernstein, B. 2004. "Social Class and Pedagogic Practice." In *The RoutledgeFalmer Reader in the Sociology of Education,* edited by S. Ball, 196–217. London: RoutledgeFalmer.

Brenner, N. 2004. *New State Spaces: Urban Governance and the Rescaling of Statehood.* Oxford: Oxford University Press.

Condron, D. 2011. "Egalitarianism and Educational Excellence: Compatible Goals for Affluent Societies?" *Educational Researcher* 40 (2): 47–55.

Dale, R. 2005. "Globalisation, Knowledge Economy and Comparative Education." *Comparative Education* 41 (2): 117–149.

Darling-Hammond, L. 2010. *The Flat World and Education: How America's Commitment to Equity Will Determine Our Future.* New York: Teachers College Press.

Espland, W. 2000. "Commensuration and Cognition." In *Culture in Mind: Toward a Sociology of Culture and Cognition,* edited by K. A. Cerulo, 63–88. London: Routledge.

Foucault, M. 1998. *The History of Sexuality Vol.1: The Will to Knowledge* London: Penguin.

Foucault, M. 2003. *Society Must Be Defended.* Translated by David Macy. London: Penguin.

Gerrard, J., and L. Farrell. 2013. "'Peopling' Curriculum Policy Production: Researching Educational Governance through Institutional Ethnography and Bourdieuian Field Analysis." *Journal of Education Policy* 28 (1): 1–20.

Grek, S. 2009. "Governing by Numbers: The PISA 'Effect' in Europe." *Journal of Education Policy* 24 (1): 23–37.

Grek, S. 2013. "Expert Moves: International Comparative Testing and the Rise of Expertocracy." *Journal of Education Policy.* doi:10.1080/02680939.2012.758825.

Hattie, J. 2008. *Visible Learning: A Syntheses of over 800 Meta-Analyses Relating to Achievement.* London: Routledge.

Hayes, D., M. Mills, P. Christie, and B. Lingard. 2006. *Teachers & Schooling Making a Difference.* Sydney: Allen & Unwin.

Head, B. W. 2008. "Three Lenses of Evidence-Based Policy." *Australian Journal of Public Administration* 67 (1): 1–11.

Henig, J. R. 2013. "Foreword." In *The Infrastructure of Accountability: Data Use and the Transformation of American Education,* edited by D. Anagnostopoulos, S. Rutledge and R. Jacobsen. Cambridge, MA: Harvard Education Press.

Hursh, D. W. 2008. *High-Stakes Testing and The Decline of Teaching and Learning: The Real Crisis in Education.* Lanham: Rowman & Littlefield Publishers.

Kallo, J. 2009. *OECD Education Policy: A Comparative and Historical Study Focusing on the Thematic Reviews of Tertiary Education, Finnish Educational Research Association.* Jyväskylä: Jyväskylä University Press.

Kelly, M. 2004. "Racism, Nationalism and Biopolitics: Foucault's Society Must be Defended, 2003." *Contretemps* 4 (September): 58–70.

Lingard, B. 2006. "Globalisation, The Research Imagination and Deparochialising The Study of Education." *Globalisation, Societies and Education* 3 (2): 287–302.

Lingard, B. 2010. "Policy Borrowing, Policy Learning: Testing Times in Australian Schooling." *Critical Studies in Education* 51 (2): 129–147.

Lingard, B. 2011. "Policy as Numbers: Ac/Counting for Educational Research." *Australian Educational Researcher* 38 (4): 355–382.

Lingard, B., and S. Rawolle. 2011. "New Scalar Politics: Implications for Education Policy." *Comparative Education* 47 (4): 489–502.

Lipman, P. 2004. *High Stakes Education: Inequality, Globalization and Urban School Reform*. London: Routledge-Falmer.

Lipman, P. 2011. *The New Political Economy of Urban Education: Neoliberalism, Race, and the Right to the City*. New York: Routledge.

Luke, A. J. Green, and G. Kelly 2010. "What Counts as Evidence and Equity?" *Review of Research in Education* 34: vii–xvi.

Luke, A., and D. Hogan. 2006. "Redesigning What Counts as Evidence in Educational Policy: The Singapore Model." In *World Yearbook of Education 2006: Education Research and Policy: Steering the Knowledge-Based Economy*, edited by J. Ozga, T. Seddon and T. Popkewitz, 170–184. London: Routledge.

Lury, C., L. Parisi, and T. Terranova. 2012. "Introduction: The Becoming Topological of Culture." *Theory, Culture and Society* 29 (4/5): 3–35.

Mayer-Schonberger, V., and K. Cukier. 2013. *Big Data: a Revolution That Will Transform How We Live, Work and Think*. New York: Houghton, Mifflin, Harcourt.

McGregor, G. Forthcoming. "Getting Beyond the 'Hotch-Potch of Competing agendas': The Need to Develop a Powerful Curriculum for *All* Young People." *Discourse: Studies in the Cultural Politics of Education*.

Menter, I., and M. Hulme. 2013. "Developing the Teacher – or Not?" In *Reinventing the Curriculum: New Trends in Curriculum Policy and Practice*, edited by M. Priestley, and G. Biesta. London: Bloomsbury.

Miller, P., and N. Rose. 2008. *Governing the Present: Administering Economic, Social and Personal Life*. Cambridge: Polity Press.

Nichols, S., and D. Berliner. 2007. *Collateral Damage: How High Stakes Testing Corrupts America's Schools*. Cambridge, MA. Harvard Education Press.

Novoa, A., and T. Yariv-Mashal. 2003. "Comparative Research in Education: A Mode of Governance or a Historical Journey?" *Comparative Education* 39 (4): 423–438.

Ozga, J. 2009. "Governing Education through Data in England: From Regulation to Self-Evaluation." *Journal of Education Policy* 24 (2): 149–162.

Ozga, J., and B. Lingard. 2007. "Globalisation, Education Policy and Politics." In *The Routledge Falmer Reader in Education Policy and Politics*, edited by B. Lingard and J. Ozga, 65–82. London: Routledge Falmer.

Porter, T. 1995. *Trust in Numbers: The Pursuit of Objectivity in Science and Public Life*. Princeton, NJ: Princeton University Press.

Power, M. 1997. *The Audit Society: Rituals of Verification*. Oxford: Oxford University Press.

Priestley, M., and G. Biesta, eds. 2013. *Reinventing the Curriculum: New Trends in Curriculum Policy and Practice*. London: Bloomsbury.

Ranson, S. 2003. "Public Accountability in the Age of Neo-Liberal Governance." *Journal of Education Policy* 18 (5): 459–480.

Rizvi, F., and B. Lingard. 2010. *Globalizing Education Policy*. London: Routledge.

Rizvi, F., and B. Lingard. 2011. "Social Equity and The Assemblage of Values in Australian Higher Education." *Cambridge Journal of Education* 41 (1): 5–22.

Robertson, S., X. Bonal, and R. Dale. 2006. "GATS and the Education Service Industry: the Politics of Scale and Global Reterritorialization." In *Education, Globalization and Social Change*, edited by H. Lauder, P. Brown, J. Dillabough, and A. H. Halsey, 228–246. Oxford: Oxford University Press.

Rose, N. 1988. "Calculable Minds and Manageable Individuals." *History of the Human Sciences* 1 (2): 179–200.

Rose, N. 1999. *Powers of Freedom: Reframing Political Thought*. Cambridge: Cambridge University Press.

Ruppert, E. 2012. "The Governmental Topologies of Database Devices." *Theory, Culture and Society* 29 (4/5): 116–136.

Rutledge, S. A., D. Anagnostopoulos, and R. Jacobsen. 2013. "The Infrastructure of Accountability: Tensions, Implications and Concluding Thoughts." In *The Infrastructure of Accountability: Data Use and the Transformation of American Education*, edited by D. Anagnostopoulos, S. Rutledge and R. Jacobsen, 213–228. Cambridge, MA: Harvard Education Press.

Sahlberg, P. 2011. *Finnish Lessons: What Can the World Learn from Educational Change in Finland?* New York: Teachers College Press.

Sassen, S. 2007. *Sociology of Globalization*. New York: W.W. Norton.

Schriewer, J. 1990. "The Method of Comparison and The Need for Externalization: Methodological Criteria and Sociological Concepts." In *Theories and Methods in Comparative Education*, edited by J. Schriewer, 25–83. Frankfurt: Peter Lang.

Sellar, S. 2013. "Transparency and Opacity: Levinasian Reflections on Accountability in Australian Schooling." *Educational Philosophy and Theory*. doi:10.1080/00131857.2013. 793924.

Sellar, S., and B. Lingard. 2013a. "Looking East: Shanghai, PISA 2009 and the Reconstitution of Reference Societies in the Global Policy Field." *Comparative Education*. doi:10.1080/03050068.2013.770943.

Sellar, S., and B. Lingard. 2013b. "Expanding PISA and the Role of the OECD in Global Educational Governance." In *Who Succeeds at PISA and Why? The Role of International Benchmarking in Emerging Global Governance*, edited by H.-D. Meyer, and A. Benavot, 185–206. Oxford: Symposium Books.

Singh, P., S. Thomas, and J. Harris. 2013. "Recontextualising Policy Discourses: A Bernsteinian Perspective on Policy Interpretation, Translation, Enactment." *Journal of Education Policy* 28 (4): 465–480.

Stobart, G. 2008. *Testing Times: The Uses and Abuses of Assessment*. London: Routledge.

Wiseman, A. 2010. "The Uses of Evidence for Educational Policymaking: Global Contexts and International Trends." In *What Counts as Evidence and Equity? Review of Research in Education*, edited by A. Luke, J. Green, and G. Kelly, 1–24. New York: AERA.

Woodward, R. 2009. *The Organization for Economic Cooperation and Development (OECD)*. Abingdon: Routledge.

Yates, L., C. Collins, and K. O'Connor, eds. 2011. *Australia's Curriculum Dilemmas: State Cultures and the Big Issues*. Carlton: Melbourne University Press.

Yates, L., and M. Grumet, eds. 2011. *World Yearbook of Education 2011: Curriculum in Today's World: Configuring Knowledge, Identities, Work and Politics*. London: Routledge.

Young, M. F. D. ed. 1971. *Knowledge and Control: New Directions for the Sociology of Education*. London: Collier-Macmillan.

Economic crisis, accountability, and the state's coercive assault on public education in the USA

Pauline Lipman

Department of Educational Policy Studies, University of Illinois at Chicago, Chicago, IL, USA

This article examines education accountability as a mechanism of coercive neoliberal urban governance in the USA. Drawing on Gramscian theory of the 'integral state' as the dialectical synthesis of coercion, consent, and resistance, the author argues that as the crisis gives the state less room to win consent, it intensifies coercion as a strategy of governance. The author discusses three aspects of coercive state responses to the crisis in relation to education: (1) cannibalizing public education as a site of capital accumulation; (2) imposition of state austerity regimes and selective abandonment of education as a mechanism of social reproduction and legitimation in African-American communities that have become zones of disposability; and (3) governance by exclusion of African-American and Latino communities through school closings, state takeovers of elected governance bodies, and disenfranchisement. Systems of accountability are integral to this process as they make schools legible for the market, mark specific schools and school districts as pathological and in need of authoritarian governance, and justify minimalist schools in areas of urban disposability. This paper concludes with the potential of emergent resistance to dominant neoliberal education policy and argues that breaking with the framework of accountability and testing is critical to a counter-hegemonic alternative.

Introduction

The state is using the structural crisis of capitalism to accelerate neoliberal restructuring of public education in the USA. Seeing an opportunity to gobble up the public sector for private gain, fractions of capital, venture philanthropists, and neoliberal ideologues have seized on the fiscal crisis of the state to attack teacher unions and further marketize public education. While these moves are legitimated through discourses of 'school failure' and framed as 'reforms,' the cultivation of consent is dialectically related to the deployment of coercive state power – disenfranchisement, expropriation of public goods, and state abandonment. Driven by intertwined logics of capital and race, African-American and Latino urban communities that are largely superfluous to corporate/financial interests and excluded from state investment are targets of a strategy to dismantle public education and essentially abandon its role in social reproduction. The state is selectively disposing of public schools and abolishing elected governance bodies in urban school districts, stripping them of democratic processes of school governance. School closings, take-overs by education management organizations, expansion of privately run charter schools, and mayoral control of school systems are the order of the day.

This coercive assault on public education can be understood in relation to broader logics of crisis and the state's response. The social contradictions created by neoliberalism have led governments to increasingly deploy coercive processes of incarceration, surveillance, and punishment to maintain order in society (Gill 2003; Wacquant 2001). In the USA, governance through coercion has been a feature of state strategy over the past two decades, apparent in a dramatic increase in surveil-lance, curtailment of civil liberties, and intensification of incarceration, policing, and containment of people of color, especially in cities, and particularly in schools. The economic crisis has intensified coercive tendencies as the state is increasingly unable to deliver on its promises and the whole of society is thrown into turmoil. This is evident in brutal police crackdowns on the Occupy movement in the USA and preemptive strikes against demonstrators attempting to exercise rights to speech and assembly.

In this paper, I examine education accountability as a mechanism of coercive neoliberal governance. The negative effects of accountability on teaching and learn-ing, teacher morale, and teaching as a profession have been well documented (e.g. Hursh 2008; McNeil 2000; Valli and Buese 2007), as have ways in which account-ability exacerbates inequality (Gillborn and Youdell 2000; Lipman 2004; Valenzuela 2005). While education accountability continues to work discursively to shape edu-cational discourse and teacher practices and subjectivities (Ball 1994), and while the ongoing struggle for hegemony is evident in efforts to construct consent for neoliberal policies and practices, consent is in dialectical relation with coercion and resistance. A pervasive audit culture of high stakes testing, performance indictors, sanctions, and competition constitute a disciplinary system of regulation and surveil-lance (e.g. Ball 2001; Suspitsyna 2010), but that is not my focus here, although I return to it in the final section of the paper. My argument is that education account-ability in the USA also plays a central role in coercive urban governance. Specifi-cally, I argue that the state is using the crisis to accelerate the expropriation of urban public schools, forced displacement of people of color, and disenfranchise-ment of African-Americans, Latinos, and other people of color, and accountability is pivotal to this project. Systems of accountability make education legible for the market and private appropriation, mark schools and school districts as pathological and in need of authoritarian governance, and justify minimalist schools in areas of urban disposability.

My argument draws on two related theoretical frames. The first is a theory of the state that accounts for both hegemony and coercion and highlights the role of coercion in neoliberal governance. The second is the proposition that education policy and neoliberal urban regimes of capital accumulation and racial domination are co-constitutive. Neoliberal education policies contribute to, and are shaped by, neoliberal urban regimes characterized by 'accumulation by dispossession' (Harvey 2003) (expropriation of territory and resources for capital accumulation), intensified exploitation (breaking unions, contingent labor, and contracting out), and racial oppression (two-tiered provision of public services, violence, and displacement, eliminating schools as anchors in disinvested communities).

I discuss three aspects of coercive state responses to the crisis in relation to education. (1) The economic crisis and fiscal crisis of the state accelerate opportunities to cannibalize public education as a site of capital accumulation while relieving the state of responsibility for portions of urban school systems. Black and Latino urban schools and students are commodified investment opportunities through privatization and financialization of the education sector. (2) The imposition of state austerity regimes (e.g. budget cuts and teacher lay-offs) suggest that the state may be *selectively* abandoning education as a mechanism of social reproduction and legitimation in African-American communities that have become zones of state abandonment and disposability. (3) School closings in African-American and Latino communities, state takeovers of urban school districts, and disenfranchisement of parents, teachers, students, and community members constitute coercive governance through exclusion. In the final section of this paper, I briefly discuss the complexity of coercion, consent, and contestation and possibilities of an emergent counter-hegemonic movement.

My analysis is grounded in eight years of ethnographic research, collection of documentary data, and participation in education justice movements in Chicago. I also draw on data and analyses of other urban US contexts, particularly the work of Kristen Buras on New Orleans (2010) and Tom Pedroni on Detroit (2011). My data include a variety of documents and participant observations collected in public meetings of teachers, union and education activists, parents, community organizers, and youth, and in public meetings of school officials. As a participant in these events, my own experiences help to inform and shape my analysis. (Much of my participation is, however, 'off limits' as a source of data as it occurs in the spirit of education activism.) The data also include formal interviews with teachers, parents, and school staff related to high stakes accountability, school closings, and markets conducted in 2006 and in 2010 (Lipman 2011; Lipman and Person 2007). Field notes, interviews, and documentary data collected for several co-authored reports and policy briefs also inform my analysis (e.g. Fleming et al. 2009; Greenlee et al. 2008; Lipman, Smith, and Gutstein 2012). In all this research, I owe a debt to the insights and contributions of community members, teachers, activists, and parents with whom I have worked.

Hegemony and coercion

In the USA, through the decades of the 1980s and 1990s, powerful social groups constructed a hegemonic alliance around the neoliberal restructuring of public education. Apple (2006) describes this hegemonic block as suturing the interests of fractions of capital committed to neoliberal, market-based education solutions to the interests of neoconservatives, religious fundamentalists (authoritarian populists), and new managerial professionals.[1] Although there are tensions within this alliance, the general goal is to create conditions for markets, choice, standards, and discipline in schools, and to orient education toward global economic competitiveness. Systems of accountability and competition have been essential to this project – to create markets as well as to define what counts as knowledge and to discipline teachers, students, and schools (e.g. Ball 2007; Ball, Bowe, and Gewirtz 1994; Lingard 2010).

Hegemony involves persuasion and relatively legitimate forms of rule. It is achieved to the extent that a hegemonic bloc wins widespread support for its values and goals (Gramsci 1971). Education accountability and markets gained popular support, in part, because they spoke to the exclusions and lack of responsiveness of public schools organized under the Keynsian Welfare State settlement (Clarke and Newman 1997). In the USA, proponents framed top-down accountability and choice as equity (i.e. No Child Left Behind [NCLB]), and the 'good sense' in this policy resonated with some parents of color and advocacy organizations fed up with persistent inequities in education and unresponsive school bureaucracies (Pedroni 2007). Accountability measures, disaggregated by race/ethnicity and other markers of difference, promised to make visible the 'achievement gap,' end the 'soft bigotry' of low expectations for students of color and second language learners, and hold teachers' and schools' feet to the fire to 'teach all children.' Some Civil Rights advocates and African-American and Latino school district superintendents initially supported NCLB[2] (e.g. Don't turn back the clock 2003). Although there was a campaign by powerful state and corporate actors to win consent, there was also tactical agency on the part of civil rights advocates and others to use the federal accountability law to draw attention to entrenched racial disparities, particularly in the absence of a robust alternative.

Hegemony requires not only ideas but also encompasses social institutions through which it is materialized and reproduced. As accountability and markets have taken hold, they have spawned an array of self-reinforcing institutional supports. Public private partnerships, firms, consortia of investors, university departments, bodies of scholarship and scholarly journals, professional degrees, corporate philanthropic institutions, product lines, for-profit supplemental educational services, non-profit services, think tanks, and more have evolved to support, elaborate, and justify this agenda.

Yet, hegemony is never complete. Ruling classes must constantly reassert moral and intellectual leadership so that dominated or subordinate classes consent to their own domination rather than being simply forced into inferior positions. In this sense, we can delineate the ongoing construction and reconstruction of neoliberal hegemony as dominant groups rearticulate subaltern claims and critiques in order to exert leadership over how people think and act on them (Apple 2006; Swalwell and Apple 2011). For example, the assemblage of media events (such as the pro-charter, anti-union *Waiting for Superman* film and massive publicity campaign), political rhetoric (e.g. Obama's 'Educate to Innovate' agenda), systems of performance measurement (paying teachers based on 'value added'), and framing teachers as the source of education problems are all designed to recruit a wide network of parents and the broad public to support expanded education markets and attacks on teacher unions.

But coincident with the ongoing construction of hegemony, another, more brutal form of governance is at work in Chicago, Detroit, New Orleans, Philadelphia, and other cities where communities of color are being stripped of their schools and their right to participate as public actors and 'citizens.' Urban scholar, Davies' (2010, 2012) theorization of the role of coercion in neoliberal urban governance is particularly useful in understanding this. Davies' analysis derives from a 'Marxist reading' of Gramsci's concept of the state as the dialectical synthesis of coercion, consent and resistance. Davies recalls Gramsci's formulation of the 'integral state' composed of 'dictatorship + hegemony' (Gramsci 1971, 239). The Gramscian integral state is a 'strategic and coercive actor' in dialectical relationship with civil society which is understood as the terrain where political classes struggle for both hegemony and domination (Davies 2010, 2). In the dialectic of hegemony and domination, although technologies of assent are critical, coercion 'remains the indispensable condition of social order' (Gramsci 1971, 57; cited in Davies 2012, 3). Davies argues that all urban governance embodies this dialectic of coercion and consent in some form.

The weakness of the hegemonic strategy is that consent of subordinated classes and social groups depends on the state cultivating expectations for social well-being and advancement that it cannot meet. Wacquant (2001), Harvey (2005), Gill (2003), and others have argued that as the neoliberal state loses legitimacy in the face of growing inequalities, deprivation, and marginalization, the state relies more on exclusion, incarceration, surveillance, repression, hierarchical imposition of authority, symbolic violence, discipline through markets, and explicit violence to maintain the existing social order. This is evident in the astounding growth of the carceral state in the USA, the expansion of surveillance and curtailment of civil liberties, and criminalization of immigration. Hegemony is further undermined by capitalism's tendency to crisis, and particularly as mature capitalism is prone to more frequent and contagious crises of accumulation (Harvey 2010). As the current economic crisis intensifies the contradictions of neoliberalism, there is a growing tendency to coercion in urban governance.

However, the disciplinary force of the state is not applied uniformly. In the USA, it targets low-income people and neighborhoods and African-Americans and Latinos, and immigrants (Wacquant 2009). Specifically in the US context, coercive urban governance is intertwined with white supremacy. Here the development of capitalism is integrally connected with slavery, the theft of native lands, conquest of part of Mexico, decades of Jim Crow laws and racial terror, and racially structured and segregated labor markets, housing, and schools. Racial oppression and capitalist exploitation are interwoven, each producing and serving the other (Brown and Lissovoy 2011). Neoliberalism is both built on and reproduces this dynamic (Lipman 2008, 2009). In the present crisis, the logics of race and capital are co-constitutive of the expropriation of the collective assets of communities of color, their commodification and disenfranchisement. Constructing consent, when it comes to these communities, does not seem to be the primary aim.

The crisis, cities, and education

Western capitalism is experiencing its deepest structural crisis since the 1930s. After nearly four years, despite talk of recovery, unemployment remains high and the global financial system is fragile, with national debt in Greece, Spain, Portugal, and Ireland threatening major banks and holders of collateral debt obligations in a house of cards of overexposed risk. With some variation, the state's response is generally to socialize the losses of investors through bank bailouts and to attempt to impose social austerity on the general populace (Harvey 2010), as mandated by the European Union and International Monetary Fund for the Greek debt crisis. In this scenario, the working and middle classes will be expected to endure repeated reductions in wages, loss of pensions and hard-won social benefits, drastic cuts in public services such as education, and decimation of personal assets, e.g. homes and other possessions. With the state unwilling to challenge corporate wealth or recoup obvious sources of federal and local revenue (e.g. taxes on the rich and corporations, reduction of military spending, taxes on financial speculation), city governments in the USA have opted to sell off public assets and impose austerity measures on working and middle classes. Budget cuts, cutbacks in public services and increases in fees, and public worker wage and benefit concessions are the order of the day. The initial, crisis-driven round of deep cuts to primary, secondary, and tertiary education are unlikely to be the last.

People of all walks of life, many heretofore unengaged in politics, have been drawn into struggle to defend their livelihoods. At the same time, those who have been suffering all along due to disinvestment and neoliberal restructuring – particularly people of color – are facing outright destitution and civic exclusion. There is a new grammar of political opposition captured by the Occupy Wall Street movement and the metaphor of the 99% vs. the 1%. The crisis has produced a new moment – ripe with both danger and opportunity – in which coercive state strategies have come to the fore in dialectical relation to grassroots mobilization against austerity and, incipiently, against capitalism itself.

Cities, which have been targets of neoliberal experimentation and resulting economic, social, and spatial inequalities and marginalization (Brenner and Theodore 2002), are a focal point of this dialectic. As critical geographers Peck, Brenner, and Theodore (2008) summarize:

> The manifestations of destructively creative neoliberalization are evident across the urban landscape: the razing of lower income neighborhoods to make way for speculative development; the extension of market rents and housing vouchers; the increased reliance by municipalities on instruments of private finance; the privatization of schools; the administration of workfare programs; the mobilization of entrepreneurial discourses emphasizing reinvestment and rejuvenation; and so forth.

Debt financing and reliance on real estate, particularly gentrification, as a pivotal sector of neoliberal urban economies, made municipal governments particularly vulnerable to the crisis. Years of failing to pay into public pension funds and entanglement of city finance in global financial markets have caught up with city and state governments as they have lost millions of dollars in revenue and cannot meet pension and other public obligations.

Because education policies are intertwined with neoliberal urban economies, education is a key site of urban contestation (Lipman 2011). Analyses of the intersection of neoliberal strategies of capital accumulation, race, and education in New Orleans (Buras, Randels, and Salaam 2010), Chicago (Lipman 2004, 2011), and Detroit (Pedroni 2011) illustrate ways in which education policies support the disinvestment and reinvestment in the urban built environment and the displacement and exclusion of working-class and low-income people of color, particularly African-Americans. In New Orleans, Chicago, and Detroit, policies of closing schools and expanding education markets have facilitated real estate development and displacement of people of color, particularly African-Americans. Racial segregation in housing, racialized labor markets, and the state's abandonment of African-American and Latino urban areas over the past three decades made these areas ripe targets of neoliberal experimentation (Wilson 2006). In turn, privatization of education in these neighborhoods is often a leading edge, discursively and materially, of the generalized privatization of public goods and services (Lipman 2011).

The fiscal crises of state and municipal governments have given new energy to neoliberal restructuring of education. Framing the financial crisis and deeper structural crisis as a crisis of public debt opens the way to specific policies (see Clarke and Newman 2010). This framing provides the rationale for broad public austerities and attacks on public sector worker unions. In education, it provides a further warrant to close public schools, turn over locally elected school boards to mayors or appointed financial managers, and to dismantle whole school districts, as is underway in the city of Philadelphia. Charter and turnaround schools, national standards, 'value added' merit pay for teachers, and demonization of teacher unions are normalized. Leading representatives of monopoly finance, information, and retail capital (e.g. Gates, Walton, Broad, and Dell), who made billions of dollars during the boom years of the 1990s and early 2000's, have deployed their enormous wealth to steer national education in this direction (Saltman 2010). At a moment when public schools face severe budget cuts,

> In state after state, men with vast personal fortunes invest in campaigns to end teachers' tenure, end seniority (now called Last In, First Out, or LIFO), and clear the way for private takeovers of public schools, where teachers work with no job rights at all. (Ravitch 2012)

Cannibalizing public schools for profit and appropriation of Black urban space

The economic crisis and interwoven fiscal crisis of the state accelerate opportunities for capital to cannibalize public education while relieving the state of responsibility for (unwanted) portions of urban school systems. In a form of 'disaster capitalism' (Klein 2007), public education has become a highly visible site of 'accumulation by dispossession' (Harvey 2003). Systems of accountability have created conditions to turn Black and Latino schools and students into investment opportunities by commodifying and financializing the education sector.

Chicago, whose system of education accountability launched in 1997 set a national trend, led the way in using performance measures to justify and facilitate markets. Referencing students' poor performance on high stakes standardized tests, in 2004, the city's mayor and corporate elites unveiled a plan to close 60–70 public schools and open 100 new schools, two-thirds as charter schools (Lipman 2011). As of Fall 2012, in African-American and Latino communities, the Chicago Board of Education has closed, phased out, or turned around 105 schools; the Academy for Urban School Leadership, a private education management organization, operates 25 'turnaround' schools; and private operators run 87 charter schools. A proposed new charter school compact, partly funded by the Gates Foundation, will give charter school operators more access school facilities and greater public funding. Chicago's mayor, Rahm Emanuel, said he hopes charter operators from around the country will 'look at this as an opportunity to set up shop' (Harris 2011). As a whole, this represents a significant appropriation of the commons in African-American and Latino areas of the city. These politics of disposability are repeated in cities across the USA as school districts close neighborhood public schools in low-income African-American and other communities of color.

In post-Hurricane Katrina New Orleans, the logics of white supremacy and capital accumulation meshed in the forcible dispossession of that city's African-American population of their homes, land, cultural institutions, and schools. For decades, city government had systematically disinvested in African-American areas of New Orleans and their schools. The performance of the city's students on state accountability measures was then used to blame students and teachers and the teachers union. This was the run-up to post-Hurricane Katrina. Capitalizing on the devastation of the storm and the forced exodus of much of New Orleans' working-class Black population, neoliberal think tanks, charter school operators, real estate investors, and those who wanted to 'revitalize' the city as a space of whiteness, pounced on the disaster as a 'golden opportunity' to 'Bring New Orleans Back,' minus its working-class African-Americans (Buras, Randels, and Salaam 2010). Dismantling and privatizing the school district was a crucial component. In the words of Lipsitz (2006), the aftermath of the hurricane ushered in an orgy of 'legalized looting to enable corporations to profit from the misfortunes of poor people' (452).

In 2008, when Arne Duncan was confirmed as US Secretary of Education, the first thing he did was fly to Detroit to tell that cash-strapped Black city[3] and struggling school system that the federal government was there to help – but only if they would do things very differently. They must follow the Chicago model: close 'failing' schools and expand privately run contracted-out charter schools or turnaround schools, disband the elected Board of Education, impose mayoral control of the school district, and run the schools like businesses. Playing to state and city revenue shortfalls, in 2008 the Obama administration's $4.35 billion federal competition for education funds (Race to the Top) made this mandate national. What followed was mass divestment and privatization of Detroit's public schools that is ongoing.

In the USA alone, elementary and secondary education is a $650 billion dollar industry, and higher education puts the education sector well over a trillion dollars. As charter schools have evolved into corporate enterprises, there is money to be made in managing them, selling them buildings and learning materials, and speculating on their growth. In a production chain that begins with a system of accountability and sanctions and ends with school closings and charter school openings, low-income children of color are the central commodity. In New York, as in Chicago, charter school expansion is accompanied by public school closings and co-location of charters in existing public schools, often with charters cannibalizing the school's best facilities and resources. Hedge funds are at the 'epicenter' of the New York charter school movement (Hass 2009). They are major financers of charter schools across the city and dominate their boards and the organizations that support charter schools. As Miner (2010) reports:

> given that most hedge funds operate on what is known as a 2–20 fee structure (a 2 percent management fee and a 20 percent take of any profits), some lucky hedge fund will make millions of dollars off of Harlem Children's Zone [charter schools] in any given year.

In addition to management fees garnered by for-profit education management organizations, charter schools can generate huge returns on investment. The New Markets Tax Credit, passed by Congress in 2000, gives a huge federal tax credit to banks and equity funds that invest in community projects in underserved communities. Investors are using the tax credit heavily to build charter schools and since this is a tax credit on money that they are lending, they are also collecting interest on the loans (Gonzalez 2010). Juan Gonzalez explains how this case of rapacious capitalism works:

> Under the New Markets program, a bank or private equity firm that lends money to a nonprofit to build a charter school can receive a 39% federal tax credit over seven years. The credit can even be piggybacked on other tax breaks for historic preservation or job creation. By combining the various credits with the interest from the loan itself, a lender can almost double his investment over the seven-year period. No wonder JPMorgan Chase announced this week it was creating a new $325 million pool to invest in charter schools and take advantage of the New Markets Tax Credit.

In the effort to construct consent for this policy, state abandonment is framed as public sector failure. The challenges of poverty, urban disinvestment, minimalized curricula, and racism register as low performance on the matrix of performance indicators. Yet parents and teachers in Chicago claim that the state produces school 'failure' as schools are stripped of resources and staff (Brown, Gutstein, and Lipman 2009; Lipman and Person 2007; Lipman, Smith, and Gutstein 2012). Once closed schools are designated for conversion to charters or turnarounds and are awarded millions of new dollars in renovations and additional staff. Over $25 million for capital improvements has been earmarked for the six schools that Chicago Public Schools (CPS) will turn over to Academy for Urban School Leadership in Fall 2012. CPS's $660 million capital budget plan for 2012 allocates almost $125 million – about one-fifth of the entire budget – to 11 schools that the district targeted to be turned around or closed and reopened by another operator (Vivea 2011).[4] In November 2010, the UNO charter school operation, led by then-Mayor Daley's chief Latino political ally, was awarded $98 million by the State of Illinois at the very time when public schools were facing cuts. UNO specializes in charter schools in Latino communities.

Especially in African-American communities that have faced the expropriation of their living space as the state has dismantled and marketized public housing and as their neighborhoods have been gentrified, education privatization is experienced as another means of seizing and commodifying Black urban space (Lipman 2011). Closing or turning around schools that are anchors in communities, further destabilizes the communities and accelerates the dislocation of African-American and Latino residents who live there. Having disinvested in these areas in the run up to the recession, capital is taking advantage of the crisis to mop up schools in communities of color just as they are mopping up foreclosed homes. 'Failing' schools are yet another form of 'distressed property' to be cannibalized for investor portfolios.

Austerity and selective abandonment of social reproduction and legitimation

Education is at the center of the 'shock doctrine' (Klein 2007) response to economic crisis. Cuts to education budgets and attacks on teacher unions are a focal point of the state's attempt to break public sector unions in general and impose severe cuts to public goods and social welfare. But schools that are most dominated by punitive accountability measures and least resourced are more deeply affected by budget cuts, teacher lay-offs, and program reductions. After 17 years of accountability mandates and threats of being closed or turned around, many Chicago public schools serving low-income African-American and other students of color are minimalist, test-prep schools, stripped of the courses and programs that constitute what has defined even a mediocre public school in the USA. Built on an historically unequal and racially segregated public school system, accountability, markets, and inequitable investment have produced what Chicago Teachers' Union President, Karen Lewis, calls an 'apartheid school system' with elite selective enrollment and well-resourced public schools in more affluent and white areas and disinvested schools concentrated in African-American and Latino neighborhoods. (Chicago public school student population is 92% of color and 86% low income.) Many elementary school students have limited access to physical education, arts, library/media instruction, science laboratories, computer science, and world language classes. In 2011, 160 of Chicago's public elementary schools did not have libraries. Only 25% of neighborhood elementary schools had both art and music teachers; 40 schools had neither and most schools are forced to choose between the two (Chicago Teachers Union 2012). Some schools do not have a full set of textbooks for each student. They lack nurses, counselors, and support staff. The economic crisis has given added impetus to, and the trope of budget deficits justifies, further disinvestment in public schools in low-income African-American communities in particular. In December 2011, the school district's Chief Operating Officer announced that the district did not intend to invest in schools that would be closed in the next 5–10 years (Ahmed-Ullah 2011).

On the other hand, there is an abundance of test preparation materials and related teacher professional development activities. As these schools are further diminished, those that are not handed over to private operators are reduced to militarized spaces of containment. The crisis is accelerating a process of sloughing off the social reproduction and legitimation function of schools in (disposable) African-American (and some Latino) communities. Charter schools and minimalist public schools in areas that are largely abandoned by the state and excluded from the life of the city reflect the further decline of the public as an avenue of opportunity or even safety in the crisis ridden, post-Keynesian welfare state (Meiners and Quinn 2011) and a shift from hegemony to governance by exclusion.

Undermining teaching as a profession and breaking teacher seniority will certainly ensure the acceleration of teacher turnover in the least resourced and most test-driven schools. A revolving door of short-term, untrained novices supplied by privately run 'alternative certification' operations will constitute the staffs of the most desperate schools or schooling will be outsourced to private providers of online learning or learning modules synched to high stakes tests. Ravitch (2012) sums up this direction:

> Teaching will become a job, not a profession. Young people will typically spend a year or two as teachers, then move on to other, more rewarding careers. Federal and state policy will promote online learning, and computers will replace teachers. Online class sizes will reach 1:100, even 1:200; the job of monitoring the screens will be outsourced, creating large economies for state budgets. For-profit companies will make large profits.

This scenario is classed and raced. While austerity measures are implemented across the board, public schools in more affluent and white areas continue to legitimate the narrative of opportunity (often with supplementary parent funding) while restricted education schools are characterized by exclusion from the historic opportunity structures that legitimated the social order. Racialized 'societal fascism' – exclusion of segments of the population from any social contract (Santos 2002) – is intensifying in a state-organized survival of the fittest. In descent into barbarism, some people (e.g. African-Americans, homeless people, some immigrants) are simply deemed disposable in a nation of high unemployment, intensified austerity, and competition for scarce resources.

Disenfranchising African-Americans: governance by exclusion

State takeovers of predominantly African-American and Latino school districts and whole cities, elimination of their elected governing bodies, and disregard for the voices of those affected exemplify coercive urban governance by political exclusion. The dismantling of the predominantly African-American New Orleans public schools and imposition of a state-run recovery district is the well-known model for this strategy. As in other cities, the state accountability system was the legitimating mechanism. Citing the city's low scores on state assessments, the state fired all 4500 public school teachers, broke the city's powerful Black-led teachers union, and dismantled the school system's administrative infrastructure (Dingerson 2008; Saltman 2007). 'Forceful explusion' of African-Americans from the city, in part, by seizing their schools (Buras, Randels, and Salaam 2010) can hardly be called hegemony through persuasion and legitimacy.

Similarly, Detroit's corporate and financial leaders are seizing on decades of disinvestment and economic decline to reshape the city for a new round of capital accumulation (Pedroni 2011) with school closings as a principle lever. Having disinvested in the city's economy for decades, in partnership with city and state officials, corporate elites see the crisis an opportunity to restructure Detroit as a global niche city, minus the economically impoverished African-Americans who along with other workers were the source of Detroit's wealth in the industrial era. The plan is to 'clear cut' disinvested Black neighborhoods and open up the land for new investment. Detroit's population is 82% African-American, and the city has the highest rate of Black home ownership in the US. School accountability is a lever to close schools, eliminating a critical anchor in distressed communities and forcing out African-American home owners. (See Pedroni 2011 for a full analysis.)

The state is facilitating this agenda by disenfranchising the city's majority Black residents. Pointing to Detroit's budget deficit, eroded tax base, fiscal 'mismanagement,' and low performance on state tests as basis, in 2009 the Michigan governor appointed an Emergency Financial Manager to oversee the school district's finances. In 2011, the Governor appointed an Emergency Manager, a former General Motors executive, to run the school system, eliminating the authority of the city's elected school board. The Emergency's Manager's agenda is to close public schools and convert others to charter schools. In the last five years, 125 public schools have been closed. By the end of the 2011–2012 school year, Detroit Public Schools will no longer operate a single neighborhood public high school. Public high schools are either selective enrollment or are part of the new State-run 'recovery district' à la New Orleans.

In April 2011, the mayor announced plans to 'downsize Detroit' by pushing out African-American residents of disinvested areas through cutting utilities, removing city roads, and reducing public services (garbage removal and street lights) (MacDonald 2011). In spring 2012, the Detroit City Council voted to accept a State-appointed financial advisory board to oversee the city's finances in order to avert a takeover by an appointed emergency manager. Disenfranchisement of Detroit's Black residents mirrors similar moves in other majority African-American cities in the State of Michigan where Detroit is located. Emergency Managers have absolute authority to unincorporate the city, sell its assets, remove its elected leaders, privatize or eliminate services, and break union contracts. Schools are central to contestation of this project. Pedroni (2011, 213) writes:

> Within this struggle over for whom the city exists, schools in Detroit play a vital role in maintaining or relinquishing one's stake in the city, which is why they are central to both the fostering of and resistance to neoliberal urbanism.

The Chicago Board of Education has closed 105 public schools in African-American and Latino working-class low-income communities since 2001, while it has expanded its 'portfolio' of charter and selective enrollment schools requiring admission tests.[5] Citing poor performance on school accountability measures, the Board has closed 80% of the schools in the historic African-American South Side Bronzeville community. These decisions are made by the mayor and his appointed school board composed of CEOs in finance, real estate, and transnational corporations, winning them the informal title of '1%ers' (the one percent wealthiest people in the USA)[6]. Their decisions are made behind closed doors, without genuine public participation. Public hearings prior to the decision have become notorious for their mockery of democracy as each member of the public is limited to two minutes to speak, evidence presented by teachers and parents is not considered, and no one in power is present. In 2012, when school communities in Chicago offered plans to transform schools threatened to be closed, the Board refused to acknowledge them. Rallies, marches, pickets, petitions, candlelight vigils, and more have spared only a handful of schools. As in Detroit and New Orleans, this is external rule with no pretense of 'citizenship' or democratic participation. Mayoral takeover of elected governance bodies, overt decision-making by financial and corporate elites, and enforced school closings continue the erosion of democratic participation instituted through the disciplinary power of top-down accountability systems, particularly affecting schools in low-income communities of color in the USA (Lipman 2004). This is perhaps why the theme of self-determination resonates in struggles to defend neighborhood public schools in Chicago.

Regimes of accountability certify the failure of schools and, by implication, the communities of which they are a part, legitimating their disenfranchisement. But this legitimation strategy has little salience for those who have seen their schools closed and neighborhoods destabilized. Residents of Chicago's, New Orleans,' and Detroit's African-American and Latino communities do not need to be told about the connection between school closings and the neoliberal restructuring of their cities. It is apparent that city plans do not include them and that closing and privatizing neighborhood schools facilitates their exclusion. They are largely disposable, and it is not necessary to obtain their consent except to the extent that their resistance necessitates concessions. This is neoliberal urban governance by exclusion, a 'form of economic, spatial and symbolic violence against the poor where hegemonic actors do not see the potential, need or possibility of organizing a more inclusionary enrolment strategy' (Davies 2010, 25).

Concluding thoughts: contestations, complexities, and possibilities

Among those directly affected, there is little consent for the punitive policies I have described, and their resistance has been fierce. More broadly, despite a richly financed and visible pro-charter, anti-teacher union campaign and the normalization of systems of accountability, the lived experience of neoliberal education policy is eroding its legitimacy. Despite the authority of numbers and metrics, the luster has worn off high stakes testing as a decade of its reductive and punitive effects have degraded teaching and learning and curriculum.[7] Accountability regimes are beginning to be the disparaged status quo with opposition to high stakes testing and corporate managerialism extending to white middle and working-class parents. Austerity measures, attacks on teaching and teacher unions, and other corporate policies are beginning to be felt across lines of class and race, setting off a backlash. Coalitions of teachers and parents, student walkouts, protests of all sorts, teacher activist organizations, and democratic stirrings in teacher unions have become a feature of US urban school districts in turmoil – so much so that corporate philanthropies are focusing on parent organizing as a counter-strategy.

In February 2012, Chicago's mayor and Board of Education high-handedly closed 19 schools and turned over six of them to private operators who received an infusion of public funds. The Board ignored protests, marches, petitions, sit-ins, and a winter sleep-out on the sidewalk in front of the Board of Education by mainly African-American and Latino parents, students, and community members. This was the culmination of eight years of ignoring pleas and demands against school closings. Meanwhile, the Board's disconnection from the educational concerns of parents and teachers has also begun to affect middle-class and white working-class schools, and the parents have mobilized and connected with organizations of people of color. The election in June 2010 of progressive leadership of the 30,000-member Chicago Teachers Union[8] has tipped the balance of social forces. A new city-wide, multi-racial, multi-class alliance of parents, community groups, and the union is emerging.

The present social conjuncture is highly volatile, marked by economic and political crisis, repression, upward redistribution, and social struggles and contestations. In the face of economic crisis, the state has fewer resources to maintain inclusive forms of urban governance associated with hegemony. Its repertoire of strategies is more limited, exposing the nexus of race and capital at its core. The combination of treating whole groups of people as disposable and the generalized failure to meet expectations undermines hegemony. Although just beginning, this is a pivotal opportunity for the formation of a counter-hegemonic education alliance. However, corporate philanthropies and heavily funded corporate school 'reform' groups are deploying massive symbolic and material resources to promote and accelerate their agenda and undermine growing opposition.[9] Internally, a counter-hegemonic alliance is complicated not only by entrenched race and class privileges of some, but also by ways in which the disciplinary power of accountability shapes resistance.

Public hearings on school closings in Chicago exemplify the persistent discursive power of testing and performance metrics to define the parameters of legitimate opposition. The hearings begin with an extensive power point presentation by a school district technocrat, meant to demonstrate in detail the school's failure to meet accountability targets. In a display of accountability metrics as a mode of regulation, the presentation's graphs, charts, and statistics reveal the school's (inferior) ranking on a matrix of performance indicators that have been defined as the 'field of judgment' (Ball 2001). This is followed by often-emotional testimonies by students, teachers, and parents proceeding from a different field of judgment. They speak of the importance of the school to the community, the human relationships it embodies, its enriching programs and dedicated teachers, its commitment to the children, their languages, cultures, and so on and the injustice of a history of inadequate resources. But there is more. They also dispute the school's performance ranking, contend 'scores are going up' or are 'better' than neighboring schools, and offer plans on how they will improve them. While they stand on ground distinct from neoliberal accountability, they also reaffirm the legitimacy of its measures, comparisons, and judgments to define the value of a school and the people who are part of it. Their testimonies are evidence of the persistent strength of accountability discourses to define teaching and learning and to discipline subjectivities and limit the terms of engagement even as resistance is growing. While accountability is contested, high stakes testing nonetheless continues to work as a discourse of containment.

The dialectic of consent, coercion, and resistance is playing out in complex ways. This is a moment of extreme tensions and contradictions. Clarke and Newman (2010, 714) note:

> Invention, innovation and revitalization of older ways of thinking and doing have been taking place around us. It is precisely the compressed co-existence of dominant, residual and emergent formations that creates the conjuncture – and the struggles among them that shape the lines of potential future development.

This is just such a moment in education in the USA. Crises tend to increase the gap between what capitalism promises and what it can deliver, leaving the state with less room to maneuver, undermining hegemony and sharpening social contradictions. Crises create new conditions for resistance, new alliances, and possibilities for coalescence around a new social vision – even as they create the impetus for an accelerated assault on public education and low-income communities of color. Breaking with the framework of accountability and testing will be critical to counter the politics of consent *and* coercion with a counter-hegemonic movement and a revitalized liberatory discourse and program.

Notes

1. Apple (2006) elaborates the interests of other social sectors: neoconservatives want a return to higher standards and a 'common' (patriarchal, Eurocentric) culture; 'authoritarian populist' religious fundamentalists are concerned about the erosion of Christian values and traditions; and a fraction of the new professional middle class benefits materially from the application of managerial strategies to the public sector (testing, business management of schools, and performance indicators).
2. The NCLB, a reauthorization of the federal Elementary and Secondary Education Act passed in 2002, mandated a system of performance indicators (disaggregated by race, English language status, socioeconomic status, and students designated for special education services), benchmarks, and sanctions.
3. Detroit's population is 82% African-American.
4. Tim Cawley, the Chief Operating Officer, is former Managing Director and Chief Finance Officer of the Academy of Urban School Leadership, the turnaround organization that would get six of the schools.
5. There are currently 675 Chicago public schools. Since 2004, the number has increased from about 500 as public schools have been closed and the students divided among smaller charter and selective schools.
6. The current seven-member Board is chaired by the CEO of the Chicago Board of Trade, a global finance institution, and five of the other six members are CEOs and leaders of major transnational corporate, financial, real estate, and marketing firms.
7. For example, more than 400 school districts in Texas, the state that pioneered high stakes accountability under then-Governor George Bush, signed a resolution to take a stand against the current testing (Cargile 2012).
8. The union's education program is a counter to accountability and corporate, market-driven policies (Chicago Teachers Union 2012).
9. For example, Stand for Children, a corporate-funded education 'reform' organization, has spent millions of dollars lobbying for anti-teacher union legislation.

References

Ahmed-Ullah, N.S. 2011, December 15. CPS: Poorer-performing schools less likely to get funds. *Chicago Tribune*. http://articles.chicagotribune.com/2011-12-15/news/ct-met-cps-buildings-20111215_1_urban-schoolleadership-cps-operating-officer-tim-cawley.

Apple, M.W. 2006. *Educating the 'right' way: Markets, standards, God, and inequality*. 2nd ed., New York, NY: Routledge Falmer.

Ball, S.J. 1994. *Education reform: A critical and poststructural approach*. Buckingham: Open University Press.

Ball, S.J. 2001. Performativites and fabrications in the education economy. In *The performing school: Managing, teaching and learning in a performance culture*, ed. D. Gleason and C. Husbands, 210–26. London: RoutledgeFalmer.

Ball, S.J. 2007. *Education plc: Understanding private sector participation in public sector education*. London: Routledge.

Ball, S., R. Bowe, and S. Gewirtz. 1994. Market forces and parental choice. In *Educational reform and its consequences*, ed. S. Tomlinson. London: IPPR/Rivers Oram Press.

Brenner, N., and N. Theodore. 2002. Cities and the geographies of 'actually existing neoliberalism'. In *Spaces of neoliberalism: Urban restructuring in North America and Western Europe*, ed. N. Brenner and N. Theodore, 2–32. Oxford: Blackwell.

Brown, A.L., E. Gutstein, and P. Lipman. 2009. The Chicago success story: Myth or reality? *Rethinking Schools* 23, no. 3: 10–4.

Brown, A.L., and N. Lissovoy. 2011. Economies of racism: Grounding education policy research in the complex dialectic of race, class, and capital. *Journal of Education Policy* 26, no. 5: 595–619.

Buras, K.L., J. Randels, K.A. Salaam, and Students at the Center, eds. 2010. *Pedagogy, policy, and the privatized city: Stories of dispossession and defiance*. New York, NY: Teachers College Press.

Cargile, E. 2012. Educators, parents fight testing system. KXAN. http://www.kxan.com/dpp/news/local/austin/educators-parents-fight-testing-system.

Chicago Teachers Union. 2012. The schools Chicago students deserve. http://www.ctunet.com/.

Clarke, J., and J. Newman. 1997. *The managerial state*. London: Sage.

Clarke, J., and J. Newman. 2010. Summoning specters: Crises and their construction. *Journal of Educational Policy* 25, no. 6: 709–15.

Davies, J. 2010. Neoliberalism, governance and the integral state. Paper presented at Critical Governance Conference, University of Warwick, December 13–14. http://www2.warwick.ac.uk/fac/soc/wbs/projects/orthodoxies/papers/.

Davies, J. 2012. Network governance theory: A gramscian critique. *Environment and Planning A*. 44: 2687–704.

Dingerson, L. 2008, August 26. New Orleans schools 3 years later. Center for community change. http://www.communitychange.org/our-projects.

Don't turn back the clock. 2003, November 18. Press release. *The Education Trust*. http://www.edtrust.org/dc/press-room/press-release/don%E2%80%99t-turn-back-the-clock%E2%80%9D-over-100-african-american-and-latino-superint.

Fleming, J., A. Greenlee, E. Gutstein, P. Lipman, and J. Smith. 2009, February. Research paper series, paper #2: Examining CPS' plan to close, consolidate, turn-around 2 schools. Data and Democracy Project: Investing in Neighborhoods. Collaborative for Equity and Justice in Education and Nathalie P. Voorhees Center for Neighborhood and Community Improvement, University of Illinois-Chicago.

Gill, S. 2003. *Power and resistance in the new world order*. New York, NY: Palgrave Macmillan.

Gillborn, D., and D. Youdell. 2000. *Rationing education: Policy, practice, reform, and equity*. Buckingham: Open University Press.

Gonzalez, J. 2010, May 7. Albany charter cash cow: Big banks making a bundle on new construction as schools bear the cost. *New York Daily News.* http://articles.nydailynews.com/2010–05-07/local/29438011_1_charter-law-albany-charter-state-aid.

Gramsci, A. 1971. *Selections from prison notebooks.* Trans. and ed. Q. Hoare and G. Nowell-Smith. London: Lawrence & Wishart.

Greenlee, A., N. Hudspeth, P. Lipman, D.A. Smith, and J. Smith. 2008. Research paper series, paper #1: Examining CPS' plan to close, consolidate, turn-around 18 schools. Data and Democracy Project: Investing in Neighborhoods. Collaborative for Equity and Justice in Education and Nathalie P. Voorhees Center for Neighborhood and Community Improvement, University of Illinois-Chicago.

Harris, R. 2011, December 6. Charter compact could bring new operators to Chicago. *Catalyst.* http://www.catalyst-chicago.org/notebook/2011/12/06/19689/charter-compact-could-bring-new-operators-chicago.

Harvey, D. 2003. *The new imperialism.* Oxford: Oxford University Press.

Harvey, D. 2005. *A brief history of neoliberalism.* Oxford: Oxford University Press.

Harvey, D. 2010. *The enigma of capital and the crises of capitalism.* London: Profile Books.

Hass, N. 2009, December 4. Scholarly investments. *New York Times.* http://www.nytimes.com/2009/12/06/fashion/06charter.html?dbk.

Hursh, D. 2008. *High-stakes testing and the decline of teaching and learning.* Lanham, MD: Rowman & Littlefield.

Klein, N. 2007. *The shock doctrine.* New York, NY: Picador.

Lingard, B. 2010. Policy borrowing, policy learning: Testing times in Australian schooling. *Critical Studies in Education* 51, no. 2: 129–47.

Lipman, P. 2004. *High stakes education: Inequality, globalization, and urban school reform.* New York, NY: Routledge.

Lipman, P. 2008. Mixed-income schools and housing: Advancing the neoliberal urban agenda. *Journal of Education Policy* 23, no. 2: 119–34.

Lipman, P. 2009. The cultural politics of mixed income schools and housing: A racialized discourse of displacement, exclusion, and control. *Anthropology & Education Quarterly* 40, no. 3: 215–36.

Lipman, P. 2011. *The new political economy of urban education: Neoliberalism, race, and the right to the city.* New York, NY: Routledge.

Lipman, P., A. Person, and Kenwood Oakland Community Organization (KOCO). 2007. *Students as collateral damage? A preliminary study of Renaissance 2010 closings in the Midsouth.* Chicago, IL: KOCO.

Lipman, P., J. Smith, and E. Gutstein. 2012. Data and democracy project: Investing in neighborhoods research paper series, paper #3. Examining CPS' plan to close, turn-around, or phase out 17 schools.

Lipsitz, G. 2006. Learning from New Orleans: The social warrant of hostile privatism and competitive consumer citizenship. *Cultural Anthropology* 21, no. 3: 451–68.

MacDonald, C. 2011, April 6. Downsizing Detroit could mean cuts to utilities and trash, removing roads. *Detroit News.* http://detnews.com/article/20110406/METRO01/104060371&t.

McNeil, L.M. 2000. *Contradictions of school reform: Educational costs of standardized testing.* New York, NY: Routledge.

Meiners, E.R., and T. Quinn. 2011. Militarism and education normal. *Monthly Review* 63, no. 3: 77–86.

Miner, B. 2010, October 20. Ultimate superpower: Supersized dollars drive 'Waiting for Superman' agenda. Not Waiting for Superman blog. http://www.notwaitingforsuperman.org/Articles/20101020-MinerUltimateSuperpower.

Peck, J., N. Brenner, and N. Theodore. 2008. City as lab. AREA Chicago, Art/Research/Education/Activism, #6 (June 7). http://www.areachicago.org/p/issues/city-as-lab/city-policy-lab/.

Pedroni, T.C. 2007. *Market movements: African American involvement in school voucher reform.* New York, NY: Routledge.

Pedroni, T. 2011. Urban shrinkage as a performance of whiteness: Neoliberal urban restructuring, education, and racial containment in the post-industrial, global niche city. *Discourse: Studies in the Cultural Politics of Education* 32, no. 2: 203–16.

Ravitch, D. 2012, March 27. The pattern on the rug. Bridging differences blog. *Education Week*. http://blogs.edweek.org/edweek/Bridging-Differences/.

Saltman, K.J. 2007. *Captializing on disaster: Taking and breaking public schools*. Boulder, CO: Paradigm.

Saltman, K.J. 2010. *The gift of education: Public education and venture philanthropy*. London: Palgrave.

Santos, B.S. 2002. Cultural and post-colonial critiques in LatCrit thoery: Nuestra America: Reinventing a subaltern paradigm of recognition and redistribution. *Rutgers Law Review* 54: 1049–86.

Suspitsyna, T. 2010. Accountability in American education as a rhetoric and technology of governmentality. *Journal of Education Policy* 25, no. 5: 567–86.

Swalwell, K., and M. Apple. 2011. Starting the wrong conversations: The public school crisis and 'Waiting for Superman'. *Educational Policy* 25, no. 2: 368–82.

Valenzuela, A. ed. 2005. *Leaving children behind*. Albany, NY: State University of New York Press.

Valli, L., and D. Buese. 2007. The changing roles of teachers in an era of high-stakes accountability. *American Educational Research Journal* 44, no. 3: 519–58.

Vivea, R. 2011, December 15. CPS lays out spending projects. *Chicago News Cooperative*. http://www.chicagonewscoop.org/cps-capital-budget-allocates-125m-to-overhaul-schools/.

Wacquant, L. 2001. The penalization of poverty and the rise of neo-liberalism. *European Journal of Criminal Policy and Research* 9, no. 4: 401–12.

Wacquant, L. 2009. *Punishing the poor: The neoliberal government of social insecurity*. Durham, NC: Duke University Press.

Wilson, D. 2006. *Cities and race. America's new black ghetto*. London: Routledge.

Raising the stakes: high-stakes testing and the attack on public education in New York

David Hursh

Warner Graduate School of Education and Human Development, University of Rochester, New York, NY, USA

Over the last almost two decades, high-stakes testing has become increasingly central to New York's schools. In the 1990s, the State Department of Education began requiring that secondary students pass five standardized exams to graduate. In 2002, the federal No Child Left Behind Act required students in grades three through eight to take math and language arts tests. Results from the state and federal tests are not only used to assess students but also to evaluate schools, with poorly performing schools facing overhaul and potentially privatization. Most recently, President Obama's *Race to the Top* competition requires evaluating teachers based on their students' test scores which, because of the way in which New York has constructed the grading curve, most teachers will be rated as 'ineffective.' Standardized testing, along with other neoliberal reforms such as granting the mayor of New York City control of the public schools, has been promoted as providing more objective assessments and increasing educational efficiency. However, I will suggest that high-stakes testing has come about as part of a larger neoliberal agenda to disparage public institutions and educators to justify reducing public expenditures and privatizing schools. Further, a brief review of testing and other policies indicates that they are neither objective nor efficient.

Introduction

Beginning in the 1980s, several states in the USA, most notably Texas (Haney 2000) and Florida (Amrein and Berliner 2002), began to administer to students not just standardized tests but high-stakes tests, tests that could prevent students, no matter how well they performed in their courses, from graduating from secondary school or advancing to a higher grade in primary school. In the 1990s, New York State similarly moved to high-stakes testing, as the New York State Board of Regents and the Commissioner of Education began the process of making graduation from secondary school contingent on passing five statewide standardized exams, one each in English, science, math, global studies and United States history.

I have described the rationale and initial consequences of these policies in previous publications (Hursh 2005, 2007, 2008; Hursh and Martina 2003). Here, I want to describe the further evolution of those education policies, in which students' scores on standardized tests are used to justify policy changes and to evaluate teachers and schools. For example, New York, as required to receive federal funding under President Obama's *Race to the Top* (RTTT) initiative, has begun using students' scores on standardized tests as the *primary* criteria in evaluating teachers. Students' test scores will be used to decide whether teachers will be rated highly effective, effective, developing, or ineffective, and those rated ineffective or developing will be required to receive additional professional development. In New York City, if a teacher receives a low rating for two consecutive years – a likely classification given the grading curve – schools can begin the process of terminating them (New York State Department of Education 2011b, 2012a; Ravitch 2012a). Standardized tests have become central to all aspects of education.

The rise of neoliberal policies

However, it is not enough to describe the events of the past decades; we also need to explain them. In doing so, I will situate high-stakes testing within the rise of neoliberal policies in the USA. Neoliberals advance a particular vision of society that promotes reducing the size of government by replacing governmental organizations with private corporations, establishing markets as the model for all economic and social transactions, and creating the entrepreneurial individual who only relies on her or himself rather than society (Olssen, Codd, and O'Neill 2004; Peters 1994). In education, neoliberal policies have focused on expanding high-stakes testing, as reflected in both state and federal policies such as *No Child Left Behind* (NCLB) and RTTT, increasing school privatization and school choice and competition. These educational reforms aim to transform education from a publicly to privately provided good.

Furthermore, by portraying teachers and schools as failing, neoliberals shift the blame for the nation's stagnant incomes and growing economic inequality away from their own policies and onto schools. We overlook that the real median earnings of full-time male workers have fallen since their peak in 1973 (Sachs 2011). Inequality has increased as incomes have risen for those with a bachelor's degree or higher and fallen for those with an associate's degree or less. Economic mobility in the USA has diminished and now lags behind almost all other developed countries (The Pew Charitable Trusts 2011).

The widening economic gap is paralleled by a widening achievement gap between our wealthiest and poorest students (Tavernise 2012). Similarly, schools in the USA have grown more spatially and economically segregated with most urban school districts overwhelmingly composed of students living in poverty and of color[1] (Kozol 2005). However, the relentless focus on test scores over the last several decades suppresses analysis and debate of economic, social, and educational policies.

Moreover, neoliberal reforms have transferred the control of schools away from the local school boards, where control has resided since the founding of public schools, to the state and federal levels, which create policies about which communities have little input but are mandated to implement (Winerip 2012). States and the federal government have managed to gain control in part by adopting a discourse of civil rights and equity, and by not imposing specific curricula on schools but, instead, leaving it to the local school districts to implement curricular policies to achieve the test score goals, what Ball (1994) describes as 'steering from a distance'

(54). For example, NCLB requires states to implement standardized testing in Reading/Language Arts and Math for grades three through eight, but left it to the states to develop and score the exams and to implement the federally required remedies, which may include converting publically funded schools into privately administered charter schools.

Similarly, 46 states and the District of Columbia (US Department of Education 2010) submitted applications for Obama's RTTT competition. Most states did so in part because they face significant declines in state and federal revenues during the current economic recession (Krugman 2012) and looked to RTTT to make up some of the shortfall.

Nineteen of the applicants, whose proposals most closely matched the Federal Department of Education's requirements, won funding. Those requirements included: (1) developing a teacher evaluation system based on student scores on standardized tests that measure 'value added,'[2] (2) significantly increasing the number of charter schools permitted in the state, if not remove the cap altogether, and (3) supporting mayoral control.

However, the federal government leaves it to the states to design and carry out, within narrow guidelines, the components of RTTT. The first requirement regarding teacher assessment is not minor. First, states must develop and administer standardized tests in every class, for every subject, including art, music, and physical education, and every grade, primary through secondary education, and use the test results as the primary criteria to rank teachers on a bell curve. The test results are to be used to determine teachers' salaries, whether they need additional professional development, and are to be tenured. In New York City, where individual teachers' ratings have been made public, if a teacher is scored as *developing or ineffective* for two consecutive years (which, because of the bell curve and scoring rubric is a likely outcome for two-thirds of the teachers), the district can begin the process of firing the teacher. Second, school districts will need to develop teacher and principal observation assessments, instruct administrators and, in some districts, teachers in how to use them, and then provide time for the assessments to be carried out. In most school districts, administrators are already overworked and have little time to take on these additional evaluation responsibilities.

Furthermore, the amounts school districts receive to implement RTTT's goals are much less than it seems. The New York State Department of Education received $700 million over four years, half of which is to be dispersed to local schools to develop and implement assessments in every subject and grade and to evaluate teachers and principals through, at minimum, two observations per year. However, dividing that sum between the state's 697 school districts over four years (with most going to the urban districts) results in the average suburban district in Monroe County, where Rochester is located, receiving $127,000 over four years (or just over $32,000 per year). Or, dividing the amount given to New York State intended for local districts by the number of students in the state, each district will receive $33.50 per student per year (Siegle 2012).

Lastly, handing over the implementation of policies to lower levels of governance makes it possible for the state and federal governments to take credit for whatever improvements result from their policies, improvements, as I will show, that are often deceptive. Conversely, whenever their policies produce negative results, they can blame someone else, usually teachers. Teachers have suffered the brunt of the blame since the publication of a Nation at Risk (1983), almost 30 years ago. Consequently, the negative portrayal of public school teachers in the USA has demoralized many educators (MetLife 2012).

The shift in policy-making from the local to the state and federal levels marks a significant change from the historical norm. For most of the history of public education in the USA, funding and school governance were located at the local level. Almost all schools in the USA are located in school districts that coincide with the geographic boundary of the village or city and are governed by an elected school board. The federal government has always played an even smaller role than either local or state governments, in large part because the US Constitution is silent on education and, therefore, reserves education to the states.

The escalating role of the federal government and New York State

However, over the last century, the federal and state governments have enlarged both their policy role and funding responsibilities. The federal government has sometimes done so to rectify unequal treatment of students, such as students with disabilities (Public Law 94-142 or the Education for All Handicapped Children Act, 1973; P.L. 101-476, 1990 or the Individuals with Disabilities Education Act) or unequal school funding at the local level. Over the last century, both states and the federal government have attempted to partially remedy the vast differences in school funding caused by differences in communities' tax base.

But, it is through implementing high-stakes standardized testing that first state governments, and then the federal government, significantly impacted primary and secondary education. In New York, students, for decades, had the choice to enroll in either the more stringent Regents courses that concluded with a statewide-standardized test that typically counted for a small portion of the course grade, or the locally developed courses that concluded with tests created by the local school districts. Students who passed a sufficient number of Regents courses were granted a Regents diploma.

But in 1994, New York State began eliminating the local option and by requiring that students pass five standardized exams to graduate, regardless of how well they performed in their classes, the exams thus became high-stakes. As a result, schools districts had little choice but to prepare their students for the tests. The Commissioner of Education and the Regents could claim that they were not telling states what to teach, but, indeed, for many schools, especially schools whose students lived in poverty and thus were less academically prepared, 'teaching to the test' became required.

Later in 2001, the passage of the federal NCLB Law mandated that states give Reading/Language Arts and Math standardized tests in grades three through eight, and that the tests be used to determine whether a school and school district made Adequate Yearly Progress or AYP. However, because the criteria for making AYP is not whether the school's aggregated test scores increase, but whether they surpass a rising minimum threshold, schools that begin with low test scores, typically urban schools with a high percentage of children living in poverty, can have improving test score results, but because they do not rise above the minimum threshold, remain classified as failing. The opposite phenomenon can occur in wealthier suburban schools where the aggregated score might stay level or fall, but as long as it does not fall below the minimum threshold, the school is classified as making progress. Ultimately, however, because NCLB requires that by 2014 essentially all students need to pass every test, almost all the schools in the USA will be found to be failing. Since declaring every school to be failing risks revealing the absurdity of the testing requirements, and the federal Congressional stalemate prevents the two political parties from passing revised educational legislation, Secretary of Education Arne Duncan has been granting States waivers from the NCLB requirements, as long as they agree to carry out his desired reforms. Consequently, the Department of Education now unilaterally decides federal education policy and funding.

New York State has also been caught up in the contradictions caused by high-stakes standardized testing. In contrast to the federal government, which only had the power to require that a greater percentage of students pass the exams each year, New York State has had the responsibility for developing the tests and grading them. Because, like with NCLB, the tests have political ramifications, New York's Commissioner of Education has manipulated the scores on the Regents exams to achieve his desired outcome, high passing rates on some exams, low passing rates on others, but generally improving results so that his policies appear successful.

Advancing neoliberal discourses of efficiency, objectivity, and global economic competition

Throughout the last fifteen years of calls for more standardized testing in New York, and at the federal level through NCLB, or for mayoral control of urban schools, the promoters have offered similar rationales. They have argued that such reforms are necessary for efficiency, to objectively assess student learning, provide accountability, achieve educational equity, and compete in the global job market.

Over the last almost three decades, neoliberals have altered the discourse regarding education to one in which schools are simultaneously blamed for the country's economic problems and described as the solution. In 1983, the Reagan administration released the report A Nation at Risk (National Commission on Excellence in Education 1983) that began by blaming schools for the economic recession of the early 1980s. In particular, it is 'the mediocre educational performance that exists today' that has placed 'Our nation … at risk. Our once unchallenged preeminence in commerce, industry, science, and technological innovation is being overtaken by competitors throughout the world' (5).

Similarly, in the 1990s, New York State's education policy-makers, including the then Chancellor of Education Carl Hayden and Commissioner of Education Richard Mills, asserted that we cannot allow students of color or those living in poverty to fail, not because they deserve a strong, thoughtful education, but because with the end of industrialization and the rise of globalization, a secondary school education is necessary for employment and to compete in the global marketplace (Hursh 2008).

The fear of falling economically behind other countries is echoed by NCLB's supporters. President Bush, in reviewing the alleged achievements gained under NCLB, stated:

> NCLB is an important way to make sure America remains competitive in the twenty-first century. We're living in a global world. See, the education system must compete with education systems in China and India. If we fail to give our students the skills necessary to compete in the world of the twenty-first century, the jobs will go elsewhere…. And therefore, now is the time for the USA to give our children the skills so that the jobs will stay here. (US Department of Education 2006, 2)

In order to compete successfully with other countries, neoliberal education reformers asserted that our schools needed to be more efficient, and that standardized exams would provide objective assessments and hold teachers and schools accountable. In New York, the Chancellor and Commissioner asserted that the state's curriculum standards were 'objectively determined' and that standardized tests provided a valid and reliable means to assessing student learning. Such objective measures were required because teachers and administrators could not be trusted to assess students objectively and accurately. Likewise, the Bush administration's *Parents Guide to NCLB* informed parents that teachers often failed to give parents objective data about how 'their children performed,' and that this would be remedied by standardized tests (US Department of Education 2003).

While criticizing teachers as self-interested and unreliable, proponents portray themselves as only interested in doing what is best for children and fighting for children's civil rights, often invoking Martin Luther King, Jr. and the civil rights movement to justify standardized tests. Bush's Secretary of Education, Rodney Paige, explicitly connected NCLB to the legacy of Martin Luther King, Jr., stating:

> Forty-four years ago, Dr. Martin Luther King, Jr., said, 'The great challenge facing the nation today is to solve segregation and discrimination and bring into full realization the ideas and dreams of our democracy.' The NCLB Act does that. (Paige and Jackson 2004, np)

More recently, New York Mayor Michael Bloomberg and Governor Andrew Cuomo have promoted their agenda of mayoral control of schools, and holding students and teachers accountable through high-stakes standardized testing, by invoking Martin Luther King, Jr. and the Civil Rights movement of the 1960s. Bloomberg and Cuomo used separate 2012 observances marking Dr. King's birthday to assail teachers as the primary cause for the failures of the city's educational system. Bloomberg, who has proposed that schools be improved by firing half the teachers and doubling salaries and class size (Strauss 2011), declared that he is 'ready to fight for the kids: I'm ready to stand up to special interests.' Similarly, Cuomo advocated: 'we have to realize that our schools are not an employment program … It is this simple: It is not about the adults; it is about the children.' Bloomberg and Cuomo portray themselves as defenders of the children's civil rights in opposition to teachers who they describe as a 'special interest.' Citing the, 1954 Brown v. Board of Education ruling, Governor Cuomo lamented that because of failing schools, 'the great equalizer that was supposed to be the public education system can now be the great discriminator' (Kaplan and Taylor 2012, A-17).

While we have had three decades of neoliberal reform discourses and policies, the evidence from New York calls into question whether the policies have improved education outcomes and whether New York's standardized tests have provided a more objective measure of student learning. There is ample evidence from the rise and fall of scores on New York's tests and the lack of improvement by New York's students on the National Assessment of Educational Progress (NAEP) that educational outcomes have not improved. Therefore, I will first provide evidence that raises doubts about whether the test scores provide more objective assessments and then turn to whether student learning has improved over the last decade.

In a recent review of the last 10 years of standardized testing in New York, Winerip (2011) recounts some of the more dubious outcomes of testing, which include administering tests that were poorly constructed, had misleading or errone-ous questions, or used a grading scale that either overstated or understated students' learning. Critics have argued that an exam's degree of difficulty has varied depend-ing on whether the State Education Department wanted to increase the graduation rate, and therefore, made the Regents exams easier, or wanted to appear rigorous and tough, and therefore, made the exam more difficult. New York State's Depart-ment of Education can raise or lower the passing rate on an exam by simply adjust-ing the cut score, turning a low percentage of correct answers into a pass or a high percentage of correct answers into a failure. In the paragraphs below, I offer only a small part of the available evidence.[3]

In exams that students are likely to take as part of the graduation requirement to pass five Regents exams in four different subjects, the State Education Department has made it easier for students to pass by lowering the cut score. For example, a decade ago, the biology or 'Living Environments' exam was criticized as being too easy, as students only needed to answer 39% of the questions correctly to earn a passing grade of 55% (Cala 2003). The practice has not substantially changed over the last decade. A current analysis of the scoring rubrics on the State Department of Education website reveals that to pass students only need correct answers on 47% of multiple choice questions on the Living Environments exam and 53% correct on the Algebra exam (New York State Department of Education 2011a).

Conversely, the exams for the advanced, non-required courses, such as physics and chemistry, have sometimes been made more difficult. In 2003, 39% of students failed the Physics exam, in order, critics charged, to make Regents testing appear more rigorous (Winerip 2003). The test results were so dubious that the State Coun-cil of Superintendents sent letters to universities urging them to disregard the test results, which Commissioner Mills defended as 'statistically sound' (Dillon 2003; Winerip 2011, 19). However, because most of the students who enroll in physics are academically successful middle-class students, the students and their parents successfully pressured the State Education Department to change the scoring (Time Out From Testing n.d.; Winerip 2003).

Furthermore, sometimes an unusually low or high failure rate may not be inten-tional, but the result of incompetence. On the June 2003 Regents Math A exam (the test students are most likely to take to meet the Regents' math requirement) only 37% of the students passed statewide. After a statewide outcry, the test scores were discarded (Arenson 2003; Winerip 2011).

While the results on the secondary schools exams have fluctuated, the scores on the primary school exams have steadily increased at rates of questionable validity. For example, in 2005, 'New York City fourth graders made record gains on the state English test, with 59 percent scoring proficient, compared with 49 percent the year before.' Similarly, in '2008 math scores for grades three through eight indicate that 89.7 percent are proficient, up from 72.7 percent in 2007' (Winerip 2011, 19).

One way to increase the percentage of students scoring at the proficiency levels is to change the cut scores/percentage correct to attain that level. Ravitch, who for most of her career advocated strongly for high-stakes standardized testing, has recently reversed her view, realizing how test scores have been used not to improve schools but, instead, for political purposes. In her book, *The Death and Life of the Great American School System: How Testing and Choice are Undermining Educa-tion* (Ravitch 2010), she points out how much easier for elementary students to score in the top three of four levels on the standardized tests. She notes:

... on the sixth-grade reading test in 2006, students needed to earn 36.2 percent of the points to attain level 2; by 2009, students in that grade need only 17.9 percent. In seventh grade math, students needed to earn 36.2 percent of the points on the test to advance to level 2 in 2006, but by 2009, they needed to earn only 22 percent. The standards to advance from level 1 to level 2 dropped so low that many students could get enough correct answers to pass to level 2 by randomly guessing. (79)

That these improvements in student learning are deceptive is also revealed when the scores on state tests are compared with students' scores on the more statistically rigorous NAEP English and Math exams, exams administered every other year to statistically representative samples of students in fourth, eighth and twelfth grades and for which the results can be compared from year to year. In 2005, only 19% of the New York City students were proficient on the eighth-grade reading test, compared to 22% two years before, and by 2009, the test results were the lowest in a decade. By November 2011, 'New York [was] one of two states in the nation to post statistically significantly declines on the National Assessment tests' (Winerip 2011, 19).

Whenever questions are raised regarding the validity of the state tests, the Commissioners and Chancellors defend them as rigorous and statistically sound. In New York City, Mayor Bloomberg used the improving test results to successfully lobby the state legislature to renew mayoral control of schools and to win re-election. However, finally, in June 2010, writes Winerip (2011) in his overview of the recent history of testing in New York, Merryl Tisch, the current chancellor of the Board of Regents, admitted that the state test scores were ridiculously inflated, should not be believed, and test scores were rescaled so that, for example, the 68.8% English proficiency rates was immediately rescaled to 42.4%.

Given the high-stakes nature of test scores and the role they can play in building or undermining careers, it should not be a surprise that scores are manipulated to serve different interests. A decade ago, Linn (2003), in his Presidential address to the American Educational Research Association conference, provided empirical evidence for how test scores unrealistically increased during a Commissioner's of Education term and then were recalibrated downward with the change in office holders. We have also witnessed superintendents in Atlanta and Washington, DC being charged with manipulating the test scores, including having teachers erase students' wrong answers and replace them with correct answers (Bello and Gillum 2011; Toppo 2011).

However, the faith in standardized test scores and the notion that all that was needed to run a school district was someone with corporate managerial experience has persisted, although increasingly challenged as the erroneous nature of those assumptions becomes increasingly apparent.

New York City and mayoral control of schools

Gewirtz and Ball (2000) and Thrupp and WIllmott (2003) describe the rise of the new managerialism in education that focuses on data, objectivity, and efficiency, and believes that educational institutions should be headed by professional managers rather than educators. In 2002, Mayor Bloomberg chose as chancellor of the New York City schools, Joel Klein, previously CEO for the global media giant Bertelsman. As chancellor, Klein employed the 'tools of business – top-down decisions, marketplace incentives, and belief in private sector solutions to public school problems' (Hancock 2007, 16). Klein operated the schools as businesses, describing them as 'key units' (17). He increased the use of standardized tests beyond that already required by the state and federal governments. Primary school students were tested every few weeks, and were required to pass the end of the year tests to be promoted to the third, fourth, and seventh grades. The schools also developed a program to pay students for attendance and high test scores (Bosman 2007).

In the fall of 2010, Klein stepped down as chancellor of the schools to return to the corporate world, and Bloomberg, confident that corporate rather than educational experience is all that is needed to successfully manage the city schools, appointed Cathleen Black chancellor, former *USA Today* publisher and head of Hearst Magazines. Because she had none of the required credentials for the position, Bloomberg had to obtain a waiver from the then state Education Commissioner David Steiner, who granted the waiver even though the committee he appointed to assess Black's preparedness voted six to two against her. Black took office on 1 January 2011, and resigned 95 days later when it became clear she had no idea how school systems worked and disrespected parents and teachers. Steiner resigned a few days later. Bloomberg replaced her with Dennis Walcott, who was deputy mayor and had worked in local community agencies, including the Urban League.

RTTT: raising the stakes

In 2008, Obama campaigned for the presidency with long-time education professor and reformer Darling-Hammond (2010) as his advisor. During the campaign, he promised fewer standardized tests and to scale back many of the Bush administration's reforms. However, after the election, he chose Arne Duncan as his Secretary of Education and used Department of Education funds to create the RTTT initiative, which aims to accomplish the opposite of what he promised in his campaign. RTTT would use money as the carrot to transform schools in Duncan and Obama's image: strong accountability for teachers, school privatization, and mayoral control of schools (Hursh 2011a, 2011b).

As mentioned, New York State applied for and was one of 19 states to win funding under President Obama's RTTT initiative. While states did not have to apply for RTTT funding, most states chose to do so in part because the current global fiscal crisis impinges most severely on state and local budgets, which, typically, by law need to be balanced.

In order to be considered for RTTT funding, states had to agree to hold teachers accountable by using students' scores on state-wide standardized tests as 20% of teacher evaluations, and increasing or removing the cap on the number of charter schools. New York State met these requirements when the legislature removed barriers to assessing teachers based on their students' test scores, and the legislature increased the maximum number of charter schools allowed from 200 to 460. In 2010, Arne Duncan, Obama's Secretary of Education, awarded New York State $700 million over a four-year period (Medina 2010).

However, the agreement that students' scores on standardized tests could compose only 20% of the teachers' evaluations was soon broken when in May 2011, 'the Commissioner of Education, Dr. John King and Gov. Andrew M. Cuomo rammed a measure through the Board of Regents making state tests worth up to 40 percent of teacher evaluation' (Winerip 2012, A-15). In response to criticism that too much weight would be given to test scores, the chancellor of the Board of Regents, Merryl Tisch, stated: 'These are not perfect tools by any means. But that being said, I believe it is important to have an objective system to evaluate teachers on a professional basis. This is the beginning of such a process' (Otterman 2011, A-17).

In response to the increase from 20 to 40%, the teachers' unions went to court and succeeded in temporarily blocking King and Cuomo. But Cuomo and Bloomberg wanted the 40% of the assessment based on state and local test scores and Cuomo threatened, if an agreement was not reached by 16 February 2012, to impose his own approach to measuring the quality of teachers' work. On that date, Cuomo and the unions reached an agreement in which testing would be used as 40% of teachers' evaluations, with teachers potentially having input on which tests might be used.

Following the agreement, schools must begin designing and incorporating what is known as an Annual Professional Performance Review (APPR) to assess every teacher based on the increase in their students' scores (described as a 'value added approach') on standardized tests and by two observations from two school administrators or an administrator and teacher (New York State Department of Education 2011c), who are trained in the evaluation process.

While this might sound objective and fair, according to the State Education Department's 'Guidance on New York State's Professional Performance Review Law and Regulations,' (2012b) fewer than half the teachers will be rated as 'effective' or 'very effective,' with most rated as 'ineffective' and 'developing.' This will occur for two reasons. First, teachers are required to be rated on a bell curve, so that 10% of teachers, whether based on test scores, observation, or other locally created criteria, must be rated as 'ineffective' and 40% as 'developing.' Second, 'before a teacher can be considered effective, her students' score growth must exceed the average for all teachers – that means based on scores, more than 50 percent of all teachers will not be effective.' (Strauss 2011, 1) Third, although the median total score will be 50 out of 100 points (remember, it is a bell curve), teachers will have to score a total of 75 points or more to be rated 'effective.' Therefore, most teachers will be found to be 'ineffective' or 'developing.' In New York City, if teachers are found to be 'ineffective overall' for two consecutive years, the district can begin the process of removing the teachers (Ravitch 2012a).

Furthermore, the scoring rubric makes it possible for a teacher to be rated as 'effective' in ALL the categories, from students' standardized test scores and administrator observations, and still not score enough points to receive an overall score of 'effective,' and, instead, be scored as 'developing.' This is comparable to passing all your tests in a course and then being told that you failed.

Similarly, a teacher who receives a low rating because his or her students score poorly on the state exams, perhaps because they are English Language Learners or have learning disabilities, but then scores 'highly effective' on the non-test score criteria, the teacher could be found to be 'ineffective overall' (Strauss 2012). This is an intended outcome of the policy that states: 'Teachers rated ineffective on student performance based on objective assessments must be rated ineffective overall' (New York State Department of Education 2012b; cited in New York State Education Department 2012b).

Ravitch (2012a), in a recent comment on the New York's Annual Performance Professional Review, noted that:

The NY press treated the agreement as a major breakthrough that would lead to dramatic improvement in the schools. The media assumed that teachers and principals in NY State would now be measured accurately, that the bad ones would be identified and eventually ousted, and that the result would be big gains in test scores. (2)

However, as should be abundantly clear by now, the tests are neither objective nor accurate. Further, the scoring guide assumes that teachers in a school or district are naturally distributed along a continuum from ineffective to very effective and that some need to be fired. Moreover, districts are now required to very quickly develop assessments for every subject in every grade and if State Commissioner of Education John King 'does not find them sufficiently rigorous, he has the unilateral power to reject them' (Ravitch 2012a, 3).

Worse yet, the New York City media, urged on by Bloomberg, won the right to publish the names and ratings of principals and fourth through eighth grade teachers of math and language arts (the only subjects for which standardized tests already exist), which occurred on 24 February 2012. The New York City teachers' union, teachers, and educational experts have criticized how the evaluations are constructed and the release of individual teacher evaluations, but the process will continue. Ravitch (2012a) succinctly summed up evaluating teachers based on their students' test scores and the grading curves thus: 'this is madness' (5).

Ravitch (2012a) also noted how President Obama either does not seem to recognize the consequences of his own policies or contradicts himself. In his 2012 State of the Union address, Obama stated 'teachers should stop teaching to the test.' But RTTT, his own program, forces teachers to teach to the test. To do otherwise is to risk being publicly shamed and fired.

The contradictions of neoliberal education policy

Over the last two decades in New York, education policy has increasingly fulfilled the neoliberal agenda. Students are subject to more standardized tests with more significant consequences. Initially, the Regents requirement to pass five standardized tests only had implications for the students' graduation. Then, using test scores to determine whether schools made Adequate Yearly Progress had implications not just for the student but also for the school and district, which might be closed or reorganized based on the students' tests scores. Currently, under RTTT, teachers' evaluations are primarily linked to their students' test scores and both teachers and students are under immense pressure for students to do well on their tests.

However, resistance to the neoliberal agenda is increasing, partly out of the neoliberals' own mistakes. Bloomberg's appointment of Cathleen Black met strong resistance in New York City and whatever management skills she had were insufficient to overcome her lack of familiarity with how school systems worked.

Similarly, mayoral control did not spread to other cities as opponents used Bloomberg's politicization of education as a cautionary tale to combat efforts to institute mayoral control, such as in Rochester (see Duffy 2010; Hursh and Henderson 2011).

Furthermore, the continuing demonization of public employees, including teachers, is meeting increased resistance. In Wisconsin, the Republican Governor Scott Walker pushed through legislation that significantly reduced the salaries of teachers and other government employees and stripped public sector employees of bargaining rights. While he was able to pass the bill over the resistance of the Democratic legislators, he has met with massive demonstrations and now faces a recall vote. The popular resistance in Wisconsin prompted similar demonstrations in other states and served as the archetype for Occupy Wall Street (Finnegan 2012).

In New York, teachers and administrators are increasingly protesting. Over a thousand New York State principals have written and signed a Letter of Concern Regarding New York State's APPR Legislation for the Evaluation of Teachers and Principals (www.newyorkprincipals.org). Further, New York City teachers, in response to the public release of teacher evaluations by teacher name, are organizing to end the process, including organizing a petition: 'Stop the public shaming and unjust firing of teachers' (http://www.change.org/petitions/stop-the-public-shaming-and-unjust-firing-of-teachers).

Beyond protesting, educators and others who care about education and equality are examining not only how other countries have created more successful educational systems, but also more equal and democratic societies. Darling-Hammond (2010) examined educational systems in Finland, South Korea, and Singapore to understand how they have become more successful than the USA. Ravitch (2012b) has compared the Finnish educational system with the USA to note that they treat their teachers as professionals, give them autonomy and decent pay, and only use one standardized test to assess how the nation is doing as a whole. Sahlberg, in *Finnish Lessons: What Can the World Learn from Educational Change in Finland?* (2011), describes how the Finnish educational system, often described as the most successful system in the world, fits into what he calls a 'competitive welfare state.'

Education in New York appears to be at a crucial point with more standardized testing, with potentially greater negative consequences for individual students, teachers, principals, and schools. On the other hand, neoliberals may have overreached with the appointment and resignation of Cathleen Black, and the release of teachers' evaluations in New York City. We shall see.

Acknowledgments

I would like to thank Camille A. Martina, Joseph Henderson, Charlie Roods, and Jody Siegle for this assistance on this manuscript.

Notes

1. See Lipman 2004, 2011, for an excellent portrayal of how this has occurred in Chicago.
2. For cautions regarding using 'value added' systems, see National Research Council (2009) and Braun of the Educational Testing Service (2005).
3. For more, see Time Out From Testing website: http://www.timeoutfromtesting.org.

References

Amrein, A.L., and D.C. Berliner. 2002. High-stakes testing, uncertainty, and student learning. *Education Policy Analysis Archives* 10, no. 18. http://www.epaa.asu.edu/epaa/v10n18/.

Arenson, K. 2003. New York math exam trials showed most students failing. *The New York Times*, August 27, C-12.

Ball, S.J. 1994. *Education reform: A critical and post-structural approach*. Buckingham: Open University Press.

Bello, M., and J. Gillum. 2011. D.C. officials to review high rates of erasures on school tests. *USA Today*, March 29. http://www.usatoday.com/news/education/2011-03-29-dcschools29_ST_N.htm?sms_ss=twitter&at_xt=4d91dceba8da77df%2C0.

Bosman, J. 2007. A plan to pay for top scores on some tests gains ground. *The New York Times*, June 9, B-1.

Braun, H.I. 2005. *Using student progress to evaluate teachers: A primer on value-added models*. Princeton, NJ: Education Testing Service. http://www.ets.org/Media/Research/pdf/PICVAM.pdf.

Cala, W. 2003, October 22. Testimony before the New York Senate Standing Committee on Education, Roosevelt Hearing Room C, Legislative Office Building, Albany, NY. http://www.timeoutfromtesting.org/testimonies.php.

Darling-Hammond, L. 2010. *The flat world and education: How America's commitment to equity will determine our future*. New York, NY: Teachers College Press.

Dillon, S. 2003. Outcry over regents physics test. But officials in Albany won't budge. *The New York Times*, July 18. http://www.nytimes.com/2003/07/18/nyregion/outcry-over-regents-physics-test-but-officials-in-albany-won-t-budge.html?pagewanted=all&src=pm.

Duffy, R.J. 2010. *Putting children first: A framework for change in school governance*. Rochester, NY: Mayor's Office.

Finnegan, W. 2012. The storm: Did a governor's anti-union crusade backfire? *The New Yorker*, March 5, 28–34.

Gewirtz, S., and S. Ball. 2000. From 'Welfarism' to 'New Managerialism': Shifting discourses of school headship in the education marketplace. *Discourse: Studies in the Cultural Politics of Education* 21, no. 3: 253–68.

Hancock, L. 2007. School's out. *The Nation*, July 9, 16–17, 20–21.

Haney, W. 2000. The myth of the Texas Miracle in education. *Education Policy Analysis Archives* 8. http://www.epaa.asu.edu/ojs/article/view/432.

Hursh, D. 2005. The growth of high-stakes testing, accountability and education markets and the decline of educational equality. *British Educational Research Journal* 31, no. 5: 605–22.

Hursh, D. 2007. Assessing the impact of No Child Left Behind and other neoliberal reforms in education. *American Educational Research Journal* 44, no. 3: 493–518.

Hursh, D. 2008. *High-stakes testing and the decline of teaching and learning: The real crisis in education*. Lanham, MD: Rowman and Littlefield.

Hursh, D. 2011a. More of the same: How free market capitalism dominates the economy and education. In *The phenomenon of Obama and the agenda for education: Can hope audaciously trump neoliberalism?* ed. P. Carr and B. Porfilio, 3–22, Charlotte, NC: Information Age Press.

Hursh, D. 2011b. Explaining Obama: The continuation of free market policies in education and the economy. *Journal of Inquiry and Action in Education* 4, no. 1: 31–47.

Hursh, D., and J. Henderson. 2011. Contesting global neoliberalism and creating alternative futures. *Discourse: Studies in the Cultural Politics of Education* 32, no. 2: 171–85.

Hursh, D., and C.A. Martina. 2003. Neoliberalism and schooling in the US: How state and federal government education policies perpetuate inequality. *Journal of critical education policy studies* 1, no. 2. http://www.jceps.com/?pageID=article&articleID=12.

Kaplan, T., and K. Taylor. 2012. Invoking King, Cuomo and Bloomberg stoke fight on teacher review impasse. *The New York Times*, January 17, A-17.

Kozol, J. 2005. *The shame of the nation: The restoration of apartheid schooling in America*. New York, NY: Crown Publishing.

Krugman, P. 2012. States of depression. *The New York Times*, March 5, A-19. http://www.nytimes.com/2012/03/05/opinion/krugman-states-of-depression.html?scp=1&sq=Krugman%20March%205&st=cse.

Linn, R. 2003. Accountability: Responsibility and responsible expectations. *Education Researcher* 32, no. 7: 3–13.

Lipman, P. 2004. *High-stakes education: Inequality, globalization, and urban school reform.* New York, NY: Routledge.

Lipman, P. 2011. *The new political economy of urban education: Neoliberalism, race, and the right to the city.* New York, NY: Routledge.

Medina, J. 2010. New York wins Race to the Top grant. *The New York Times*, August 24. http://www.cityroom.blogs.nytimes.com/2010/08/24/new-york-wins-race-to-the-top-grant/?scp=1&sq=NEw%20York%20Race%20to%20the%20Top&st=cse.

MetLife. 2012. *Met life survey of the American teacher: Teachers, parents, and the economy.* New York, NY: Metropolitan Life Insurance Agency. http://www.metlife.com/about/corporate-profile/citizenship/metlife-foundation/metlife-survey-of-the-american-teacher.html?WT.mc_id=vu1101.

National Commission on Excellence in Education. 1983. *A nation at risk: A report to the nation and the Secretary of Education.* Washington, DC: US Department of Education.

National Research Council. 2009, October 5. Letter report to the US Department of Education on the Race to the Top fund. http://www8.nationalacademies.org/onpinews/newsitem.aspx?RecordID=12780.

New York State Department of Education. 2011a, January 25. The information booklet for scoring regents examinations in the sciences. http://www.nysedregents.org/livingenvironment/20110125rg.pdf.

New York State Department of Education. 2011b, May. Regarding the Annual Professional Performance Review (APPR). http://www.regents.nysed.gov/meetings/2011Meetings/May2011/511bra4.pdf.

New York State Department of Education, 2012a. Chancellor Tisch and Commissioner King praise evaluation agreement. http://www.oms.nysed.gov/press/ChancellorTischandCommissionerKingPraiseEvaluationAgreement.html.

New York State Department of Education. 2012b. New York State teacher and principal evaluation 2012–13 and beyond: Summary of revised APPR provisions. http://www.engageny.org/wp-content/uploads/2012/03/nys-evaluation-plans-guidance-memo-march-2012.pdf (accessed 8 March, 2012).

New York State Department of Education. 2012c, August 13. Guidance on New York State's Annual Professional Performance Review for teachers and principals to implement education law 3012c and the Commissioner's regulations. http://www.engageny.org/wp-content/uploads/2012/05/APPR-Field-Guidance.pdf.

Olssen, M., J. Codd, and A.M. O'Neill. 2004. *Education policy: Globalization, citizenship and democracy.* Thousand Oaks, CA: Sage.

Otterman, S. 2011. Teacher reviews will put more focus on state tests. *The New York Times*, May 13, A-17.

Paige, R., and A. Jackson. 2004, November 8. *Education: The civil-rights issue of the twenty-first century.* Hispanic Vista. http://www.hispanicvista.com/HVC/Opinion/GuestColumns/1108Rod_Paige-Alponso_Jackson.htm.

Peters, M. 1994. Individualism and community: Education and the politics of difference. *Discourse: Studies in the cultural politics of education* 14, no. 2: 65–78.

Ravitch, D. 2010. *The death and life of the Great American school system: How testing and choice are undermining education.* New York, NY: Basic Books.

Ravitch, D. 2012a. No student left untested. *New York Review Blog*, February 21. http://www.nybooks.com/blogs/nyrblog/2012/feb/21/no-student-left-untested/.

Ravitch, D. 2012b. Schools we can envy. *New York Review of Books* 49, no. 4: 19–20.

Sachs, J. 2011. *The price of civilization: Reawakening American virtue and prosperity.* New York, NY: Random House.

Sahlberg, P. 2011. *Finnish lessons: What can the world learn from educational change in Finland?* New York, NY: Teachers College Press.

Siegle, J. 2012, March 12. Personal communication from the Executive Director of the Monroe County School Boards Association.

Strauss, V. 2011. Are half of New York's teachers really 'not effective?' *The Washington Post*, December 7. http://www.washingtonpost.com/blogs/answer-sheet/post/are-half-of-new-yorks-teachers-really-not-effective/2011/12/05/gIQAhDXyaO_blog.html.

Strauss. V. 2012. You are so smart ... why did you become a teacher? *The Washington Post*, February 19. www.washingtonpost.com/blogs/answer-sheet/post/you-are-so-smartwhy-did-you-become-a-teacher/2012/02/19/gIQA2vBNNR_blog.html#pagebreak.

Tavernise, S. 2012. Education gap grows between rich and poor, studies show. *The New York Times*, February 10, A1.

The Pew Charitable Trusts. 2011, November. Does America promote mobility as well as other nations? http://www.economicmobility.org/assets/pdfs/CRITA_FINAL.pdf.

Thrupp, M., and R. WIllmott. 2003. *Education management in manageralist times: Beyond the textual apologists*. Buckingham: Open University Press.

Time Out From Testing. n.d. Timeline of New York State Regents Fiascos. http://www.time-outfromtesting.org/timeline.php.

Toppo, G. 2011. Schools marred by testing scandals in 2011. *USA Today*, December, 29. http://www.usatoday.com/news/education/story/2011-12-29/schools-test-scandal/52274708 /1.

US Department of Education. 2003. *NCLB: Parents guide to NCLB: What to know and where to go*. Washington, DC: US Department of Education.

US Department of Education, Office of the Press Secretary. 2006. *President Bush discusses No Child Left Behind*. Washington, DC: US Department of Education, Office of the Press Secretary. http://www.ed.gov/news/releases/2006/10/20061005-6.html.

US Department of Education. 2010, August 24. Nine states and the District of Columbia win second round Race to the Top grants. http://www.ed.gov/news/press-releases/nine-states-and-district-columbia-win-second-round-race-top-grants.

Winerip, M. 2003. Passing grade defies laws of physics. *The New York Times*, March 12, A22 & B7. http://www.nytimes.com/2003/03/12/nyregion/on-education-when-a-passing-grade-defies-laws-of-physics.html?src=pm.

Winerip, M. 2011. 10 years of assessing students with scientific exactitude. *The New York Times*, December 19, A-24.

Winerip, M. 2012. In Race to the Top, the dirty work is left of those on the bottom. *The New York Times*, January 22, A-15.

'Gap talk' and the global rescaling of educational accountability in Canada

Wayne Martino and Goli Rezai-Rashti

Faculty of Education, The University of Western Ontario, Ontario, ON, Canada

In this paper, we undertake a particular policy critique and analysis of the gender achievement gap discourse in Ontario and Canada, and situate it within the context of what has been termed *the governance turn* in educational policy with its focus on policy as numbers and its multi-scalar manifestations. We show how this 'gap talk' is inextricably tied to a neoliberal system of account-ability, marketization, comparative performance measures and competition within the context of a globalized education policy field. The focus initially is on how the gender achievement gap has emerged in the Organisation for Economic Co-operation and Development's (OECD) publication of the *2009 Program For International Student Assessment Results*, but attention is drawn to questions and categories of equity that are used to define and measure socio-economic disadvantage. We illustrate that such measures and *categories in use* function to eschew important aspects of maldistribution, with important conse-quences for understanding the significance of the interlocking influences of race, social class, gender and geographical location, where there is evidence of spatial concentrations of poverty and histories of cumulative oppression. In the second part of the paper, we focus on the Canadian data to illustrate the multi-scalar dimensions of global/national/provincial 'policyscapes' through a politics of numbers. Contrary to the ways in which Canada and specifically Ontario have been marketed and celebrated by OECD and other stakeholders for their *high performing, high quality* education system in terms of achieving equitable out-comes for diverse student populations, we illustrate how the 'failing boys' dis-course and achievement 'gap talk' have actually functioned to produce a misrecognition of the gender achievement gap, with boys emerging as a disad-vantaged category in the articulation of equity policies.

Introduction

In this paper, we undertake an analysis of the case of the gender achievement gap in Ontario and Canada as an exemplary instance of misrecognition in eliding systemic inequalities related to the effects of social class and racial differences in the education system. Such an investigation is situated within the context of what has been identified as a global education policy field with attention being accorded to the particular role of Organisation for Economic Co-operation and Development's

(OECD) *Program For International Student Assessment* (PISA) constituting a space of equivalence for measuring comparative performance across nation states, with implications for further neoliberal forms and marketization of education systems (Ball 2012; Grek 2009; Lingard 2011; Lingard and Rawolle 2011; Ozga 2009). We focus specifically on policy-making processes and discourses from within the Ontario Ministry of Education and also the role of *Pan Canadian Assessment Program* (PCAP) (Council of Ministers of Education Canada [CMEC] 2011), which is administered under the authority of the Council of Ministers of Education in Canada, who through the mobilization of what Gillborn (2008) refers to as 'gap talk', are concerned to steer educational policy designed to address boys' underachievement.[1] This influence and attempt to steer educational policy are particularly noteworthy, given that education in the Canadian context falls within the jurisdiction of the provinces and not the federal government.[2] Attention is drawn to the increasing use of numbers and a particular 'policy habitus' (Lingard and Rawolle 2011, 496; Ozga 2009), defined in terms of a meta-narrative of 'failing boys', which is framed within a gender achievement gap discourse.[3] In following Power and Frandji (2010) in the UK and Lingard, Creagh, and Vass (2012) in Australia, we illustrate the extent to which policy as numbers, as driven by forms of neoliberal governance in the education field in the Canadian context, has also contributed to powerful instances of *policy misrecognition*. This misrecognition has resulted in the displacement of a politics of redistribution and a failure to attend to racial inequality in terms of bleaching a more considered contextual analysis of schooling and the reality of the impact of material disadvantage on student participation and achievement in schooling. In short, we emphasize that such policy articulation, in terms of 'gap talk' and use of numbers, overshadows a commitment to addressing and tackling 'the underlying causes of educational failure' related to what Power and Frandji identify as the 'uneven educational outcomes' for various minority and economically disadvantaged populations which can best be explained in terms of 'maldistribution' (394).[4] Such policy misrecognitions in Canada and elsewhere have actually displaced previous commitments by education policy makers to addressing racism and social class inequality.

We draw on the literature from within the field of policy sociology in education (Ball 1994), which deals with the politics of numbers (Grek 2009; Lingard 2011; Ozga 2009) and that which addresses questions of biopower and classificatory systems in relation to neoliberal governance and accountability (Ball 2012; Hacking 2006; Miller and Rose 2008; Rose 1999). In so doing, our purpose is to highlight the political processes and practices that have enabled the phenomenon of *struggling* or *failing* boys to emerge as a target of policy-making within the field of education in Ontario with its multiscalar dimensions. The particular significance of this phenomenon of the gender achievement gap in the Ontario context in relation to a global education policy field and regimes of neoliberal accountability and audit cultures as central to evidence-based policy is highlighted (Jordan 2010; Wiseman 2010). Attention is also drawn to the role of the media and how it functions as a particular technology in setting both the terms and limits of a social imaginary that endorses or fuels a neoliberal policy regime with all of its distorting consequences for measuring and understanding educational inequality. In short, we are concerned to foreground the effects of such policy frames and meta-narratives about 'failing boys' in their capacity to displace a fundamental politics of redistribution, particularly as it relates to the persistence of race and class inequalities in education (Fraser 1997; Gillborn 2008; Rothstein 2004).

Our analysis is set against a broader national and global scalar policy context in which testing regimes such as PISA and PCAP serve as a legitimating basis for accountability-driven, evidence-based policy in terms of defining, framing and explaining the limits of educational inequality (Ball 2003; Jordan 2010; Lingard and Rawolle 2011).[5] What is needed, we argue, is more sustained policy engagement with an informed research base and onto-epistemological frameworks that attend to the theoretical bases and norms underpinning what Lucas and Beresford (2010) refer to as 'the categories in use'. Hacking (2006) refers to this phenomenon as 'making up people' in the sense of constituting and classifying populations, which have implications for the framing of policy discussions on education and inequality, specifically as they pertain to questions of socio-economic status, race, ethnicity, gender, and sexuality and their intersectionality:

> ... empirical research offers little to social analysts and policy makers: theory is essential for drawing proper inferences from the research. Yet the wide set of plausible theories, and strategies of analysis that are not designed to eliminate nonviable theories, can ultimately render social science evidence of little value to policy. (Lucas and Beresford 2010, 26)

In this paper, therefore, we draw on both the empirical and theoretical literature pertaining to the gender achievement gap to highlight the problem of misrecognition and displacement in the *failing boys* policy discourse. Our specific case is located in Ontario, Canada. Furthermore, we elaborate on the non-viability of certain theoretical frameworks and epistemologies that underpin the authoritative assertions about the constitution and reconstitution of boys as the *new disadvantaged* (Lingard and Douglas 1999) within the limits set by what has been termed by Ball (2012) as a neoliberal imaginary.

The global policy field and the governance turn: PISA, questions of equity and the gender achievement gap

The particular polemics about *failing boys* need to be understood in relation to the imperatives of globalization and the governance turn in terms of the neoliberal education policy regime that has come to define the nature of policy-making within the field of education (Ball 2008; Rizvi and Lingard 2010). Within this new neoliberal education policy regime, Ball (2008), for example, identifies new managerialism, markets and performativity as the three central technologies of governance (see also Lingard, Creagh, and Vass 2012, 315–316). Boys have emerged at the provincial, national and global levels as a specific target of policy intervention in education and we argue that this emergence needs to be understood and reconsidered in light of the global education policy field, with PISA functioning as another layer in the technology of governance in further directing and enhancing policy makers' attention to a comparative focus on 'failing boys' both within and across nations. Through PISA and its use in the Canadian context, for example, we see this rescaling and relocation of political authority in terms of policy effects within the nation state. As both Lingard (2011) and Grek (2009) have pointed out, it is important to understand the role of PISA as a technology of neoliberal governance in setting the terms for ushering in a culture of performativity and competitiveness among nations desiring to achieve 'world-class standards' (OECD 2010a, 4). In other words, the nation is constituted as a 'space of equivalence' with

Finland, Shanghai, and Canada, specifically Ontario, being held up as exemplary in their performance on PISA tests. As we will illustrate later, by the OECD promoting and marketing Ontario as a high quality/high performing jurisdiction, in terms of highlighting the achievement of high school students in spite of their family background and immigrant status, important questions of misrecognition and maldistribution for minority populations in the Canadian context are eschewed and elided (see Anisef et al. 2010).

Such marketing of nations by OECD as top-performers draws attention to the ways in which political authority is being mobilized beyond the nation state, as we will illustrate later in the paper through the Canadian case of CMEC and other networks, including the media, in their attempt to steer education policy regarding 'failing boys' in the Ontario context. As Rose (1988) highlights, numbers in conjunction with the human sciences establish 'a regime of visibility' and 'a grid of codeability' for creating a navigable space of commensurability, equivalence and comparative performance, thereby rendering the population amenable to administration, statistical mapping and governance (187; see also Desrosieres 1998). Power (2004), in fact, argues that 'much has to be done to render diverse phenomena countable' or calculable, and that 'measurement is based on classification systems that ignore "inessential differences" and reduce complexity' (767). This is not to ignore the importance of quantification measures, but rather to highlight, as Rose (1999) explicates, the politics of numbers and 'the complex technical work' that is required to render phenomenon amenable to measurement and, hence, government, particularly with regard to 'the complex array of judgements and decisions that go into a measurement, a scale, a number' (208). Moreover, Lingard (2011) highlights that numbers as inscription devices with their classificatory potential are not able to capture the messy, hybrid realities of people's lives today and can elide the complexity of schools in their variable contexts (see also Jordan 2010; Luke, Green, and Kelly 2010; Wiseman 2010).

Thus, it is important to understand the role of PISA in terms of the execution of a neoliberal governmental rationality and analytics of governmentality, which is inextricably tied to norms for establishing grids of intelligibility that are rendered amenable to administration through calculable practices. Miller and Rose (2008), for example, point out that rationalities and technologies of markets have been extended 'to previously exempt zones such as health and education' (18). They argue for an approach to policy analysis that takes account of the 'complex and heterogenous assemblage of conditions that makes it possible for objects of policy to be problematized, and rendered amenable to administration' (28). It is in this sense that we are interested to investigate how 'boys' and broader questions of equity are treated as *objects of government,* which we set against this analysis of a rescaling of educational politics and policy making. Our position is that there is a need to attend to the global, national and local dimensions of education policy making. This requires that we draw attention to the marketization of education, which is connected to cultures of performativity and accountability influenced by transnational policy actors, ministries and ministers of education, the media, administrative bodies and economic organizations such as OECD.

Eschewing important questions of equity and redistribution

In its document, *PISA 2009 results: Overcoming social background (Volume II),* the OECD (2010a) aims to address equity in learning opportunities and outcomes and highlight the significance of socio-economic background and the inequitable distribution of educational resources as key factors impacting student performance. However, the thrust of the data analysis in the second PISA 2009 volume is to draw attention to the fact that 'educational equity can be achieved in diverse socio-economic contexts' (32). To support such claims, data are used to illustrate that countries with similar levels of income inequality do not necessarily show similar patterns of distribution in terms of learning outcomes and performance on PISA measures. Rather, what is more closely correlated is the performance of education systems and the share of poorly performing students, identified as those who fail to reach the PISA baseline Level 2 of reading proficiency (33). In short, the OECD (2010a) supports the position that, while there is a link between socio-economic background and student performance, such an impact can be ameliorated by an effective school system, appropriate policies and increased educational resources. Moreover, the data reveal that 'there are students from disadvantaged backgrounds who show high levels of performance', which further supports the position that performance on PISA cannot be reduced solely to a student's socio-economic back-ground (33). Within the context of such a framing and discussion of performance measures on PISA, equality in learning outcomes is defined as both the relative 'difference between high and low performing students', and in terms of the propor-tion of those students who perform at a baseline level of proficiency. This enables attention to be focused on 'the absolute proportion of students who fall below a baseline level of performance', which represents those students 'who have not acquired the fundamental knowledge or mastered the basic skills that will enable them to progress further in education and beyond' (38). Thus, both relative and absolute measures of equality in learning outcomes are flagged as important because of their capacity to 'provide insight into *the extent to which a school system fails to provide* all students with equal and adequate levels of knowledge' (38) (our empha-sis). While we do not deny that the quality of teachers and schooling can make a difference and may lead to better educational outcomes for some economically disadvantaged students and that not all disadvantaged students necessarily perform badly, there is some concern that such a position can lead to an overzealous empha-sis on school-based reform and the centrality of teachers at the expense of a more considered engagement with a broader societal politics of redistribution – a point which we explicate more fully later in the paper (also see Condron 2011).

Two aspects of this framing of equity and relative performance gaps within coun-tries in terms of schools failing to ensure equality in learning outcomes emerge as troubling. The first relates to how gender is inserted into a grid of intelligibility regarding measures of educational equity. The second pertains to the *categories in use* that are deployed to measure the effect of socio-economic background on student performance. Included in Figure 11.1.4 on page 34, for example in the OECD (2010a) document, is a summary of PISA measures of educational equity for all OECD and partner countries ranked in terms of their mean scores. Gender as a category, disaggregated in terms of the percentage of boys and percentage of girls scoring below reading proficiency Level 2, comprises two of the columns represented with other criteria in separate columns, such as percentage of variance in student performance explained by students' socio-economic background also being represented. What is foregrounded in the presentation and tabulation of such data is the stark gender achievement gap across nations, with more than twice as many boys (14%) than girls (6%) in Canada, for example, performing below Level 2 proficiency. In Finland and Australia, the difference is even greater with over three times as many boys failing to meet Level 2 proficiency and these are the results for some of the most highly ranked countries. In the UK, which performs just slightly above the OECD average mean reading score, the gender gap is still quite significant with 21% of boys and 14% of girls failing to meet Level 2 proficiency in reading. In the US, the numbers are 23% of boys vs. 14% of girls. Such disaggregation of data to include a specific focus on gender elides a more thoughtful and nuanced consideration of race and class inequalities in performance gaps, which significant literature in the field has shown to be much greater than any gender gap, particularly in countries such as the UK, US and Canada (AAUW 2008; Anisef et al. 2010; Gillborn 2008; Mead 2006; Rothstein 2004; Toronto District School Board [TDSB] 2006). The problem is that such measures of equity, which direct attention to a gender achievement gap, do so at the expense of a consideration of how other important socio-economic and demographic variables interlock and overlap, with significant consequences for certain visible minority populations – both boys and girls.

This focus on the persistence of race inequalities of achievement as 'a locked in' phenomenon is highlighted by Gillborn (2008). He discusses the effects of privileging both class and gender underachievement in terms of eschewing important questions of maldistribution. Gillborn argues for a more careful disaggregation of performance data and draws on data sources from within the Department for Education and Skills in England, which are disaggregated by class, race and gender to reveal the extent of different achievement gaps. The mapping of such data reveals the extent to which race and class achievement gaps are far greater than any gender achievement gap. However, Gillborn is concerned to draw further attention to the significance of an intersectional analysis of these achievement data, which uses a more sophisticated indicator of ethnic background to reveal important variations within these class- and gender-based trends. For example, a close reading of the data shows that white non-Free School Meal (FSM) students outperform their peers from the same gender from different ethnic groups with the largest disparity existing between White students and their Black Caribbean counterparts: 'White non-FSM girls outperform their Black Caribbean counterparts by 9.7 percentage points' while the achievement gap between 'White non-FSM boys' and Black Caribbean students is 17.2% points (56).

Gillborn uses such data analysis to challenge the discourse of white failure, which was generated by the media coverage at the time in England, which tended to portray white boys as being left behind by the education system. There was also much sensationalized newspaper coverage of white working-class boys specifically as 'the worst performers in schools' (56), which tended to rely on moral panic and crisis associated with the familiar 'failing boys' rhetoric, which has 'tended to emphasize the scale of class inequalities as if they were a common factor', rather than unevenly distributed across race and ethnic lines (55). This focus on the practices of journalists in contributing to the mediatization of educational policy (Lingard and Rawolle 2004), as we will illustrate later specifically in relation to the Ontario context, is central to understanding the role of the media in how boys continue to be constituted as particular objects of government in which they are rendered as knowable and calculable subjects, and hence amenable to systematic and programmatic intervention (Miller and Rose 2008, 30). The rendering of boys into such a discourse of moral panic and crisis (Titus 2004) eschews important questions about the persistence of 'locked-in' racial inequalities in education. As

Gillborn (2008) illustrates, while both Black and White students' achievement has improved over a period of 15 years since 1989 in England, the Black/White achievement gap was far greater in 2004 (at 21% points) than it was 15 years earlier (at 12% points) (59).

Such an illustration of disaggregated data use and its capacity to draw attention to more complex interactions between gender, social class and race influences, in terms of how they impact educational achievement for various populations, raises important questions about what counts as evidence and equity. Moreover, such data usage draws attention to important epistemological and political issues underscoring approaches to measuring, explaining and defining inequality in educational policy and practice (Luke, Green, and Kelly 2010, vii; Martino and Rezai-Rashti 2012). For example, while the OECD (2010a) does acknowledge the relationship between family and socio-economic background factors and the unequal distribution of social and financial resources among various school locations, in terms of its impact on school performance, data are employed to show that there are indeed 'weaker relationships between background characteristics and reading performance in some countries compared to others [which] signal that inequalities in educational opportunity are not inevitable' (43). Here, we witness, once again, an exemplary instance of how numbers, rankings and comparisons are used with implications for 'new geographies of governance' particularly in terms of their capacity to steer policy related to educational and school-based reform within nations (Lingard 2011, 357).

More significantly, this focus on measuring certain background factors instead of others relates to the second concern mentioned above about *categories in use* governing the measurement of such variables and their potential influence on students' reading performance. For instance, PISA mentions collecting 'detailed information on various aspects related to the economic, social and cultural status' of students' families, and indicates that measurement is based on indices such as 'the education level and occupational status of students' fathers and mothers and their access to cultural and educational resources at home'. However, it does offer the following cautionary note in drawing attention to what is not being measured:

> The relationship between socio-economic background and performance does not necessarily reflect inequalities that occur within the boundaries of the school; inequities also hinge on societal arrangements for family healthcare, income maintenance, housing and children, to name just a few factors. Indeed, some of these factors, or *their interaction with socio-economic background*, may have as much or a greater impact on performance than schools. *While PISA did not collect information about these factors*, it is worth keeping them in mind when interpreting the results reported here. (43, our emphasis)

In short, PISA acknowledges that 'the average performance of students depends on the education system and the overall social, economic and political institutions that influence student performance', which include 'government institutions that improve children's material conditions, like housing nutrition and health care', but that 'differences in these conditions across countries are not taken into account' (56). These limitations have serious implications for being able to address the full extent to which any school is able to overcome socio-economic disadvantages and, hence, the *locked-in inequality* related to these structural determinants, which we know affect variously positioned populations differently, given histories of race-relations and maldistribution in terms of accessing to resources such as good quality housing in urban locations and employment, etc. (Anyon 1997; Condron 2011; Dumas 2009; Lipman 2004). Anyon (1997), for example, argues that school reform initiatives are simply not enough to overcome 'decades of accumulated want and despair that impede students every day' in urban schools '… until the economic and political systems in which the cities are enmeshed are themselves transformed so they may be more democratic and productive for urban residents, educational reformers have little chance of effecting long-lasting educational changes in city schools' (13). Failing to account for such socio-economic factors and generational poverty enables overzealous attention to be focused on the role of school-based and pedagogical reform interventions in their capacity to improve the quality of education, while overlooking the devastating impact of generational poverty and its concentration in certain urban locations and among specific populations.

Rothstein (2004) challenges policy makers' *commonsense* positions that schools can make a difference, which he indicates can easily slip into attributing the achievement gap to the fault of 'failing schools' (and we would add, poor teachers) and with which he associates the current emphasis on high stakes testing regimes – a practice clearly related to the emergence of quasi market forces in education associated with the rise of neoliberal governance and performance management systems (1) (see Lingard 2011; Ozga 2009). As Ball (2012) points out, 'education is just one manifestation of a global reworking of the economic, social, moral and political foundations of public service provision and the development of new kinds of responses to social disadvantage' (15). Grek (2009) has well highlighted the role of PISA as a 'governing device', which has enabled the OECD to constitute a space of equivalence for the emergence of a global education policy field (27). In short, the OECD (2010a) argues that 'in a global economy, the yardstick is no longer improvement by national standards alone, but how education systems perform internationally'; they further argue that PISA is a means by which nations across the globe can be evaluated and can evaluate themselves in terms of ascertaining 'the quality, equity and efficiency of school systems' (3). As we have witnessed, this rescaling of educational politics and political authority (Lingard and Rawolle 2011) has produced a degree of competition amongst nations and has led to certain education systems in countries such as Finland, Canada (Ontario) and China (Shanghai) being marketed as exemplary models to be emulated by other nations or at least as providing lessons for other nations to learn about what lies behind the success of each country (Tucker 2011).[6]

The policy steering capacity of PISA as a technology of neoliberal governance in education

With regard to the use of PISA results, there is some disturbing evidence that the data on reading performance lend themselves to being co-opted by neoliberal influences and forms of governance in relation to driving particular educational reform initiatives that ignore important effects of poverty and their impact on the provision of quality education. Riddile (2010) in her article, 'It's poverty not stupid', for example, reports that the US Secretary of Education, Arnie Duncan, issued a statement upon the release of the PISA 2009 scores, which he claimed heralded 'a massive wake-up call' because they 'show American students holding relatively steady in the middle of the pack of the developed nations taking the international exam'. Here, we witness the scalar effects of PISA as a technology of governance in steering educational reform and policy initiatives at the national level. In light of such data, Riddile claims that Duncan is advocating for 'more charter schools, more reliance on competition and free market strategies, more testing, more use of test scores to evaluate teachers, more firing of principals and teachers, more closing of low scoring schools'. The US is clearly responding to concerns about its ranking on PISA measures for designating 'high performing education systems' across the globe with the potential for nations to both being marketed and to market themselves as world leaders. Tucker (2011), for example, highlights that performance on PISA measures is about 'compet[ing] in the global economy' (16), with scholars such as Mehta and Schwartz (2011) drawing specific attention to Canada, which 'looks a lot like US but gets much better results', as having *high quality* and *high equity* systems (141) (see also Luke 2011).

Riddile (2010), however, includes commentary from the National Association of Secondary School Principals' Executive Director, Dr Tirozzi, who offers a scathing critique of PISA by re-using the statistics to direct renewed attention to the correlation between performance on PISA reading scores and concentrations of school populations of students living in poverty, measured in terms of identifying those schools with a higher or lesser percentage of students who receive free and reduced cost lunch. He shows that schools with a less than 10% poverty rate had an average PISA score of 551, while those with a poverty rate of greater than 75% had an average score of 446. In fact, using these measures, Tirozzi shows US schools with a poverty rate between 10 and 24% do better than 10 comparable nations (including Canada), with a top ranking PISA score of 527 and asserts that:

> The problem is not so much with our education system as it is with our high poverty rates. The real crisis is the level of poverty in too many of our schools and the relationship between poverty and student achievement. Our lowest achieving schools are the most under-resourced schools with the highest number of disadvantaged students. (Riddile 2010)

This use of disaggregated data draws attention once again to the categories in use in the generation and analysis of data as numbers, as well as to the fact that 'the very measurement of educational inequality itself is also not a given' (Lucas and Beresford 2010, 25). As Tirozzi illustrates, how equity in education is defined changes how nations are ranked according to PISA reading scores and can lead to a shift in the reform focus away from blaming or reforming schools as a policy solution or problematic to one which requires serious consideration of a politics of redistribution. This is an argument also proffered by Condron (2011). As Riddile (2010) argues, 'Of all the nations participating in PISA assessment, the US has, by far, the largest number of students living in poverty – 21.7%'.

Given the influence of such scalar regimes of standardization and marketization within the context of the global policy-making field in education, Rothstein (2004) also offers caution to policy makers, who in their concern to close the achievement gap for low-income and minority students have directed inordinate attention to school reform efforts, which have focused on raising the quality of teaching with the effect of eschewing 'the greater importance of reforming social and economic institutions if we truly want children to emerge from school with equal potential' (9). Such a position is consistent with that advocated by Fraser (1997), who argues for the need to move beyond a politics of recognition as a basis for addressing social injustice and directing attention to the politics of redistribution in looking to remedy, or at least ameliorate, socio-economic disadvantage for minoritized populations (Power and Frandji 2010). Rothstein, for example, highlights the need for reform strategies that are focused more broadly on redistribution and highlights the following salient points about socio-economic disadvantage and its impact:

- The 'full array of socio-economic differences' need to be considered and cannot be measured solely in terms of income and parental education levels (52);
- No more than one-third of student achievement variation can be attributed to school effects which tend to be overstated (56) – differences in home literacy support, social class differences in childrearing practices, differential access to out-of-school experiences such as summer camp, health conditions, housing and social mobility, racial discrimination which are exacerbated by living in poverty and the accumulated, generational and persistent effects of such factors over time for specific populations and cannot be overcome by contending that higher quality teachers and schools can compensate for such structural deficits: 'simply improving the quality of teaches without having to worry about the social and economic causes of low achievement' cannot close the achievement gap for economically disadvantaged students (69);
- Low expectations that teachers and schools have of black and Latino students, while playing a role cannot offer an adequate explanation of black underachievement – the cumulative effects of poverty, overcrowded and unstable or inadequate housing conditions, levels of support in terms of completing homework and for literacy learning outside of school and how these are ambitions are exacerbated or frustrated by repetitive experiences of racism in terms of labour market access and success for these specific minoritized populations need to be considered (35);
- There are significant social class differences between blacks and whites with similar incomes – 'income is an inexact proxy for the many social class characteristics that differentiate blacks from whites whose current year income is the same' because 'blacks whose incomes are near the poverty line are more likely to have been poor for several years than whites whose poverty is more often episodic' (47);
- Significant differences also exist between blacks and whites with middle-class incomes – 'white middle-class families are more likely than black middle-class families to have adequate and spacious housing, even when annual incomes are similar, because white middle-class families are more likely to have received capital contributions form their own parents' whereas the Black middle-class parents are more likely to be the first generation in their families to have acquired middle-class status (49).

Overall, Rothstein (cf. Condron 2011) is concerned to emphasize the need for economic reform in achievement gap discourse, which must also address important questions of race and intersectionality as they relate to the cumulative effects of various socio-economic determinants of generational poverty, health, well-being, adequate residential security and stability, childrearing and access to educational experiences and opportunities outside of school, etc. For example, he claims that 'if black students expect their academic efforts to be unrewarded, it is because the weight of historical experience has been that black efforts in fact have been unrewarded' and that, in spite of their 'force of will and determination' to overcome the weight of such history, 'teachers and schools cannot transplant ambition into students who are not ready to adopt it' (51). It is in this sense that Rothstein argues for an approach which takes into account both a politics of recognition and how it is intertwined with economic considerations and, hence, a need to attend to a politics of redistribution in addressing educational reform concerned to address the black–white achievement gap (see Fraser 1997). Thus, an interactional or intersectional analysis that takes into account questions of identity, culture, race and social class is needed when interpreting test scores. Such an analysis would take into account background characteristics and differences related to long-term family income, provision of social and cultural capital through childrearing practices, quality of housing, access to health care services, nutrition and health differences amongst various populations, generational poverty, parents' educational levels and occupational status. This approach is consistent with Fraser's (1997) argument about addressing both a cultural politics of difference/recognition and a politics of social equality/redistribution, when it comes to dealing with injustices that are simultaneously both racial (cultural) and socio-economic (economic) and which amount to 'theorizing the ways in which economic disadvantage and cultural disrespect are currently entwined with and support one another' (12).

These discussions about the use of categories and interpretation of test score data, along with engagement with epistemological and conceptual matters regarding issues of redistribution and recognition, further highlight the need for methodologically sophisticated and nuanced considerations in the use of data and analysis. In short, we need to attend more closely to the 'theoretical bases of the categories in use' in interpreting test score data and in engaging with policy-generating discourses about the achievement gap, particularly in terms of addressing 'the complexity of defining and classifying persons along assumed equity-relevant dimensions' (Lucas and Beresford 2010, 25, 27). In this sense, we support Connolly's (2008) position regarding need for policy-making discussions involving the measurement of achievement gaps to 'engage adequately with substantive theoretical and empirical literature' (249), particularly 'concerning the content of sociodemographic categories as well as the phenomena those categories collectively reference' (Lucas and Beresford 2010, 73).

PISA's focus on the gender achievement gap in reading performance

The OECD (2010b) draws specific attention to *tackling both gender and socioeconomic inequalities*, but in ways which forget the need for the sort of disaggregation that has been illustrated by scholars in the field such as Gillborn (2008) and Rothstein (2004) and which we have dealt with to this point. It asserts, for example, that 'Girls outperform boys in reading in all countries assessed by PISA' and draws specific attention to 'underachievement among disadvantaged boys' (85). While the OECD (2010b) acknowledges the importance of socio-economic background's effect on reading performance and that such differences 'are often compounded by racial and ethnic differences in achievement' (86), there is no focus on such disaggregated performance measures on PISA which, as Gillborn (2008) illustrates, provides a more accurate picture of which boys and which girls are most at risk of underachieving (AAUW 2008; Collins, Kenway, and McLeod 2000; Lingard, Martino, and Mills 2002; Martino and Rezai-Rashti 2012; TDSB 2006). For example, such disaggregated data tend to highlight that middle-class boys perform much better than girls from disadvantaged backgrounds and that the race gap in achievement is much greater than any gender gap (Martino 2008; Mead 2006). However, the PISA focus is on highlighting that, *on average*, girls 'have better reading skills than boys' and that particular attention needs to be focused on the wide gender gap among low-achieving students, given that 'boys greatly outnumber girls among those students who lack basic reading skills' and, hence, those who fail to attain Level 2 in reading proficiency (86). The effect of the use of such numbers is to illuminate the 'fact' that this group of boys is most at risk.

However, in disentangling the influences behind both gender and class dispari-ties in reading performance on PISA, the OECD (2010b) identifies *reading habits* and *interests* as key explanatory factors, claiming that 'when boys enjoy reading, when they read widely and adopt learning strategies extensively, they can attain higher levels of performance reading than girls' (86). Much of the explanatory discourse behind boys' lower reading proficiency throughout the specific chapter devoted to the topic in the third *PISA 2009 Results* volume tends to highlight that 'boys enjoy reading substantially less than girls' and, moreover, that they 'have less extensive knowledge about effective summarizing strategies than girls', which, it is argued, 'explains a large part of the gender gap in reading performance in most countries and economies' (89). It is mentioned that even in Finland, one of the highest ranking performing countries on PISA reading measures, 'boys score an average of 55 points lower than girls'.

In addition, disadvantaged boys are compared with socio-economically advan-taged girls in terms of their differential reading performance on PISA to assert that if these boys' enjoyment of reading matched those of the latter group and if these boys had the same levels of awareness of effective summarizing strategies, the achievement gap would indeed be significantly narrower (OECD 2010b, 95). Questions about comparing disadvantaged boys with advantaged girls, rather than disadvantaged girls with middle-class and more affluent boys need to be posed, because they draw attention to the space of equivalences that are constituted through numbers. They also draw attention to PISA as a technology of governance for steering and endorsing educational policy-making discussions that further endorse a discourse of *failing boys* and moral panic in their capacity to eschew important questions of male and white privilege (Connolly 2008; Gillborn 2008). In short, the troubling nature of such framing of boys' literacy underachievement data is that it lends itself easily to being co-opted by a *recuperative masculinity politics* and, in so doing, tends to eschew important questions of class privilege that exists for middle-class boys and those boys from more affluent backgrounds.[7] More importantly, this emphasis on gender achievement gaps tends to oversimplify complex issues, not only in terms of eliding how race and ethnicity *intersect* with gender and social class to impact on groups of students differently vis-à-vis their reading achievement, but also in terms of lending itself to an overzealous emphasis on pedagogical reform that ignores the significance of structural determinants, such as access to resources and the material conditions with which many students in poverty have to contend.

These systemic influences, as Rothstein (2004) and Condron (2011) emphasize, cannot be compensated for by pedagogical and school-based interventions alone that are committed to motivating boys and engaging their interest in reading. For example, to emphasize that the 80% of gender achievement gap can be explained in

terms of 'the extent to which boys and girls enjoy reading and are aware of strategies to summarize information', and to further frame the problematic as a question
of 'the untapped potential of boys' as 'represented by their unsatisfactory levels of
internal motivation to read' (90), is to minimize the significance and impact of
socio-economic conditions and family circumstances. This impact is particularly
pertinent for those most at-risk students living at or below the poverty line, that is,
those students who fail to attain Level 2 reading proficiency. Ultimately, closing the
achievement gap, in fact, is reduced to a matter of 'changing attitudes and
behaviours' and to providing 'equal access to high quality teachers and schools',
the former being identified as 'inherently more difficult' (99):

> In the short term, this may require catering to boys' reading preferences, such as their
> relatively strong interest in reading newspapers and reading online, rather than
> designing a single model of engagement in reading. Over the longer term, *shrinking
> the gender gap* in reading performance will require the concerted efforts of parents,
> teachers and society at large to change stereotyped notions of what boys and girls
> excel in doing and what they enjoy doing. (OECD 2010b, 99, our emphasis)

Here, questions of gender identification are singled out for boys as inhibiting their
engagement with literacy. While clearly masculinity intersects in very important
ways with boys' engagement and participation in literacy (Alloway et al. 2002;
Martino 2001), such gender achievement *gap talk* suffers from many of the blind
spots identified by Gillborn (2008) in terms of ignoring the significant variations
that exist within broad class- and gender-based trends in achievement (55). More
specifically, the question of how certain dispositions are acquired and the sorts of
social, cultural and economic capitals that are associated with high performance in
reading and active participation in schooling are simply minimized (Bourdieu
1986). In short, in its treatment and discussion of reading achievement, PISA tends
to rely on a *politics of misrecognition,* rather than engaging substantively with *a
politics of redistribution* and how both the former and latter are intimately
intertwined in very complex ways (Fraser 1997) and need to be a focus of
government policy.

Along these lines, what is also important to highlight is that many of the most
at-risk students in school systems in Canada, for example, are not included in the
PISA sample, simply because they have already dropped out of the system due to
the cumulative effect of a range of socio-demographic and structural influences
which intersect with race (see Anisef et al. 2010; TDSB 2006). For example, as
Bouchard, Boily, and Proulx (2003) indicate, 'extremes in achievement do not
divide solely along gender lines'; nor can social class differences be adequately
accounted for without attending to significant questions of race and ethnicity, in
addition to a consideration of the historical legacy of colonialism and its impact on
Aboriginal populations in countries such as Canada to produce conditions of *locked
in* inequalities that cannot be easily ameliorated through a reliance on school based
reform interventions: 'In Quebec, for example, 77.4% of Aboriginals starting high
school have already failed at least one year: In outlying regions, 87.9% of
Aboriginal youth leave school before getting their high school diploma [Translation]
(Larose et al. 2001, 153)' (57). In addition, such performance data also need to be
coupled with an analysis of post-school outcomes and trajectories for boys and girls
in terms of their participation in the labour market and also earning capacity. Such

data have the capacity to further highlight the scale of structural disadvantages for specific groups of both boys and girls (Collins, Kenway, and McLeod 2000).

Overall, this discussion and analysis highlight the extent to which the OECD (2010b) employs and frames an analysis of PISA performance data regarding the gender achievement gap in reading, to steer educational policy-making in a direction that is marred by significant blind spots, as it relates to prioritizing a discourse of *failing boys*. In this capacity, it needs to be understood as a technology of governance in terms of *making up* boys as a specific category and target (Hacking 2006), which enables them to be made amenable to administration and policy-making through an orchestrated use of numbers (Miller and Rose 2008). Hacking highlights the role of statistical analysis and its function in the classification of 'classes of people' or specific groups defined as having 'definite properties'. The ways in which boys are constituted within the commensurate space of the global policy-making field, and the role of the OECD and specifically PISA, draw attention to the use of both numbers and onto-epistemological frames of reference that are deployed to render the thinkable problem of 'failing' boys. In this capacity, PISA functions as 'a vast statistical apparatus through which this domain [of underachieving boys] can be inscribed, tabulated and acted upon' (Miller and Rose 2008, 36). The political effects of such a technology in terms of treating boys as a target of government through a politics of misrecognition is further highlighted in the following section with our analysis of the achievement gap discourse in the pan Canadian context.

PCAP and the focus on the gender achievement gap: an exemplary case of misrecognition

As already pointed out, the governance of education in Canada falls under the jurisdiction of specific provinces. However, the CMEC was formed in 1967 by the ministers themselves 'to provide a forum in which they could discuss matters of mutual interest, undertake educational initiatives cooperatively, and represent the interest of provinces and territories with national educational organizations, the federal government, foreign governments and international organizations' (CMEC 2011, i). CMEC also claims to be 'the national voice for education in Canada' and, hence, positions itself as an administrative conduit for the provinces and territories 'to work collectively on common objectives' (i). CMEC devised a PCAP, which is designed to generate 'comparative Canada wide data' on the achievement levels of Grade 8 students in Mathematics, Science and Reading and is specifically designed to 'inform educational policies to improve learning' (1). Through such a statistical apparatus, the Ministers of Education have strategically attempted to influence education policy as it relates to the problem of boys' underachievement. In conjunction with the Federal government of Canada – namely The Department of Human Resources and Skills Development – and Statistics Canada – CMEC has also produced a report which details how Canadian results on the 2009 OECD PISA study 'measure up' (Human Resources and Skills Development Canada 2010). Both reports are posted on the CMEC website and are concerned to draw attention to gender achievement gaps. In fact, both reports highlight that girls continue to outperform boys in reading, and that boys tend to outperform girls in mathematics and science, although it is emphasized that in these latter two domains, the gender gap is less pronounced (Human Resources and Skills Development Canada 2010, 39).

What is significant about the PCAP results is that for each province, test score data are disaggregated solely along the lines of gender and the two official languages, English and French. This specific focus on gender is justified in terms of 'policy makers (including educators at all levels, parents, and other interested parties)' as having a particular interest 'in reducing disparities in educational performance' (29). Throughout the report, gender comparisons are noted for each of the subject areas across all provinces and territories. However, given this concern with the gender achievement gap, CMEC is concerned to emphasize that in Mathematics, for example, while boys tend to do better overall, the gap is not as large as it is for reading performance, and, moreover, that in some subdomains, such as 'Patterns and Relationships' and 'Data Management and Probability', girls have actually caught up to boys, so that there is no significant difference in favour of boys (31). In addition, the PCAP results also reveal that the mean score of girls in Science is significantly higher than the mean score of boys. A bar graph is also strategically included on page 128 of the report to represent gender and language differences in reading with regard to reading score comparisons on both the 2007 and 2010 PCAP tests. The graph shows that reading performance for both girls and boys has declined – by seven points for girls (from 522 in 2007 to 515 in 2010) and by 12 points for boys (from 501 in 2007 to 489 in 2010). The representation of data in these terms draws attention to the extent to which the gender gap has widened over time – in 2007, there was 21-point difference in mean scores between girls and boys, while in 2010 it had increased to a 26-point difference.

The use of such disaggregated data and their representation in bar-graph form is designed to illuminate the phenomenon of 'failing boys'. This immediately produces a significant blind spot in terms of significant disparities in achievement that exist for minority populations and in terms of socio-economic background, which, as already pointed out, is far greater than any gender gap (Anisef et al. 2010; Jordan 2010; Rothstein 2004). In short, reducing achievement to a politics of gender disparities is to fundamentally *misrecognize* and eschew what counts as evidence and equity (Fraser 1997; Luke, Green, and Kelly 2010), particularly in terms of the need to consider economic disadvantage and intra-group variability regarding 'the importance of race, class, and culture in measuring student outcomes' (Jordan 2010, 150). As Jordan (2010) highlights, racial and socio-economic equity is actually hindered when investigated through neoliberal- and performance-driven educational accountability discourses (164). In this sense, as Rose (1999) points out, numbers are deployed as 'inscription devices' and 'actually constitute the domain they appear to represent', such as the problematic of 'failing boys' thereby rendering boys as 'representable' and 'amenable to the application of calculation and deliberation' (198).

What is also interesting to note is that the 'measuring up' report, which was published in 2010 by CMEC and the Canadian Government prior to the release of the PCAP report in 2010, reflects an exemplary instance of the rescaling of political authority that results in the constitution of a particular 'policy habitus', which Lingard and Rawolle (2011) claim 'enhances cross field effects between the global educational policy field and specific national fields' (496). In fact, CMEC (2011) explicitly states that one of the key purposes of PCAP 'was to align itself with international assessments such as the OECD PISA' (37). The cross-field policy effects, particularly in terms of the emphasis on the gender achievement gap, are also evidenced by the mediatization of policy (Lingard and Rawolle 2004), with the role of journalists immediately reporting on the release of the PCAP results to spin a familiar discourse of moral panic about 'failing boys'. For example, upon the release of the PCAP results, a journalist for the *Globe and Mail*, Canada's National newspaper, published an article with the sensationalized headline: 'Boys' poor results in reading feared to be spreading to math, science' (Hammer 2011, Boys Poor Results in Reading Feared to be Spreading to Math, Science. *The Globe and Mail*, http://www.theglobeandmail.com/news/national/education/primary-to-secondary/boys-poor-results-in-reading-feared-to-be-spreading-to-math-science/article2254436/?utm_medium=Feeds%3A%20RSS%2FAtom&utm_source=Home&utm_content=2254436). The heading immediately mobilizes the rhetoric of disadvantaged boys, who are now also at risk of underachieving in other areas of the curriculum, where traditionally they have performed well. The notion of their failure 'spreading' conjures up the spectre of an epidemic that risks inflicting boys across core curriculum subjects such as mathematics and science. In short, it is a phenomenon that is not confined only to reading: 'The results raise questions whether struggles with reading are having a domino effect on boys' academic performance. Whether an isolated event, or a sign of something bigger, they raise a red flag for education' the journalist, Hammer, asserts. This newspaper report, published upon the 2010 release of the PCAP results, provides an exemplary instance of the mediatization of policy production. This mediatization is manifested particularly in terms of endorsing a particular policy narrative about 'failing boys' that is consistent with the one being promulgated through the use of numbers by CMEC for conferring a certain degree of political legitimacy regarding the existence of a gender achievement gap.

The role of media within a scalar network of cross-field policy effects has also been highlighted by coverage of the *Globe and Mail* newspaper on the subject of 'failing boys', which spanned an entire week in 2010. This particular topic was identified as one of the eight most pressing issues that will challenge Canada in the next decade, alongside the future of the military and the provision of public health-care (Abraham 2010, Part 1: Failing boys and the powder keg of sexual politics. *The Globe and Mail*, October 15, http://www.theglobeandmail.com/news/national/time-to-lead/failing-boys/part-1-failing-boys-and-the-powder-keg-of-sexual-politics/article1758791/). The article introducing the topic began with the following asser-tion: 'There's a new gender gap in education: Around the world, boys rank behind girls by nearly every measure of scholastic achievement' (Abraham 2010). Splashed across the bottom of the two full-page feature articles was a series of graphs drawn from the 2006 PISA results, which disaggregated achievement data solely on the basis of gender for science, reading and math across a number of OECD countries, including Canada. What immediately becomes apparent is evidence of a rescaling of authority as set against a particular policyscape (Ball 1998) in which the interplay of national and the global forces is mobilized around the recuperative masculinity interests of proliferating a particular social imaginary about boys as the 'new disadvantaged' through the mediatization of policy production (Lingard and Rawolle 2011; Martino and Rezai-Rashti 2012). As we have illustrated in this section, the mass media has functioned in very significant ways within a network of policy-making effects and practices, as evidenced by both the role of CMEC and OECD to constitute a particular policy habitus, particularly in relation to the endorsement of a gender achievement gap and the mobilization of discourses about failing boys in the Canadian context.

Equity and gender achievement gap talk in Ontario

Ontario, along with Finland, Singapore and Shanghai-China, has been identified as having one of the highest performing education systems (Luke 2011; Tucker 2011). In short, PISA enables the national, provincial and global city aspects to be highlighted as part of the subnational, national and global rescaling of education policy field (Lingard and Rawolle 2011). On the OECD website, a promotional video of Ontario is included, along with those of other top-performing nations identified as *successful reformers in education*. Luke (2011) specifically attributes Ontario's success to 'a distinctive commitment to equity, to multiculturalism' as 'core Canadian values' (374). He also draws attention to the high quality of teacher candidates in universities and the investment in ongoing professional development for teachers. He also mentions the significance of a 'less prescriptive curriculum and 'low-moderate emphasis on standardized testing', which he attributes to the push for educational reform that was instigated under Ben Levin, as 'one of its key architects' (373) (see Anderson and Ben Jaafar 2003; Dei and Karamanchery 1999; Rezai-Rashti 2003, 2009 for an alternative interpretation of education reform in Ontario). The OECD promotional video, which is entitled *Making Sure Students From All Backgrounds and Origins Can Fulfill Their Potential*, follows along these celebratory lines and markets Ontario as an *exhibit* or exemplification of achieving equity for all students, especially those students from immigrant backgrounds: 'Ontario shows how high-school students can do well whatever their family background, first language or place of birth' (OECD web site, *Strong Performers and Successful Reformers in Education*). While there has indeed been a commitment to equity policy in Ontario that has been influenced by the *Charter of Human Rights* as an overarching framework for policy-making both in education and across over fields of governance, the marketing of Ontario in these terms eschews and, we would argue, contributes to a fundamental misrecognition of the historical legacy of inequality that persists in Ontario for specific immigrant and visible minority populations. The impact of standardized testing regimes and forms of neoliberal accountability mechanisms such as those instigated under the previous Harris conservative government and continued under the McGuinty liberal government should not be minimized or downplayed (Martino and Rezai-Rashti 2012).

Such blind spots are orchestrated in the promotional video through the inclusion of a public school in Unionville, Ontario, as an exemplary case which illustrates the success of immigrants in the Ontario education system. What is not mentioned in the video is that Unionville, which is a district in Markham, located 33 kms north of downtown Toronto, is one of the most affluent areas in the Greater Toronto Area with an average household income of $127,900 (http://en.wikipedia.org/wiki/Unionville,_Ontario). The immigrants who live in this geographical location differ from those living in other locations in Toronto in government-subsidized housing, and where there have high concentrations of economic disadvantage and poverty. Analyses of TDSB data provided by Anisef et al. (2010), as well as data provided by the TDSB (2006) itself, tend to offer a different picture of the situation in Ontario for immigrant students. Anisef et al. (2010), for example, document the phenomenon of early school leaving among immigrants in Toronto secondary schools and emphasize that this is 'strongly influenced by socio-economic status as well as such factors as country of origin, age at arrival, generational status, family structure, and academic performance' (104). Moreover, these scholars show that not all immigrants are successful in school and that 'the substantially higher incidence of poverty' for certain immigrant populations means that they are 'likely to face greater obstacles to academic success that may in turn have detrimental, long-term consequences' (104). In addition, a TDSB study found that students who speak Spanish, Portuguese or Somali are at a higher risk than any other group of students failing the Grade 10 literacy test. Furthermore, students from the Caribbean, Central or South America and Eastern Africa have significantly higher dropout rates than the rest of the population (TDSB 2006). This example of policy as numbers highlights the need to address which groups of students are most at risk, and clearly, data generated by local school boards such as the TDSB provide a more informed account of the structural inequalities that continue to impact on differently positioned populations in relation to their socio-economic and immigrant backgrounds.

Such analysis needs to be set against a problematic policy-making context within the Ontario Ministry of Education, which in 2009 launched its *Equity and Inclusive Education* policy, which states 'an explicit commitment to reducing achievement gaps' and includes the category of boys as a designated targeted population, along with 'recent immigrants', 'children from low income families', 'Aboriginal students' and 'students with special education needs' as being 'at risk of lower achievement' (Ontario Ministry of Education 2009, 5). Prior to the insertion of boys into official equity policy as a designated disadvantaged group, the Ministry also produce a guide for facilitating boys' literacy engagement in Ontario schools, which endorsed, for the most part, problematic 'boy friendly' approaches grounded in essentialist mindsets regarding the need to cater for stereotypical boys' interests as basis for pedagogical intervention. The guide was also used as a template or policy frame for directing school-based research, funded by the Ontario Ministry of Education, as a basis for generating evidence-informed policy for effective interventions in addressing the problem of boys' literacy achievement in schools. We have written about such policy initiatives with their implications for actually exacerbating questions of equity, which we have highlighted here as thwarting a politics of redistribution and a more sophisticated politics of recognition that does not resort to endorsing a recuperative masculinity politics (see Martino and Rezai-Rashi 2012). We refer briefly to such policy interventions here only because they further highlight the importance of contextualization in producing a counter narrative that interrupts the celebratory discourses of equity and multiculturalism that have come to characterize the ways in which Ontario is currently being marketed, based on its performance on PISA measures, as a high quality world-class education system. This has the effect of blinding the schooling system to ongoing inequalities in and through schooling.

Conclusion

In this paper, we have drawn on policy sociology and substantive theoretical and empirical literature in undertaking an analysis of PISA's focus on equity and achievement gaps as basis for explicating the scalar dimensions of the policy habitus of 'failing boys' within the Canadian context. In drawing on Fraser (1997), Miller and Rose (2008) and Lingard's (2011) scholarship on policy as numbers, we have illuminated how the OECD's PISA functions as technology of governance, which is imbricated in policy-making at the national and local levels, using Canada as a specific case in point. In the first part of the paper, we concentrated on OECD and PISA 2009 to provide a critique of the use of numbers and its scalar effects, particularly in terms of endorsing a gender achievement gap which eschews important questions of intersectionlity, particularly with regards to race, culture, ethnicity and social class. We have drawn attention in this analysis to the theoretical bases of the categories in use that are deployed by OECD in *tackling* gender and socio-economic inequalities in reading. Our analyses highlight the categories in use behind the measurement of educational inequality, which as Lucas and Beresford (2010, 25) highlight, should certainly not be taken as a given.

In the second part of the paper, we focus specifically on the use of numbers in the Canadian context and draw attention to how such numbers, particularly as they relate to the gender achievement gap, are implicated in a global education policy field with OECD's PISA results as a pivotal reference point. This analysis has highlighted the extent to which national and provincial administrative bodies such as PCAP and the Ontario Ministry of Education function within a global web of networks in which Ontario features as reference society for marketing itself as a high-achieving/ high-equity performer in the global education market place. In highlighting this global reworking of national and provincial policyscapes through a politics of numbers, we have drawn attention to the problematics of misrecognition that potentially result from the use of such comparative data sets, which fail to account for the complexity of socio-economic disadvantage and its cumulative effects across generations for specific visible minority populations in the Canadian context. We conclude on the basis of our critique that the OECD, through PISA, is able to endorse a focus on school-based interventions and the role of quality education systems in their capacity to ameliorate socio-economic disadvantages by ignoring significant structural dimensions of inequality and a politics of redistribution. In addition, we have been concerned to highlight how the rescaling of authority that has been granted to the validity of performance measures on PISA as an indicator of achieving quality and equity is intertwined with broader effects of globalization and neoliberal systems of accountability. It is through such technologies of governance with their capacity for producing 'a globalizing empiricism' (Torrance 2006) that 'failing boys' have been made more amenable to administration.

Overall, the critiques offered in this paper suggest a cautionary note for education policy makers in respect of relying too heavily on PISA measures as a basis for decision-making regarding questions pertain to equity as they relate to maldistribution. What is needed, then, is more engagement with data generation from the *bottom up,* which includes both quantitative and rich qualitative data that are generated at school board and local school level and disaggregated in multiple ways. Such data generation has the capacity to better account for the contextual specificity of schooling, as well as the influence of specific background characteristics and their effects for particular populations in specific school communities. What is also flagged as necessary – for both policy makers and those involved in the conduct of research into equity and social justice matters within the field of education – is the need for a detailed consideration of the extent to which onto-epistemological standpoints impact on both interpretive frameworks that are employed to generate and make sense of performance data and their methodological implications. As we have illustrated throughout this paper, both the conduct of research and the sort of theoretically informed empiricism that comes to count as legitimate evidence are what that need critical interrogation, particularly as they relate to 'gap talk' within the global education policy field.

Acknowledgement

This paper is based on a SSHRC (Social Sciences Humanities Research Council of Canada)-funded project entitled: *Beyond the crisis of failing boys: Investigating which boys and which girls are underachieving* (410-2010-0599).

Notes

1. Our critique of 'gap talk' is informed by engagement with Gillborn (2008) who argues that "talk of 'closing' and/or 'narrowing' gaps operates as a discursive strategy whereby statistical data are deployed to construct the view that things are improving and the system is moving in the right direction" (65). Within the context of this paper our concern is to highlight how 'gap talk' is deployed politically to steer education policy in directions which eschew careful attention to performance gaps between multiple and intersecting categories of analysis such as race, ethnicity, gender, class, geographical location. It is not that achievement gaps should not be the focus of policy intervention. Rather we argue that attention needs to be devoted to the categories in use and the epistemological frameworks that govern the use of numbers.
2. In Canada education remains the exclusive responsibility of each province with each province appointing its own Minister of Education. There is no Federal or National Minister of Education.
3. The 'policy habitus' refers specifically to a particular field and interconnected networks of relations and flows of discourses in which policy making is implicated. As Lingard, Rawolle, and Taylor (2005) explicate a policy habitus refers to dispositional tendencies of policy makers and emphasizes the sedimentation of history, structure and culture in individual disposition to practice (764). With regards to 'failing boys' as an object of the education policy making field, we identify a particular logics of practice governing policy making as it relates to the constitution of a gender achievement gap and the designation of boys as a disadvantaged group which has a particular history in terms of its backlash against feminism and recuperative impetus and is implication in certain value systems and discourses. These value systems are reflected in certain dispositional tendencies of policy makers and are connected to a broader masculinity politics. For example, numbers and 'gap talk' function politically and are used by both policy makers and the media to establish the terms for policy intervention and there are scalar aspects to such flows of discourses and logics about gender achievement gaps. OECD PISA data and publications, for example, function as a reference point and technology of governance within a global education policy field, with effects for steering equity education policy within nations and also at the provincial level, and are governed by a particular logics of practice pertaining to the designation of boys as a disadvantaged category. It is such logics of practice that characterize the policy habitus of boys' education.
4. Power and Frandji (2010) draw on Fraser (1997) who explicates the need to attend to the politics of both redistribution and recognition in addressing fundamental questions of social injustice.
5. PCAP is administered by the Council of Ministers of Education Canada (CMEC) who set up a working group in 2003 comprising representatives from various jurisdictions and an external authority on measurement theory to develop a large scale assessment tool and program that has been administered to a sampling of 13 year old students in all provinces and territories. Students were assessed in Mathematics, Science and Reading in 2003 and 2010 and this testing regime needs to be understood as part of elaborating federalism in Canadian schooling.
6. It is important to note here that while PISA is an international comparison of national system performance, in Canada we are dealing with provinces, with Ontario's education system being singled out as high performing. Similarly with the case of China, it is Shanghai, as highlighted by Sellar and Lingard (Forthcoming).
7. Lingard and Douglas (1999) coined this term which refers to a backlash and defensive gender politics committed to reinstalling traditional notions of masculinity and patriarchal power relations.

References

AAUW. 2008. *Where the Girls Are: The Facts about Gender Equity in Education*. Washington, DC: AAUW Educational Foundation.

Alloway, N., P. Freebody, P. Gilbert, and S. Muspratt. 2002. *Boys, Literacy and Schooling: Expanding the Repertoires of Practice*. Melbourne: Curriculum Corporation.

Anderson, S., and S. Ben Jaaffar. 2003. *Policy Trends in Ontario Education 1990–2003*. ICEC Working Paper, OISE. http://fcis.oise.utoronto.ca/~icec/policytrends.pdf.

Anisef, P., R. S. Brown, K. Phythian, R. Sweet, and D. Walters. 2010. "Early School Leaving among Immigrants in Toronto." *Canadian Review of Sociology* 47 (2): 103–128.

Anyon, J. 1997. *Ghetto Schooling: A Political Economy of Urban Educational Reform*. New York, NY: Teachers College Press.

Ball, S. 2012. *Global Education Inc.: New Policy Networks and the Neo-liberal Imaginary*. London: Routledge.

Ball, S. 2008. *The Education Debate*. Bristol: The Policy Press.

Ball, S. 2003. *Class Strategies and the Education Market: The Middle Classes and Social Advantage*. London: Routledge.

Ball, S. 1998. "Big Policies/Small World: An Introduction to International Perspectives in Education Policy." *Comparative Education* 34 (2): 119–130.

Ball, S. 1994. *Politics and Policy Making in Education: Explorations in Policy Sociology*. London: Routledge.

Bouchard, P., I. Boily, and M. Proulx. 2003. *School Success by Gender: A Catalyst for Masculinist Discourse*. Ottawa: Status of Women Canada.

Bourdieu, P. 1986. "The Forms of Capital." In *Handbook of Theory and Research for the Sociology of Education*, edited by J.G. Richardson, 241–258. Westport, CT: Greenwood Press.

Collins, C., J. Kenway, and J. McLeod. 2000. *Factors Influencing the Educational Performance of Males and Females in School and their Initial Destinations after Leaving School*. Canberra: Department of Education, Training and Youth Affairs.

Condron, D. 2011. "Egalitarianism and Educational Excellence: Compatible Goals for Affluent Societies?" *Educational Researcher* 40 (2): 47–55.

Connolly, P. 2008. "A Critical Review of some Recent Developments in Quantitative Research on Gender and Achievement in the United Kingdom." *British Journal of the Sociology of Education* 29 (3): 249–260.

Council of Ministers of Education, Canada (CMEC). 2011. *PCAP – 2010: Report on the Pan-Canadian Assessment Program of Mathematics, Science, and Reading*. Toronto: CMEC.

Dei, G., and L. Karamanchery. 1999. "School Reforms in Ontario: The "Marketization of Education" and the Resulting Silence on Equity." *Alberta Journal of Educational Research* 45 (2): 111–131.

Desrosieres, A. 1998. *The Politics of Large Numbers*. Harvard: Harvard University Press.

Dumas, M. 2009. "Theorizing Redistribution in Urban Education Research: 'How do we get Dictionaries at Cleveland?'" Chapter 3 In *Theory and Educational Research*, edited by J. Anyon, 81–107. New York, NY: Routledge.

Fraser, N. 1997. *Justice Interruptus*. New York, NY: Routledge.

Gillborn, D. 2008. *Racism and Education: Coincidence or Conspiracy?* London: Routledge.

Grek, S. 2009. "Governing by Numbers: The PISA 'Effect' in Europe." *Journal of Education Policy* 24 (1): 23–37.

Hacking, I. 2006. "Making up People." *London Review of Books* 28 (16): 23–26.

Human Resources and Skills Development Canada, CMEC and Statistics Canada. 2010. *Measuring up: Canadian Results of the OECD PISA Study: The Performance of Canada's Youth in Reading, Mathematics and Science*. Ottawa: Statistics Canada.

Jordan, W. 2010. "Defining Equity: Multiple Perspectives to Analyzing the Performance of Diverse Learners." *Review of Research in Education* 34: 142–178.

Lingard, B. 2011. "Policy as Numbers: Ac/counting for Educational Research." *Australian Educational Researcher* 38: 355–382.

Lingard, B., and P. Douglas. 1999. *Men engaging Feminisms: Profeminism, Backlashes and Schooling*. Buckingham: Open University Press.

Lingard, R., S. Creagh, and G. Vass. 2012. "Education Policy as Numbers: Data Categories and two Australian Cases of Misrecognition." *Journal of Education Policy* 27 (3): 315–333.

Lingard, B., and S. Rawolle. 2011. "New Scalar Politics: Implications for Education Policy." *Comparative Education* 47 (4): 489–502.

Lingard, B., W. Martino, M. Mills, and M. Bahr. 2002. *Addressing the Educational Needs of Boys*. Canberra: Department of Education Science and Training.

Lingard, B., S. Rawolle, and S. Taylor. 2005. "Globalizing Policy Sociology in Education: Working with Bourdieu." *Journal of Education Policy* 20 (6): 759–777.

Lingard, B., and S. Rawolle. 2004. "Mediatizing Educational Policy: The Journalistic Field, Science Policy, and Cross Field Effects." *Journal of Education Policy* 19 (3): 361–380.

Lipman, P. 2004. *High Stakes Education: Inequality, Globalization, and Urban School Reform*. New York, NY: Routledge Falmer.

Lucas, S., and L. Beresford. 2010. "Naming and Classifying: Theory, Evidence, and Equity in Education." *Review of Research in Education* 34: 25–84.

Luke, A. 2011. "Generalizing Across Borders: Policy and the Limits of Educational Science." *Educational Researcher* 40 (8): 367–377.

Luke, A., J. Green, and G. Kelly. 2010. "What Counts as Evidence and Equity?" *Review of Research in Education* 34: vii–xvi.

Martino, W., and G. Rezai-Rashti. 2012. "Neo-liberal Accountability and Boys' Underachievement: Steering Education Policy by Numbers in the Ontario Context." *International Journal of Inclusive Education* 16 (4): 423–440.

Martino, W. 2008. *Boys' Underachievement: Which Boys are we Talking about?* Toronto: Ontario Ministry of Education.

Martino, W. 2001. "Boys and Literacy: Investigating Boys' Reading Preferences and Involvement in Literacy." *Australian Journal of Language and Literacy* 24 (1): 61–74.

Mead, S. 2006. *The Truth about Boys and Girls*. New York, NY: Education Sector.

Mehta, J. D., and R. B. Schwartz. 2011. "Canada Looks a lot like us but gets much Better Results." In *Surpassing Shanghai: An Agenda for American Education Built on the World's Leading Systems*, edited by M. S. Tucker, 141–165. Cambridge, MA: Harvard Education Press.

Miller, P., and N. Rose. 2008. *Governing the Present*. Cambridge: Polity.

OECD. 2010a. *PISA 2009 Results: Overcoming Social Background*. 2 vols. Paris: OECD.

OECD. 2010b. *PISA 2009 Results: Learning to Learn* 3 vols. Paris: OECD.

Ontario Ministry of Education. 2009. *Ontario's Equity and Inclusive Education Strategy*. Toronto: Queens Printer for Ontario.

Ozga, J. 2009. "Governing Education through Data in England: From Regulation to Self-evaluation." *Journal of Education Policy* 24 (2): 149–162.

Power, M. 2004. "Counting, Control and Calculation: Reflections on Measuring and Management." *Human Relations* 57 (6): 765–783.

Power, S., and D. Frandji. 2010. "Education Markets, the new Politics of Recognition and the Increasing Fatalism towards Inequality." *Journal of Education Policy* 25 (3): 385–396.

Rezai-Rashti, G. 2009. "The assault of neo-liberalism on education reform, restructuring, and teaching in Ontario secondary schools." In *Canadian Perspectives on the Sociology of Education*, edited by C. Levine-Rasky, 307–321. Toronto: Oxford University Press.

Rezai-Rashti, G. 2003. "Equity Education and Educational Restructuring in Ontario: Global and Local Policy and Practice." *World Studies in Education* 4 (1): 29–44.

Riddile, M. 2010. *PISA: It's Poverty not Stupid.* 'The Principal Difference', National Association of Secondary School Principals (NASSA). http://nasspblogs.org/principaldifference/2010/12/pisa_its_poverty_not_stupid_1.html.

Rizvi, F., and B. Lingard. 2010. *Globalizing Education Policy.* London: Routledge.

Rose, N. 1999. *Powers of Freedom: Reframing Political Thought.* Cambridge: Cambridge University Press.

Rose, N. 1988. "Calculable Minds and Manageable Individuals." *History of the Human Sciences* 1 (2): 179–200.

Rothstein, R. 2004. *Class and Schools: Using Social, Economic, and Educational Reform to Close the Black–White Achievement gap.* Washington, DC: Economy Policy Institute.

Sellar, S., and Lingard, B. Forthcoming. "Looking East: Shanghai, PISA and the Reconstitution of Reference Societies in the Global Education Policy Field." *Comparative Education.*

Titus, J. 2004. "Boy Trouble: Rhetorical Framing of boys' Underachievement." *Discourse* 25 (2): 145–169.

Toronto District School Board. 2006. *Research Report: The TDSB Grade 9 Cohort Study: A Five-year Analysis, 2000–2005.* Toronto: Toronto District School Board.

Torrance, H. 2006. "Globalising Empiricism: What, if Anything, can be Learned from International Comparisons of Educational Achievement?" In *Education, Globalisation and Social Change*, edited by H. Lauder, P. Brown, J. Dillabough, and A. H. Halsey, 824–834. Oxford: Oxford University Press.

Tucker, M. S. 2011. *Surpassing Shanghai: An Agenda for American Education built on the World's Leading Systems.* Cambridge, MA: Harvard Education Press.

Wiseman, A. 2010. "The uses of Evidence for Educational Policymaking: Global Contexts and International Trends." *Review of Research in Education* 34: 1–24.

The paradox of the education race: how to win the ranking game by sailing to headwind

Hannu Simola[a], Risto Rinne[b], Janne Varjo[a] and Jaakko Kauko[a]

[a]University of Helsinki, Helsinki, Finland; [b]University of Turku, Turku, Finland

In this article, we experiment with the idea of combining path dependency, convergence and contingency in explaining Finnish distinctiveness in education policy and politics since the early 1990s. The focus of this paper is on quality assurance and evaluation (QAE) in comprehensive schooling. We elaborate on and contextualise the Finnish QAE model by analysing the particular and somewhat ambiguous ways in which global QAE practices have – or have not – been received and mediated in Finland.

Introduction

Media visibility and the political use of global rankings have highlighted the topicality and relevance of comparative studies in education. This importance has not entailed the development of theoretical instruments in the field, however. Contemporary research is criticised, e.g. for a lack a historical perspective and contextualisation (Kazamias 2009; Steiner-Khamsi 2009), for too optimistic a view about transfer (Cowen 2000), and for suffering 'unbearable narrowness of the national view' (Dale 2009a, 2009b; Kettunen 2008; Strange 1997). An eminent comparativist of education, Cowen (2009, 963), crystallised the situation when stating that comparisons are too often just like train spotting: 'collecting train numbers: interesting only if you are already hooked on the hobby'. There is a risk that comparison will become only a tool for identifying differences and similarities, and hence will eventually become trivial. To sum up, comparative education is suffering from serious methodological deficits and under-theorisation, while at the same time having bigger political and media weight than ever (Nóvoa and Yariv-Mashal 2003; Simola 2009; Simola and Rinne 2011; Simola, Varjo, and Rinne 2011a, 2011b).

It is evident that greater global interconnectedness and a nascent global educational community, mediated, translated and recontextualised within national and local education structures is creating a certain resemblance among educational policies across nations (e.g. Lingard 2000). The waves of global policy reforms (travelling policies) have a tendency to diffuse around the globe and reshape socially and politically different societies with dissimilar histories. It is clear that these transnational trends and tendencies do not simply shape the regional, national or local policies, but they rather collide and intertwine with 'embedded policies' to be found in 'local' spaces (national, provincial or local) where global policy agendas come up against existing practices and priorities (see, e.g. Ozga and Jones 2006).

This narrowness of the national view easily creates a blind spot in terms of how interactions and comparisons reconstruct the national or the local: how transnational interactions and crossings constitute the national parties of these relationships. Here we come to the crucial role of comparative practices as a mode of reflexivity that (re)shapes individual and collective agency (Grek et al. 2009). In pursuance of an understanding of such a complex phenomenon as the relationship between the global, the regional, the national and the local in education policy formation, it is vital to consider the theoretical conceptualizations from a both/and rather than an either/or point of view. A good and illuminating example here is the controversy among researchers of nationalism and the frequently observed confrontation between understanding nationalism as 'the invention of traditions' by the elite (e.g. Hobsbawm 1990) or as creating prerequisites and limits for ethnic identities (e.g. Smith 1995). From the perspective of comparative research, nationalism as an elite strategy and nationalism as a socio-cultural frame are both necessary. This requires analyzing comparative actions *both* as economic, political and cultural practices and international exhibitions of national competitiveness in the global educational zmarket place.

Anyhow the educational comparisons as well as ranking lists introduced by the supranational organisations such as the OECD are here to stay and show by numbers and calculations the positions of the nation states in the world order of education. Accountability and managerialism in education have been likened to a juggernaut that is gathering momentum as a global force of standardization and uniformity in education. Its main engines are benchmarking and efficiency studies carried out by international organizations (IOs) and management consulting groups, issuing in international rankings in which the world's school systems are held up and compared to a small band of top-performers. As OECD itself says: 'For more than 40 years the OECD has been the world's largest and most reliable source of comparable statistics, and economic and social data' (Spring 2009, 56). Through international assessments such as PISA, the OECD creates global standards and standardized data, ranking scales, indicators and benchmarks (Lawn and Grek 2012, 10–1, 69–70, 83–4; Martens 2007, 49; Spring 2009, 62) and is emerging as a leading force in the neoliberal movement, enacting ideologies of technocratic rationality and causing countries with diverse traditions and cultures to assimilate their educational practices to seemingly unassailable standards of technocratic rationality, economic competitiveness and market growth.

Although being the winner of PISA, Finland is the country, whose educational practices are running in many areas counter to the vast main stream mantra of accountability. Rather than being the gloss scarp of the OECD, Finland is in this respect a kind of model case against it succeeding in spite of that in the international race for benchmarking by avoiding to play the same game by the same rules.

The main aim of this article is to understand how it has been possible for the Finnish Comprehensive School (*Peruskoulu*) to go against the mainstream in policy terms and – in spite or just because of it – become a 'poster-boy' in global educational spectacles such as PISA.[1] Since this small peripheral Nordic nation rocketed to fame in the PISA studies during the 2000s, it has veered to the hope to all the educationalists still believing in two things. They believe, on the one hand, in the possibility of combining quality and equity at a reasonable financial cost. What is even more noteworthy, on the other hand, they believe that this is possible without school inspection, standardized curriculum and high-stakes student assessments, test-based accountability, and a race-to-the-top mentality in terms of educational change (Sahlberg 2011).

Our theoretical explanation and contribution to overcoming difficulties for comparative education works with three concepts. Path dependency and convergence are among the conventional conceptualisations of transnational and national policy relations, while contingency is a more recent theorisation. Path dependency and convergence are often conceptualized as a simple dualism in comparative studies: the former is taken to refer to major national specificities and the latter refers to international tendencies. This false dichotomy is perhaps more apparent in these global and late-modern times (Joas 2008; Joas and Knöbl 2009). Kettunen (2008, 21) proposes that by integrating these two dimensions – path dependency and contingency on the one hand, and path dependency and convergence on the other – we may develop more reflexive and sophisticated comparative studies.

Indeed, despite increasing international interdependence, which seems to generate pressures toward convergence, the advanced industrial societies continue to exhibit differences in their institutional practises. As Andy Green (1999, 56) points out:

> As regards education, there is very little evidence across the globe that nation states are losing control over their education systems or ceasing to press them into service for national economic and social ends, whatever the recent accretions of internationalism. In fact the opposite may be true. As governments lose control over various levers on their national economies and cede absolute sovereignty in foreign affairs and defence, they frequently turn to education and training as two areas where they do still maintain control.

Green (1999, 69) further points out that while there is evidence of policy convergence within Europe around a range of broad policy themes, including decentralization in regulation and governance and increasing use of quality assurance and evaluation (QAE) mechanisms, this does not appear to have led to convergence in structures and processes.

If convergence is disputed, path dependence is somewhat stronger as an analytical concept. According to Pierson (2000, 251), the idea of path dependency is generally used to support a small number of key claims, namely: that specific patterns of timing and sequence matter; that starting from similar conditions a wide range of social outcomes are possible; that large consequences may result from relatively 'small' or contingent events; that particular courses of action, once introduced, can be most difficult to reverse; that, consequently, political development is often punctuated by critical junctures that shape the basic contours of social life.

However there is no single definition of path dependence. Levi (1997, 28) highlights the difficulty of exiting from the chosen path:

> Path dependence has to mean, if it has to mean anything, that once a country or a region has started down a track, the costs of reversal are very high. There will be other choice points, but the entrenchments of certain institutional arrangements obstruct an easy reversal of the initial choice.

The concept of contingency carries a double meaning: on the one hand, it signifies *coincidence* or *conjunction*, and on the other, *free will* or *volition* (Joas 2008, 209). In the first dimension, the uncertainty of contingency emphasizes the fact that events are essentially haphazard and random: things often happen by accident. In the second dimension, the freedom of contingency may be understood as the ability to manage the contingent characteristics of reality. According to eminent Finnish political scientist Palonen (1993, 13), polity and policy refer to attempts to regulate contingency, but politicization opens new aspects to it and politicking can be understood as 'the art of playing with the contingency'.

In this article, we first describe the supranational mainstream of education politics change. Then we draw the picture of the particular opposite Finnish Education Evaluation Model (FEEM) and trace the trajectory of this model. We are throwing also some light to the understanding, why this counter model was able to be established particularly in Finland. In that historical and social context, we also discuss about theoretical possibilities for understanding more profoundly the mixed and contradictory pressures and processes of international convergence and national path dependency in the field of education politics by harnessing it to the use of the concept of contingency.

The supranational mainstream of education politics in the audit society

Over the latest decades a new global neoliberal policy paradigm has emerged. There are several reasons behind this. One of the most crucial was the rejection of the ideas of the Keynesian welfare state. Governments have increasingly praised a minimalist role for the state in education, greater trust on market mechanisms and new public management (NPM) principles and have become unwilling to pay the costs for ever increasing educational expansion. This new globalization policy normalizes a 'growth-first approach', naturalizes the market logics and individual choices, privatisation, deregulation and competitive regimes of resource allocation as the only true social imaginary or There Is No Alternative-thinking (TINA) with its images, myths, parables, stories legends and narratives (Mundy 2007, 26; Rizvi and Lingard 2010, 3, 31–4, 37; Soguel and Jaccard 2008, 1).

The reasons behind the reassessment of governance might be listed as: economic recession and diminishing public expenditures, globalisation and new games without frontiers, disappointed achievements of national governments and distrust of them, an ideological shift towards the market and the rise of the NPM movement (de Boer, Enders, and Schimank 2008, 36–7).

According to Leuze, Martens, and Rusconi (2007, 3), the changes in education today can be attributed to two main trends: (1) the growing activity of IOs in education policy making and (2) the increasing marketization of the field of education. Education has been transferred into the field of international policy making beyond national boarders and regionally or universally applicable models for education have been produced. Increasing marketization is turning education into a tradable commodity and adding private providers as well as competition for students.

Neoliberal policies have brought attempts to stimulate market forces by making schools behave more like businesses, through giving them greater autonomy and encouraging parents to behave more like customers, through relaxing admissions policies and diversifying types of schools. One of the strongest and most discussed matters has been publishing of league tables, because they expose the uneven distribution of educational attainment and the worth of the schools in educational market (Power and Frandji 2010, 385–6).

When considering the new roles of nation states and supranational organisations, Dale (2009b, 122–7) argues that there have long prevailed three false methodological assumptions of 'isms' producing misunderstanding when discussing and comparing education. These are 'nationalism', 'statism' and 'educationism'. Nationalism means that we still think that the nation states strongly work on their own and the regions follow the nations. Statism means the thinking that the state is the source and means of all governing activity, which is taken for granted, though it is essentially contingent. Educationism refers 'to the tendency to regard education as a single category for purposes of analysis, with an assumed common scope, and a set of implicity shared knowledges, practices and assumptions'. Education is often treated as 'abstract, fixed, absolute, ahistorical and universal' (see also Dale and Robertson 2007; Robertson and Dale 2008).

The role of supranational organisations such as the OECD has been most crucial in the formation of the new supranational educational politics and the new politics of 'governance by comparison' (Martens 2007, 40). But it is crucial, however, to recognize that 'there is no zero-sum relationship between global and national or subnational forms of governance. IOs do not replace nation states, but create additional and informal structure of authority and sovereignty besides and beyond the state' (Dale and Robertson 2007, 222). As Nóvoa and Yariv-Marshal (2003) write: 'the global eye works together with the national eye today in both education policy and governance' (quoted in Rizvi and Lingard 2010, 56).

There are also ambivalent effects for nation states and the role of supranational organisations has been controversial compared to the role of national governments. We night say that 'Nation states, IOs and markets might be hostile siblings in the governance of education' (Weymann et al. 2007, 238). Martens and Wolf describe this controversy elegantly using metaphors in their article 'Boomerangs and Trojan Horses: The Unintended Consequences of Internationalising Education Policy Through the EU and the OECD' (2009). In their example of the EU it was just the governments who wanted to ask for advice of international organisations for their educational politics and strengthen their national reformative position at home and to defuse the domestic opposition, but by no means weaken governmental influence at any level. But the boomerangs went astray from the throwers and weakened their power. In the example of the OECD and especially indicators and PISA, national governments wanted to make a comparison between nation states to strengthen their power, but as the unintended consequence the Trojan horse opened the gates and now these governments are in a totally new situation of regular comparative assessments of their performance in educational politics. In this respect, the new standard setting of the supranational organisations has challenged the traditional ideas of national meritocratic competition, and nation sates are losing their power to define standards and to control the key features of their national education with all the nation state functions including the educational selection (Rinne and Ozga 2011, 68). Education has traditionally been regarded as the most national of activities. 'It is the institution through which new members of the society are socialized into its ways and understandings, and learn the values and the rules of appropriateness of the society' (Dale and Robertson 2007, 217). Now the times have changed. The OECD, before the 'debating club', the 'toothless tiger', the 'eminence grise' the 'global office' is rating and ranking nations and telling them the orthodox answers, how to classify, how to measure and how to produce 'best practices'.

We have stepped into the 'audit society', 'steering at a distance' society, where the audit culture is closely linked to the NPM and accountabilities and summative assessment and evaluation (Power 1999, 2003). This fundamental change has been analysed through the metaphors of 'quality revolution', the 'evaluation industry', and the 'audit explosion' (Lawn and Grek 2012, 85). We have become the citizens of the 'evaluative state', but all the more of the evaluative 'suprastate' (cf. Maroy 2008; Neave 1998). We have become 'governed by numbers' (Grek 2009; Rose 1999) or 'self-capitalizing individuals' (Rose 1999) or 'self-responsbilizing individuals' (Rizvi and Lingard 2010, 98–9, 119, 138). A kind of 'metrological mood' has become the mechanism through which education systems are measured and made accountable (Lawn and Grek 2012, 119; cf. Power 2004, 766). 'Less government and more governance' has become the widely shared cred. (de Boer, Enders, and Schimank 2008, 35; cf. Frederickson 1999, 705). We may make the starting point of 'governmentality' (Foucault 1991) and end up with a new imperative in neoliberal governance – 'agile bodies' – the person as an enterprise (Gillies 2011). We have seen the 'governance turn' as a shift in strategy that 'is highly dependent on the appearance of deregulation, but that is equally marked by strong central steering through various policy technologies' and 'sophisticated instruments of steering of policy – standardisation quality benchmarking and data harmonisation' (Ozga 2009, 150, 158). 'Governing needs data and is legitimated by them' (Lawn and Grek 2012, 85). 'Through all of its work the OECD is part of and helped constitute the new form of global governance in education, as well as within nations' (Rizvi and Lingard 2010, 133).

Neoliberalism paradoxically re-asserts the state's role when attempting to reduce its financial responsibilities in the public sector – it centralizes and decentralizes the state at the same time. Of utmost importance for neoliberalism is 'the development of techniques of auditing, accounting and management that enable a market for public services to be established autonomous from central control' (cf. Barry, Osborne, and Rose 1996, 14; Webb 2011, 736).

Neave (2009, 24) names 'Quality, Efficiency and Enterpreneurdom' as 'Liberalisms Holy Trinity'. QAE together with the efficiency has become the core of the new supranational educational apostle (Lawn and Grek 2012, 97). Neave argues that already in 1980s, this new liberal formation of global educational politics was clearly to be seen at least in the field of Higher Education. Concerning Finland, we came on a late train, but in the field of Higher Education we have also clearly seen this new dawn of the enterprise university (Clark 1998) and academic capitalism (Slaughter and Leslie 1997). In the field of the comprehensive school, however, there is still the national road to go, although something has happened also in this respect in Finland.

In the new global audit or assessment building, we may categorize some interconnected central features of the new supranational mainstream of QAE practices and technologies of educational politics on primary and lower secondary school level based on earlier literature (Maroy 2008, 17–20; Ozga et al. 2011, 124–5; Power and Frandji 2010, 385–6; Rinne 2001; Rinne and Ozga 2011):

(1) *Strong marketisation* which is understood to lead to excellence:

- large sector of independent schools,
- strive for individualisation and excellence.

(2) *Choice and visibility* enhancing marketisation:

- consumer and parental choice,
- high local accountability including intelligent accountability,
- large assessment enterprises.

(3) Ranking and classification supporting visibility:

- national testing systems,
- league tables, ranking lists.

(4) *Control* promoting visibility:

- growing inspection and monitoring system,
- strong quality assurance regulation,
- control, sanctions and rewards on the basis of collected assessment data.

We argue in this article for a particular Finnish Model of QAE in Basic Education, which clearly seems to differ from the mainstream of international and global evaluation policies. This has its roots in two historical developments: the Finnish path-dependency in egalitarianism, which has been challenged by the converging market-liberalism, and the path-dependency of deregulation, which had its spur in converging international education policies.

Finnish path-dependent egalitarianism and the radical decentralisation

In terms of path dependency, it is hard to over-emphasise the fact that Finland was among the last countries in Europe to establish compulsory education. Six-year elementary education was made compulsory by law only in 1921. In addition, the expansion of the primary school was slow even after the law, and compulsory education was not fully implemented until just before World War II (Ramirez and Boli-Bennett 1982; Rinne 1984; Rinne and Salmi 1998, 27; Simola and Rinne 2011).

Because of the late formation of the educational system, educational gaps between older and younger generations are among the widest in Europe (Simola and Rinne 2011). All this is witness to the fact that the Finnish success story in education is very recent. As an indicator of the symbolic power of traditional social democratic-agrarian *equality* in Finnish educational discourse, there is no analogous concept of *equity*, even though it would be easy to find one (*oikeus, oikeudenmukaisuus*). The concept of equality is used in two contrasting ways. These two conceptions were connected in a major document published by the Finnish Educational Evaluation Council (FEEC 2004, 15):

> The economic and social welfare of Finnish society is based on an egalitarian public system of schooling. Its mission is to guarantee for every citizen both educational opportunities of good quality regardless of his/her sex, dwelling place, age, mother

tongue and economic position and the right to tuition accordant with his/her capabilities and special needs and his/her self-development. (Emphasis added)

The 1987 Prime Minister Harri Holkeri's cabinet aimed to bring about a fundamental change in Finnish politics. For the first time since World War II, the conservative National Coalition Party held the post of Prime Minister and its two decades in opposition were over. As far as education was concerned, this marked the end of the deal between the Central and Social Democratic parties in the Ministry of Education (ME) and the National Board of Education (NBE), and the right wing was set to dominate State educational discourse for more than a decade. The posts of Ministers of Education also went to right-wing ministers. The changes in education were part of a general wave of decentralization and deregulation in Finland. The process started with the Free Municipality Experiment (Law 718/1988), which gave local authorities in experimental municipalities more freedom to make independent decisions.

The recession in 1991–1993 heralded the deepest peacetime crisis in Finland's economy until then. According to many indicators, the Finnish crisis was the sharpest and deepest among the industrialised countries facing economic problems during the 1990s and it was comparable only with the Great Recession of the 1930s and the late economic crisis in 2000s (Kiander and Virtanen 2002; Rinne et al. 2002; Simola et al. 2002).

The Recession of the 1990s not only speeded up the change. It also revitalized the Nordic egalitarian ethos so the comprehensive idea survived thanks to it. For example, Ahonen (2003) argues that the recession altered the political atmosphere in favour of market liberalism back to traditional Nordic welfare values, and thus, defence of the common comprehensive school. Another totally unexpected event was the Finnish success in PISA. This success, on the one hand, has stifled pressures for change in municipal and school autonomy and, on the other, buffered other market-liberal innovations.

The Act on Central Government Transfers to Local Government (Law 705/1992) and the Local Government Act (Law 365/1995) radically increased local autonomy and strengthened the judicial position of the municipalities. The new system granted funding according to annual calculations per pupil, lesson or other unit, and liberated the municipalities from the detailed 'ear-marked' funds through the allocation of lump-sums which could be freely used by the municipalities according to their priorities.

It is widely accepted among the political and economic elites that without shifting decision-making to the local level the municipalities could not have been required to cut spending as much as they did during the recession. Thus the new decentralized and deregulated mode of governance was moulded around the economic principles of savings and cutbacks. The Recession radicalized decentralization and deregulation:

> The decentralisation level of the educational administration in Finland is one of the highest in Europe, according to the information of the OECD. (Temmes, Ahonen, and Ojala 2002, 129, 92)

After the deregulation, the first attempt to apply a strong evaluation system was the Curriculum Framework of 1994, which included a detailed *Structural Model of Evaluation* emphasising effectiveness, efficiency and economy, summed up in 33 issues to be evaluated. This was dropped from the final version, however (Simola 1995, 297). The Framework for Evaluating Educational Outcomes (NBE 1995) was published a year later. The change in regime of the 1990s is tangible in the NBE's framework – or at least in the rhetoric: the three E's are the cornerstones of the NPM doctrine (e.g. Lähdesmäki 2003, 65–9).

The fundamental role of evaluation was formalized in the Basic Education Act of 1999 (Law 628/1998). A statutory evaluation system was considered necessary in the move from norm steering to the control and evaluation of outcomes. The new purpose of evaluation was said to be 'to support the development of education and improve conditions of learning'. Guided by the ME, the NBE decided on the means by which to accomplish the evaluation procedures. The organizers (mainly the municipalities) are obliged to evaluate the education they provide and to submit to external evaluations of their operations. Moreover, as a common but vaguely articulated norm, the results should be public: 'The main results of evaluations shall be published' (Law 628/1998, §21).

In 1999 the NBE published 'The criteria for graduating evaluation in basic education' (NBE 1999). The introduction refers to the need for equality in evaluation that serves as a basis for placement in subsequent education. The same kinds of criteria were published for early and middle-stage evaluation in the 2004 Framework Curriculum (NBE 2004). In fact, this could be seen as the only direct mechanism of evaluation at classroom level.

Thus despite the amount of evaluation activity, whether 'QAE – apart from traditional pupil assessment [is] a fundamental part of everyday schoolwork in Finland' (Rinne et al. 2011), remains an open question. Reports from the local level have shown that practices vary, to say the least. The NBE conducted two surveys (Löfström et al. 2005; Rajanen 2000) of QAE implementation at the local level. According to the 2000 survey (Löfström et al. 2005, 19), only one-third of the providers of comprehensive education said they had *some* system of evaluation underpinning their work (Rajanen 2000, 31). Only a few of the respondents to the later (2005) survey used the models Association of Finnish Local and Regional Authorities (AFLRA) had been promoting for a decade, such as ISO, Quality Awards, Balanced Scorecard and EFQM, while a quarter of those using some model referred to the NBE's Efficiency Model of Educational Evaluation. The great majority (more than 70%) said they capitalized on 'their own application of different models', which could mean anything from a genuinely new model to no evaluation at all.

The Committee for Education and Culture of the Finnish Parliament concluded in 2002:

> Evaluation has had very small effects at the level of municipalities and schools. Nation-level evaluations have been implemented to a creditable extent, but there is no follow-up on how these evaluations affect the actions of the evaluated and the development of the schools. … [o]nly evaluation of the biggest providers of schooling seems to be systematic enough and based on a system provided by the present model of administration. Many municipalities are at the very beginning in the evaluation of education (CEC 2002)

Finland is one of the few European countries in which there is no direct control from the national to the school level (Eurydice 2004). This created space for AFLRA in the field of education policy. According the AFLRA, municipalities are no longer mere education providers executing top-down, national level decisions, but true political actors possessing an intent of their own – and, thus, a vast amount of *Spielraum* in this peculiar twofold system, where the nation-state *and* municipalities are the main actors in education policy (Kauko and Varjo 2008; Sarjala 2002). On the one hand the ME and the NBE consider QAE from the perspective of the education system and the associated legislation, and on the other the AFLRA and the Ministry of the Interior – often accompanied by the Ministry of Finance – see it in terms of municipal service production and legislation. Both have attempted to assume the leading role in determining the discourse of evaluation in the context of education (Simola et al. 2009).

It is thus obvious that the radical municipal autonomy, spurred and deepened contingently by the Recession of the 1990s, was one of the factors that have buffered the implementation and technical development of QAE in Finnish comprehensive schooling. If the role of radical municipal autonomy has been against convergent tendencies, other contingent factors have supported egalitarian path dependency. Those are the re-valorization of the comprehensive idea and the Finnish PISA Miracle itself.

There are four doctrines in this FEEM, which are essential to understand in Finnish practices in their context and history. Those special characteristics or policy outlines are national doctrines that are commonly accepted and shared:

(1) QAE data are intended first and foremost for administration and decision-making at national and municipal levels – and only secondly, if at all, for other interest groups, i.e. pupils and their parents.
(2) The purpose of QAE in education is quite purely dedicated to develop education – not to control, sanction or allocate resources.
(3) No to nationwide test apparatuses upon different school grades in QAE. Sample-based few assessments of learning are favoured over mandatory national testing of the whole age cohort.
(4) No to the ranking lists. There is no basis or need to publish school-based ranking lists but to protect the evenness of the images of the schools.

All of these doctrines are against the supranational mainstream described above. The QAE measured do not aim to control; they do not produce visibility in terms of ranking, classification and enabling choice. The opposition for such trends lies in path dependencies of the tradition of equality and deregulation. This all leads to a situation, where the marketization of schooling is much more difficult. We further elaborate these doctrines referring to Finnish policy texts, processes and interviews.

Data and Information for administration only

During and after the Depression of the 1990s, new education legislation was drafted in Finland in 1993–1996 in two consecutive Working Parties, the second of which defined the purpose of evaluation as to produce information primarily for the education authorities (ME 1996, 85). Families needing information in order to make their school choices are only referred to incidentally. Neither the Basic Education Act (Law 628/1998) nor the Decree on the Evaluation of Education (A 150/2003) make reference to families, parents or customers as having an interest in evaluation beyond the school achievements of their own children. There are no statements about the need for evaluation results in relation to school choice. The administration is the target group for the production of information, an impression strengthened by a recent Ministry publication (ME 2007a, 12–3).

The stands taken in the most important legislation are symbolic of the opposition to promoting visibility to enable choice, due to the embedded egalitarianism. The choices differed for instance from the views of the OECD (1992), which supported the public availability of all information.

The use of QAE for developmental purpose only

The second doctrinal truth concerns the absence of sanctions in Finnish QAE. According to a Ministry Working Party in 1990, the aim of evaluation was to 'set a solid foundation for intentional and open development of education' (ME 1990, 30). Since the middle of the 1990s, official texts have repeatedly stated that evaluation is 'for developing educational services and not an instrument of administrative control' (e.g. ME 1995, 55, 1996, 85). The Basic Education Act of 1999 (Law 628/1998, 21 §) stated that '[t]he purpose of the evaluation of education is to ensure the realization of the purpose of this law and to support the development of education and improve the prerequisites of learning'. Since then, this definition of policy has been absorbed into education legislation with strong political support. The Committee for Education and Culture of the Parliament of Finland stated that: 'The evaluation system is a vital component in the development of education, not a tool of administrative surveillance' (CEC 3/1998).

This emphasis on development has meant that the interpretation of evaluation results and the allocation of resources – or any other kind of administrative reward or sanction – are divorced from one another (ME 1997). The Administration Committee of the Parliament of Finland concluded that the evaluation of basic services implemented by the Regional State Administrative Agencies is not an instrument of administrative control (AC 8/2000, 2).

Also, since its formation in 2003 the FEEC has highlighted the developmental character of evaluation:

> Educational evaluation promotes the social effectiveness of education by providing policy-makers, developers, practitioners and interest groups in the field with reliable information, which clarifies the underlying values and supports the qualitative development of education. (2005, 17)

In our interviews, a central actor in Finnish QAE concluded that: 'what was actually a sacred issue for us was that we are not creating any control system but the information we produce, it will be for developmental work' (FabQ Interviewee 2, 2007).[2] On the one hand, this viewpoint beautifully crystallises the deep-rooted opposition to rankings, which is consistent with the egalitarian ideas. On the other hand, it is created in the narrow choice situation of the national level. Due to the deregulation, the best way to affect the local is through soft governance.

No national testing

There has been consensus among education politicians and state level officials that thematic, focused and sample based research is sufficient for controlling school performance. To run national testing was unanimously seen as too expensive, besides bringing negative side effects, well-known from the Anglo-American research literature. However the Confederation of Finnish Industries and Employers (CIE), in pamphlets published throughout the 1980s and early 1990s, made new demands to make compulsory education into a real asset in international economic competition. In the *Productivity of Education* (CIE 1990) the measurement of learning outcomes, optimal resource allocation and consumer satisfaction were advocated. The CIE also supported final national examinations (Purhonen 2005, 63). In the first draft of the 1999 education legislation, the idea of national achievement tests in compulsory education appears:

> It has been considered that there would be uniform nation-wide achievement tests conducted annually at various subjects. Based on the results of these exams, the level of teaching and the accomplishment of educational aims at municipalities and schools would be evaluated. (Numminen 1994, 105–6)

However, Finland did not follow the Anglo-Saxon accountability movement in education. The path dependencies prevailed as traditionally, the evaluation of student outcomes has been the task of each teacher and school. The only standardised high-stakes assessment is the matriculation examination at the end of upper-secondary school before students enrol in tertiary education. Prior to this, no external national tests or exams are required (Aho, Pitkänen, and Sahlberg 2006, 12). *A Framework for Evaluating Educational Outcomes in Finland* (NBE 1995, 36) confirmed this policy. NBE's Framework defines sample-based *national exams* as the Finnish equivalent to general *achievement tests*.

No school ranking lists

Practically no education official or politician has supported the provision of ranking lists or making schools transparent in competition by comparing them in terms of performance indicators (CEC 3/1998) Paradoxically, antipathy to ranking may be supported by the Finnish bureaucratic tradition (see, for example Pekonen 2005; Tiihonen 2004), according to which administrative innovations are considered to support the system rather than to inform citizens.

The Finnish Education Evaluation Council highlighted the developmental features of evaluation and the anonymity of schools in its evaluation strategy:

> In publicising evaluation results schools will not be ranked, nor will schools or teachers be labelled as of high or low standard on the basis of one-sided evidence. When reporting upon an analysis based on a nationwide sample, no data identifying individual schools will be given, but in cases concerning only a small group of schools, a national evaluation report may also include information on a single school. A prerequisite for so doing is that the evaluation takes place in co-operation with the school and is made for expressly developmental purposes. (FEEC 2005, 36)

Obviously there has been antipathy towards ranking, in both the central and local administration. The informal consensus at the municipal level not to study schools in a way that would enable the results to be used to produce rankings is a good example here (Simola et al. 2009).

In relation to school ranking, two separate appeals in 2000 and 2003 were made to regional administrative courts against municipal education authorities' decisions not to publish school-specific information. In both cases, the focus of the appeals was on school-specific school performance indicators that, it was argued, were essential for parents to make their school choice decisions. Both cases were located in large Finnish cities (Turku and Vantaa) and behind the appealing party in both cases were big media corporations (Simola 2006). In the first case, the Turku Administrative Court took the side of municipal education authorities and refused to require them to hand over the evaluation results of individual schools for publication. In the second case, the Helsinki Administrative Court decided the opposite. It ordered Vantaa educational authorities to hand over the school-specific evaluation results to the appealing party. The municipality of Vantaa took the case to the Supreme Administrative Court and asked for the appeal to be dismissed. The Supreme Administrative Court ordered Vantaa to hand over the school-specific evaluation results to the appealing party (Simola 2006). However, only a couple of provincial newspapers have published school-specific evaluation results or taken any actions in that direction. The silence here is very meaningful and indicates something about the Finnish ethos concerning league tables and school-specific evaluation results in general.

The uncertain future of FEEM

All in all, since the early 1990s there has been a strong contradiction between *convergence* and *path dependence* in Finnish education policy. After decades of *Finlandisierung* there was an extremely strong push towards convergence: to be accepted as a Western advanced liberal society. At the same time, there was strong path dependence in social and educational decisions based on traditional social democratic and agrarian values of equality.

Finland's position between east and west framed most of its international cooperation until the fall of the Berlin Wall and the collapse of 'Real Socialism' in Europe in the 1990s. Openness to the influence of the OECD and the west came late, and openness to neoliberal system redesign even later. The collective narrative of education as a national enterprise and comprehensive provision was weakened during the 1990s. According to the *Proposal of the NBE for a structural programme of education* (NBE 1992), the development of the Finnish comprehensive school was to be characterised by 'decentralised and consumer-based accountability', 'result-based public funding' and 'self-responsible individual learning'.

Finland became the OECD's 'model pupil' (Rinne 2007; Rinne et al. 2004), but through technical and incremental policy, rather than through making strong neoliberal declarations. A leading ex-politician characterized it as a 'tiptoeing education policy change' (Rinne et al. 2001). OECD's own account of Finland stated: 'Finland has a record of heeding the advice of past OECD education reviews. The review seems likely to continue that pattern, helping to shape the future of a dynamic education sector' (OECD 2003).

The titles of some publications (published only in Finnish) of the NBE and the Ministry of Foreign Affairs reveal the positive and highly respectful attitude to OECD: *Learning from the Analysis of the OECD* (Laukkanen and Kyrö 2000); *OECD – Firm Base for Decision-Making* (1999); *OECD – Directions for Policy-making in the 21st Century* (2001); *OECD Resources for Decision Making in the Era of Globalisation* (2005). The exceptionally receptive stance of the Finnish education policy elite towards the OECD has been noted by various commentators. Interviewees in Niukko's (2006) study, for example, refer to mutual respect especially following the recent attention given to Finland after its national success in PISA (Grek et al. 2009, 17, 14).

Among other things, PISA taught Finnish education politicians and officials the 'market value' of international comparisons. Interview data make it apparent that OECD is seen as a transcendent carrier of reason (see also Niukko 2006, 112). It may be seen as creating a consensual community (Weber 1981), a discourse of truth (Foucault 1989), a style of reasoning (Hacking 1990). Interviewees described the importance and meaning of OECD meetings and texts as follows: 'OECD-doctrine' (Niukko 2006, 122 and 126), 'up-dated themes' (Ibid., 111), 'magic of numbers' (Ibid., 117), 'the only table where Finland can sit with the G8-countries' (Ibid., 130); 'a council of the sages' (Ibid., 131); 'guiding member states in the same direction', 'peer and moral pressure' (Ibid., 143); 'moral commitment', 'indirect effect' (Ibid., 144), 'the economic as the primary nature of education' (Ibid., 161–4); 'tuning sentiment and sympathy' (interview 10, April 2007), 'modernization' (Finnish policy actor 3).

There have also been some attempts to break the consensus on FEEM. The policy as administrative, developmental, non-testing and non-ranking has also been questioned and challenged. The economic recession of the early 1990s changed education policy, and a committee presented a Bill (ME 1996) emphasising the 'viewpoint of social solidarity'. The new Basic Education Act (Law 628/1998) confirmed parents' free choice throughout the country, but the municipalities retained the right to restrict parents' choice of school by stating that such a choice must not supersede the right of other children to attend the school designated by the municipal authorities. In the education commission of parliament, this right was formulated as the right to attend one's neighbourhood school (Ibid., 172–3, 175) and this has obvious limiting effects on choice. In some big cities, most of the smaller towns and all country municipalities there is no real school choice and thus no demand for school based QAE information (cf. Seppänen 2003, 2006).

In relation to the doctrine of QAE for development, the Regional State Administrative Agencies (e.g. ME 1996, 98) and the Ministry of Finance (e.g. ALFRA and MoF 1998, 13) were against the exclusively developmental emphasis, as was AFLRA, which argues that all evaluation implemented in municipal organizations contributes to municipal evaluation, which means that it is a tool of municipal management and control (Granö-Suomalainen and Lovio 2002, 7).

Recently, the future of national sample-based learning-result assessment has become uncertain, as the right-wing officer Timo Lankinen's statement just before he was appointed to the post of the Director General of the NBE makes clear:

> The follow-up of learning results will be carried out as web-based examinations in all schools. These exams would assess what learning goals have been attained and give an overall diagnosis of the state of education. The aim is to give up the sample-based learning result assessments and produce evaluation information and feedback for the whole age cohort and all appropriate teachers. (ME 2007b, 194)

The new Green Paper on *Basic Education 2020 – The national general objectives and distribution of lesson hours*, chaired by Lankinen, emphasises criteria for assessment so strongly that the opposition and the Social Democrat Party state that the implementation of the Green Paper will bring performance ranking to Finland (ME 2010, 207).

In this light, the FEEM looks less solid than it used to be. According to one of our interviewees, the internationalisation of Finland and its people is obviously challenging the old ways:

> But, if you listen to well-educated parents, you will notice that is it quite commonly understood that there are good schools and there are bad schools. And we have the right to know. And there should be means to find out that difference. It might not be that frequent yet, but it does exist much more than in 1990s. It might be crucial, because this kind of parents have a great deal of power in our society. And it concerns also globalisation, because they are well aware what is happening in other countries. Under these circumstances, they don't perceive the situation of their children at the context of Finnish education policy and its tradition. They consider: if it is allowed elsewhere, why not here in Finland. (FabQ Interviewee 11, 2007)

Thus, on one hand, the Finnish trajectory of evaluation of education manifests itself as a combination of an unarticulated consensus about the direction of advancement, and the endogenous origins of the reform, and a passive but persistent resistance to global models of education restructuring. The extent of path dependency is a different question: despite national definitions of policy, it is difficult to see the trajectory as a functional entity, coordinated and directed normatively.

The aim of this article was threefold. First we analyzed the supranational mainstream of education politics and global QAE policy in the audit society in order to locate Finland in the global context and to mirror it against that. Secondly and explicitly, we tried to make Finnish QAE policy more comprehensible by using the concepts of convergence, path dependency and contingency. These concepts and above all their combination did shed light on the Finnish case. An extremely strong contradiction emerged between the convergent pursuit of international acceptance as a consenting adult in the Western advanced liberal family and deep rooted path dependence on traditional social democratic and agrarian egalitarianism, that made Finnish QAE policy remarkably double-layered. This analysis does not, of course, completely explain the Finnish case, and we have outlined some other significant historical factors elsewhere (Rinne et al. 2002; Simola 1993, 2005; Simola and Rinne 2011; Simola et al. 2002). Thirdly, what might be even more important, however, is that our conceptual experiment may be seen as supporting a conceptualization and theorisation that might be useful in other cases, too.

Notes

1. This text owes to our earlier elaborations, e.g. Simola, Varjo and Rinne (2010) and Simola, Varjo, and Rinne (2011a, 2011b).
2. Other two were, according to the interviewee that '(...) we will never create ranking lists. We will not produce information that make possible to build ranking lists. (...) the next principle was independence (...) and one is this principle of publicity' (FabQ Interviewee 2, 2007).

References

A 150/2003. Valtioneuvoston asetus koulutuksen arvioinnista [Decree on the Evaluation of Education].

AC 8/2000. Hallintovaliokunnan mietinnön HaVM 8/2000 vp. [Memorandum from the Administrative Committee]. Hallituksen esitys laiksi lääninhallituslain 2 ja 4 §:n muuttamisesta.

Aho, E., K. Pitkänen, and P. Sahlberg. 2006. *Policy development and reform principles of basic and secondary education in Finland since 1968*. The World Bank Education: Working paper series no. 2. Washington, DC: The World Bank.

Ahonen, S. 2003. *Yhteinen koulu: tasa-arvoa vai tasapäisyyttä* [Common school: Equality or leveling off?]. *Koulutuksellinen tasa-arvo Suomessa Snellmanista tähän päivään*. Tampere: Vastapaino.

ALFRA and MoF. 1998. *Julkisten palveluiden laatustrategia* [The quality strategy for public sector]. Helsinki: Suomen Kuntaliitto. Valtiovarainministeriö.

Barry, A., T. Osborne, and N. Rose. 1996. *Foucault and political reason: Liberalism, neo-liberalism, and rationalities of government*. Chicago, IL: University of Chicago Press.

CEC 3/1998. Sivistysvaliokunnan mietintö SiVM 3/1998. [Memorandum from Committee for Education and Culture]. Hallituksen esitys koulutusta koskevaksi lainsäädännöksi.

CEC 11/2002. Sivistysvaliokunnan mietintö SiVM 11/2002 [Memorandum from Committee for Education and Culture]. Hallituksen esitys laeiksi eräiden koulutusta koskevien lakien sekä Opetushallituksesta annetun lain 4 §:n muuttamisesta.

CIE. 1990. *Koulutuksen tuottavuus* [The productivity of education]. Helsinki: Suomen Työnantajain Keskusliitto.

Clark, B.R. 1998. *Creating entrepreneurial universities: Organizational pathways of transformation. Issues in higher education*. Oxford: Pergamon Press for International Association of Universities.

Cowen, R. 2000. Comparing futures or comparing pasts? *Comparative Education* 36, no. 3: 333–42.

Cowen, R. 2009. Editorial introduction: New thinking. In *International handbook of comparative education – part 2*, ed. R. Cowen, A.M. Kazamias, and E. Unterhalter, 961–4. Dordrecht: Springer.

Dale, R. 2009a. Contexts, constraints and resources in the development of European education space and European education policy. In *Globalisation & Europeanisation in education*, ed. R. Dale and S. Robertson, 23–43. Oxford: Symposium Books.

Dale, R. 2009b. Studying globalization and Europeanisation in education: Lisbon, the open method of coordination and beyond. In *Globalisation & Europeanisation in education*, ed. R. Dale and S. Robertson, 121–40. Oxford: Symposium Books.

Dale, R., and S. Robertson. 2007. New arenas of global governance and international organisations: Reflections and directions. In *Transformations of the state and global governance*, ed. K. Martens, A. Rusconi, and K. Lutz, 217–28. London: Routledge.

de Boer, H.F., J. Enders, and U. Schimank. 2008. Comparing higher education governance systems in four European countries. In *Governance and performance of education systems*, ed. N.C. Soguel and P. Jaccard, 35–54. Dordrecht: Springer.

Eurydice. 2004. *Evaluation of schools providing compulsory education in Europe*. No. D/2004/4008/2. Directorate-General for Education and Culture. Brussels: European Commission.

FEEC. 2004. Koulutuksen arvioinnin uusi suunta. Arviointiohjelma 2004–2007. *Koulutuksen arviointineuvoston julkaisuja* 1.

FEEC. 2005. *New directions in educational evaluation. Evaluation programme 2004–2007*. Publications of the Finnish Education Evaluation Council 3. Jyväskylä: The Finnish Education Evaluation Council.

Foucault, M. 1989. *The order of things: An archaeology of the human sciences*. London: Routledge.

Foucault, M. 1991. 'Governmentality', trans. Rosi Braidotti and revised by Colin Gordon. In *The Foucault effect: Studies in governmentality*, ed. Graham Burchell, Colin Gordon, and Peter Miller, 87–104. Chicago, IL: University of Chicago Press.

Frederickson, H.G. 1999. The repositioning of American Public Administration. 1999 John Gaus Lecture. *PS: Political Science & Politics* 32, no. 4: 701–11.

Gillies, D. 2011. Agile bodies: A new imperative in neoliberal governance. *Journal of Education Policy* 26, no. 2: 207–23.

Granö-Suomalainen, V., and M. (toim.) Lovio. 2002. *Mihin me pyrimme? Miksi arvioida kunnan koulutus- ja kirjastopalveluja* [Where are we aiming to? Why to evaluate municipal education services?]. Helsinki: Suomen Kuntaliitto.

Green, A. 1999. Education and globalization in Europe and East Asia: Convergent and divergent trends. *Journal of Education Policy* 14, no. 1: 55–71.

Grek, S. 2009. Governing by numbers: The PISA effect in Europe. *Journal of Education Policy* 24, no. 1: 23–37.

Grek, S., M. Lawn, B. Lingard, J. Ozga, R. Rinne, C. Segerholm, and H. Simola. 2009. National policy brokering and the construction of the European Education Space in England, Sweden, Finland and Scotland. *Comparative Education* 45, no. 1: 5–21.

Hacking, I. 1990. *The taming of chance*. Cambridge: Cambridge University Press.

Hobsbawm, E. 1990. *Nations and nationalism since 1780: Programme, myth, reality*. Cambridge: University Press.

Joas, H. 2008. Kontingenssin aikakausi [The era of contingency]. *Sosiologia* 45, no. 3: 203–12.

Joas, H., and W. Knöbl. 2009. *Social theory. Twenty introductory lectures*. Cambridge: Cambridge University Press.

Kauko, J., and J. Varjo. 2008. Age of indicators – changes in the Finnish education policy agenda. *European Educational Research Journal* 7, no. 2: 219–31.

Kazamias, A.M. 2009. Padeia and politeia: Education, and the polity/state in comparative education. In *International handbook of comparative*, ed. R. Cowen and A.M. Kazamias, 161–8. Dordrecht: Springer.

Kettunen, P. 2008. *Globalisaatio ja kansallinen me* [Globalisation and national us]. Tampere: Vastapaino.

Kiander, J., and S. Virtanen. 2002. *1990s economic crisis: The research programme on the economic crisis of the 1990s in Finland: Final report*. Helsinki: Valtion taloudellinen tutkimuskeskus.

Lähdesmäki, K. 2003. *New Public Management ja julkisen sektorin uudistaminen* [New Public Management and reforming public sector management]. Vaasan yliopisto: Acta Wasaensia 113.

Laukkanen, R., and M. Kyrö, eds. 2000. *Oppia OECD:n analyyseista* [Learning from the analysis of the OECD]. Helsinki: Opetushallitus.

Law 718/1988. Laki vapaakuntakokeilusta [The law on free municipality experiment].

Law 705/1992. Laki opetus- ja kulttuuritoimen rahoituksesta [The act on central government transfers to local government].

Law 365/1995. Kuntalaki [The local government act].

Law 628/1998. Perusopetuslaki [The basic education act].

Lawn, M., and S. Grek. 2012. *Europeanizing education. Governing a new policy space*. Oxford: Symposium Books.

Leuze, K., K. Martens, and A. Rusconi. 2007. New arenas of education governance – the impact of international organizations and markets on education policy making. In *New arenas of education governance – the impact of international organizations and markets on educational policy making*, ed. K. Martens, A. Rusconi, and K. Leuze, 3–15. New York, NY: Palgrave Macmillan.

Levi, M. 1997. A model, a method and a map: Rational choice and historical analysis. In *Comparative politics: Rationality, culture and structure*, ed. M. Lichbach and A. Zuckerman, 19–41. Cambridge: Cambridge University Press.

Lingard, B. 2000. It is and it isn't: Vernacular globalization, educational policy and restructuring. In *Globalization and education: Critical perspectives*, ed. N. Burbules and C. Torres, 79–108. London: Routledge.

Löfström, E., J. Metsämuuronen, E. Niemi, K. Salmio, and K. Stenvall. 2005. *Koulutuksen paikallinen arviointi vuonna 2004* [The local evaluation of education in 2004]. Arviointi 2/2005. Opetushallitus: Helsinki.

Maroy, C. 2008. The new regulation forms of educational systems in Europe: Towards a post-bureaucratic regime. In *Governance and performance of education systems*, ed. N. C. Soguel and P. Jaccard, 13–34. Dordrecht: Springer.

Martens, K. 2007. How to become an influential actor – the 'comparative turn' in OECD education policy. In *New arenas of education governance – the impact of international organizations and markets on educational policy making*, ed. K. Martens, A. Rusconi, and K. Leuze, 40–56. New York, NY: Palgrave Macmillan.

Martens, K., and K.D. Wolf. 2009. Boomerangs and Trojan Horses: The unintended consequences of internalising education policy through the EU and the OECD. *Higher Education Dynamics* 26, no. 2: 81–107.

ME. 1990. *Koulutuksen tuloksellisuuden arvioinnista. Arviointimenettelyä selvittäneen työryhmän muistio* [On evaluation of educational outcomes]. Opetusministeriön työryhmien muistioita 1990:23. Helsinki: Opetusministeriö.

ME. 1995. *Koulutusta koskevan lainsäädännön kokonaisuudistus* [The reform of education legislation]. Helsinki: Opetusministeriö.

ME. 1996. *Koulutuksen lainsäädännön kokonaisuudistus. Lausunnot komiteamietinnöstä 1996:4* [The reform of education legislation. Comments for memorandum 1996:4]. Helsinki: Opetusministeriö.

ME. 1997. *Koulutuksen arviointistrategia* [Evaluation strategy for education]. Helsinki: Opetusministeriö.

ME. 2007a. *Koulutuksen arviointijärjestelmän kehittämistyöryhmän muistio* [Memorandum from working group developing national system of educational evaluation]. Opetusministeriön työryhmämuistioita ja selvityksiä 2007:27. Helsinki: Opetusministeriö.

ME. 2007b. *Opetushallituksen asema, rooli ja tehtävät sekä koulutustoimialan ohjaus muuttuvassa toimintaympäristössä* [The position, role and tasks of Finnish National Board of Education and the steering of the educational branch in a changing operating environment]. Opetusministeriön työryhmämuistioita ja selvityksiä 2007:46. Helsinki: Opetusministeriö.

ME. 2010. *Perusopetus 2020 – yleiset valtakunnalliset tavoitteet ja tuntijako* [Basic education 2020 – the national general objectives and distribution of lesson hours]. Opetus- ja kulttuuriministeriön työryhmämuistioita ja selvityksiä 2010:1. Reports of the Ministry of Education and Culture, Finland. Helsinki: Opetus- ja kulttuuriministeriö.

Mundy, K. 2007. Educational multilateralism – origins and indications for global governance. In *New arenas of education governance – the impact of international organizations and markets on educational policy making*, ed. K. Martens, A. Rusconi, and K. Leuze, 19–39. New York, NY: Palgrave Macmillan.

NBE. 1992. *Opetushallituksen ehdotus opetustoimen rakenneohjelmaksi* [Proposal of the National Board of Education for a Structural Programme of Education]. Helsinki: Opetushallitus.

NBE. 1995. *Koulutuksen tuloksellisuuden arviointimalli* [A framework for evaluating educational outcomes in Finland]. Arviointi 9/1995. Helsinki: Opetushallitus.

NBE. 1999. *A framework for evaluating educational outcomes in finland*. Evaluation 8/1999. Helsinki: National Board of Education.

NBE. 2004. *National core curriculum for basic education*. Helsinki: National Board of Education.

Neave, G. 1998, September. Quatre modèles pour l'Université. Courrier de l'UNESCO. http://www.unesco.org/courier/1998˙09/uk/dossier/intro12.htm.

Neave, G. 2009. The Bologna process as alpha or omega, or, on interpreting history and context as inputs to Bologna, Prague, Berlin and beyond. In *European integration and the governance of higher education and research*, ed. A. Amaral, G. Neave, C. Musselin, and P. Maassen, 17–58. Dordrecht: Springer.

Niukko, S. 2006. *'Yhteistyötä ilman riskejä'?: OECD:n rooli Suomen koulutuspolitiikassa* ['Cooperation without risks'? The role of the OECD in Finnish education policy]. Turku: Annales Universitatis Turkuensis C:251.

Numminen, J. 1994. *Koulutuspolitiikan vaihtoehdot* [The alternatives of education policy]. Helsinki: Otava.

Nóvoa, A., and T. Yariv-Mashal. 2003. Comparative research in education: A mode of governance or a historical journey? *Comparative Education* 39, no. 4: 423–39.

OECD. 1992. *Education at a glance. OECD indicators*. Paris: OECD.

OECD. 1999. *Suomen OECD-edustusto OECD – tukeva pohja päätöksenteolle* [OECD – firm base for decision-making]. UM Taustat 1/1999. Helsinki: Ministry of Foreign Affairs.

OECD. 2001. *Suomen OECD-edustusto. OECD – Suuntaa päätöksenteolle 21.* vuosisadalla. Suomen OECD-edustusto, Pariisi, syyskuu 2001 [OECD – directions for policymaking in the 21st century]. Ulkoasiainministeriön julkaisuja 10/2001. Helsinki: Ministry of Foreign Affairs.

OECD. 2003. Country and thematic policy reviews in education. http://www.oecd.org/document/27/0,2340,en_2649_34511_2744219_1_1_1_1,00.html.

OECD. 2005. *Suomen OECD-edustusto – eväitä päätöksenteolle globalisaation aikana* [Resources for decision making in the era of globalisation]. Helsinki: Ulkoasiainministeriön julkaisuja.

Ozga, J. 2009. Governing education through data in England: From regulation to self-evaluation. *Journal of Education Policy* 24, no. 2: 149–62.

Ozga, J., P. Dahler-Larsen, C. Segerholm, and H. Simola, eds. 2011. *Fabricating quality in education. Data and governance in Europe*. London: Routledge.

Ozga, J., and R. Jones. 2006. Travelling and embedded policy: The case of knowledge transfer. *Journal of Education Policy* 21, no. 1: 1–17.

Palonen, K. 1993. Introduction: From policy and polity to politicking and politicization. In *Reading the political: Exploring the margins of politics*, ed. K. Palonen and T. Parvikko, 6–16. Helsinki: The Finnish Political Science Association.

Pekonen, K. 2005. *Suomalaisen hallitsemiskäsitteistön historiaa* [On the history of Finnish administrative concepts]. Helsinki: Yliopistopaino.

Pierson, P. 2000. Increasing returns, path dependence and the study of politics. *American Political Science Review* 94, no. 2: 251–67.

Power, M. 1999. *The audit society: Rituals of verification*. Oxford: Oxford University Press.

Power, M. 2003. Evaluating the audit explosion. *Law & Policy* 25, no. 3: 185–203.

Power, M. 2004. Counting, control and calculation: Reflections on measuring and management. *Human Relations* 57: 765–83.

Power, S., and D. Frandji. 2010. Education markets, the new politics of recognition and the increasing fatalism towards inequality. *Journal of Education Policy* 25, no. 3: 385–96.

Purhonen, K. 2005. Eteläranta peruskoulun ja yksityiskoulujen puolesta. In *Yhtenäisen peruskoulun menestystarina* [The succes story of common comprehensive school], ed. K. Hämäläinen, A. Lindström, and J. Puhakka, 61–5. Helsinki: Yliopistopaino kustannus.

Rajanen, J. 2000. *Selvitys koulutuksen paikallisen tason arvioinnin tilasta* [The state of local level evaluation]. Arviointi 11/2000. Helsinki: Opetushallitus.

Ramirez, F.O., and J. Boli-Bennett. 1982. Global pattern of educational institutionalization. In *Comparative education*, ed. P.G. Altbach, R.F. Arnove, and G.P. Kelly, 15–38. New York, NY: Macmillian.

Rinne, R. 1984. *Suomen oppivelvollisuuskoulun opetussuunnitelman muutokset vuosina 1916–1970. Opetussuunnitelman intentioiden ja lähtökohtien teoreettis-historiallinen tarkastelu* [The changes in national curriculums of Finnish compulsory school between years 1916–1970. A theoretical-historical examination of intentions and premises for national curriculums]. Turku: Turun yliopiston julkaisuja, Annales Universitatis Turkuensis C: 44.

Rinne, R. 2001. Koulutuspolitiikan käänne ja nuorten syrjäytyminen [Cuff of education policy and the social exclusion of adolescents]. In *Koulutuspolitiikka Suomessa ja ylikansalliset mallit*, ed. A. Jauhiainen, R. Rinne, and J. Tähtinen, Vol. 1, 91–138. Turku: Suomen kasvatustieteellinen seura, Kasvatusalan tutkimuksia.

Rinne, R. 2007. The growing supranational impacts of the OECD and the EU on national educational policies and a case of Finland. Paper presented to the NERA conference at Turku University, March 15–17, in Finland.

Rinne, R., J. Kallo, and S. Hokka. 2004. Too eager to comply? OECD education policies and the Finnish response. *European Educational Research Journal* 3, no. 2: 454–85.

Rinne, R., J. Kivirauma, and P. Hirvenoja. 2001. Nordic educational policy under siege: Educational politicians tell their stories. In *Listening to education actors on governance and social integration and exclusion*, ed. B. Lindblad and T.S. Popkewitz, 77–132. Uppsala: University of Uppsala, Department of Education, Uppsala Reports on, Education 37.

Rinne, R., J. Kivirauma, and H. Simola. 2002. Shoots of revisionist education policy or just slow readajustment? The Finnish case of educational reconstruction. *Journal of Education Policy* 17, no. 6: 643–58.

Rinne, R., and J. Ozga. 2011. Europe and the global: The role of the OECD in education politics. In *Fabricating quality in education – data and governance in Europe*, ed. J. Ozga, P. Dahler-Larsen, C. Segerholm, and H. Simola, 66–75. London: Routledge.

Rinne, R., and E. Salmi. 1998. *Oppimisen uusi järjestys: Uhkien ja verkostojen maailma koulun ja elämänmittaisen opiskelun haasteena* [The new order of learning: The world of risks and networks as a challenge for lifelong learning]. Tampere: Vastapaino.

Rinne, R., H. Simola, M. Mäkinen-Streng, S. Silmäri-Salo, and J. Varjo. 2011. *Arvioinnin arvo. Suomalaisen perusopetuksen laadunarviointi rehtoreiden ja opettajien kokemana* [The value of evaluation. Quality assurance and evaluation of Finnish comprehensive education in the eyes of principles and teachers]. Suomen kasvatustieteellinen seura: Kasvatusalan tutkimuksia 56.

Rizvi, F., and B. Lingard. 2010. *Globalizing education policy*. London: Routledge.

Robertson, S., and R. Dale. 2008. Researching education in a globalizing era: Beyond methodological nationalism, methodological statism, methodological educationism and spatial fetishism. In *The production of educational knowledge in the global era*, ed. J. Resnik, 19–32. Rotterdam: Sense Publications.

Rose, N. 1999. *Governing the soul: The shaping of the private self*. London: Free Association Books.

Sahlberg, P. 2011. *Finnish lessons: What can the world learn from educational change in Finland?* New York, NY: Teachers College, Columbia University.

Sarjala, J. 2002. Arvioinnin merkitys koulutuspolitiikassa [The meaning of evaluation in education policy]. In *Koulutuksen arviointi. Lähtökohtia, malleja ja tilannekatsauksia* [The evaluation of education. Starting points, models and snapshots], ed. E. Olkinuora, R. Jakku-Sihvonen, and E. Mattila, 9–13. Turku: University of Turku. Publications of the Faculty of Education B:70.

Seppänen, P. 2003. Patterns of 'public-school markets' in the Finnish comprehensive school from a comparative perspective. *Journal of Education Policy* 18, no. 5: 513–31.

Seppänen, P. 2006. *Koulunvalintapolitiikka perusopetuksessa. Suomalaiskaupunkien koulumarkkinat kansainvälisessä valossa* [School-choice policy in comprehensive schooling – school markets of Finnish cities in the international perspective]. Turku: Finnish Educational Research Association: Research in Educational Sciences 26.

Simola, H. 1993. Educational science, the state and teachers. Forming the corporate regulation of teacher education in Finland. In *Changing patterns of power: Social regulation and teacher education reform in eight countries*, ed. T.S. Popkewitz, 161–210. Albany, NY: State University of New York Press.

Simola, H. 1995. *Paljon vartijat. Suomalainen kansanopettaja valtiollisessa kouludiskurssissa 1860-luvulta 1990-luvulle* [The guards of plenty. The Finnish school teacher in educational state discourse from 1860s to tke 1990s]. Helsinki: University of Helsinki. Helsingin yliopiston opettajankoulutuslaitoksen tutkimuksia 137.

Simola, H. 2005. The Finnish miracle of PISA: Historical and sociological remarks on teaching and teacher education. *Comparative Education* 41, no. 4: 455–70.

Simola, H. 2006. Globalisation of Finnish educational governance – school performance indicators and their publication as a case in point. In *Supranational regimes and national education policies. Encountering challenge*, ed. J. Kallo and R. Rinne, 337–52. Research in Educational Sciences 24. Turku: Finnish Educational Research Association.

Simola, H. 2009. Trans-national technologies, national techniques and local mechanisms in Finnish university governance. A journey through the layers. *Nordisk Pedagogik* 29, no. 1: 6–17.

Simola, H., and R. Rinne. 2011. Education politics and contingency: Belief, status and trust behind the Finnish PISA miracle. In *PISA under examination: Changing knowledge, changing tests, and changing schools*, ed. M.A. Pereyra, H.-G. Kotthoff, and R. Cowen, 225–44. Rotterdam: Sense Publisher.

Simola, H., R. Rinne, and J. Kivirauma. 2002. Abdication of the education state or just shifting responsibilities? The appearance of a new system of reason in constructing educational governance and social exclusion/inclusion in Finland. *Scandinavian Journal of Educational Research* 46, no. 3: 237–46.

Simola, H., R. Rinne, J. Varjo, J. Kauko, and H. Pitkänen. 2009. Quality assurance and evaluation (QAE) in Finnish compulsory schooling: A national model or just unintended effects of radical decentralisation? *Journal of Education Policy* 24, no. 2: 163–78.

Simola, H., J. Varjo, & R. Rinne. 2010. Vasten valtavirtaa – kontingenssi, polkuriippuvuus ja konvergenssi suomalaisen perusopetuksen laadunarviointimallin kehityskuluissa. [Against the flow: Path dependence, convergence and contingency in understanding the Finnish QAE model]. *Hallinnon tutkimus [Administrative Studies]* 29, no. 4: 285–302.

Simola, H., J. Varjo, and R. Rinne. 2011a. Contra la corriente: dependencia del camino, convergencia y contingencia en la comprensión del modelo finlandés de la garantía de la calidad en educación (QAE) [Against the flow: Path dependence, convergence and contingency in understanding the Finnish QAE model]. *Profesorado – Revista de currículum y formación del profesorado* 15, no. 1: 211–27.

Simola, H., J. Varjo, and R. Rinne. 2011b. À contre-courant: dépendance au sentier, convergence et contingence. Vers une meilleure compréhension du modèle finlandais d'assurance-qualité et d'évaluation [Against the flow: Path dependence, convergence and contingency in understanding the Finnish QAE model]. *Éducation et Sociétés: Revue internationale de sociologie de l'éducation* 28, no. 2: 35–51.

Slaughter, S., and L.L. Leslie. 1997. *Academic capitalism. Politics, policies and the entrepreneurial university*. Baltimore: The Johns Hopkins University Press.

Smith, P. 1995. On the unintended consequences of publishing performance data in the public sector. *International Journal of Public Administration* 18, nos. 2 & 3: 277–310.

Soguel, N.C., and P. Jaccard. 2008. Introduction: Governance and performance of education systems. In *Governance and performance of education systems*, ed. N.C. Soguel and P. Jaccard, 1–10. Dordrecht: Springer.

Spring, J. 2009. *Globalization of education. An introduction*. London: Routledge.

Steiner-Khamsi, G. 2009. Comparison: Quo Vadis? In *International handbook of comparative education – part 2*, ed. R. Cowen, A.M. Kazamias, and E. Unterhalter, 1143–58. Dordrecht: Springer.

Strange, S. 1997. The future of global capitalism – or, will divergence persist forever? In *Political economy of modern capitalism. Mapping convergence and diversity*, ed. W. Streek and C. Crouch, 182–92. London: Sage.

Temmes, M., P. Ahonen, and T. Ojala. 2002. *Suomen koulutusjärjestelmän hallinnon arviointi* [Evaluation of the Finnish education administration]. Helsinki: Opetusministeriö.

Tiihonen, S. 2004. *From governing to governance. A process of change.* Tampere: Tampere University Press.

Webb, P.T. 2011. The evolution of accountability. *Journal of Education Policy* 26, no. 6: 735–56.

Weber, M. 1981. *General economic history.* New Brunswick, NJ: Transaction Books.

Weymann, A., K. Martens, A. Rusconi, and K. Leuze. 2007. International organizations, markets and the nation state in education governance. In *New arenas of education governance – the impact of international organizations and markets on educational policy making*, ed. K. Martens, A. Rusconi, and K. Leuze, 229–41. New York, NY: Palgrave Macmillan.

'Catalyst data': perverse systemic effects of audit and accountability in Australian schooling

Bob Lingard and Sam Sellar

School of Education, The University of Queensland, Brisbane, Australia

This paper examines the perverse effects of the new accountability regime central to the Labor government's national reform agenda in schooling. The focus is on National Assessment Program – Literacy and Numeracy (NAPLAN) results that now act as 'catalyst data' and are pivotal to school and system accountability. We offer a case study, with two embedded units of analysis, in which NAPLAN has become high stakes testing for systems. The first involves the relationships between the federal government and three States (Victoria, New South Wales and Queensland) in negotiating performance targets on NAPLAN for reward payments in respect of a national agreement to improve literacy and numeracy. We show how Victoria used 2009 data as baseline, set ambitious targets and failed to meet them, while Queensland set much less ambitious targets, met them and was rewarded. New South Wales created targets that combined literacy and numeracy scores, obfuscating the evidence, and met their targets. The second focuses specifically on Queensland and the ramifications of the poor performance of the State on the 2008 NAPLAN. This resulted in a review commissioned by the Premier, a Report on how to improve performance, and the introduction of Teaching and Learning Audits and State-wide targets for improvement on NAPLAN. This unit of analysis focuses on the perverse effects of this highly politicized agenda. This paper shows how States seek to protect their 'reputational capital' and as such, 'game' the system. The data for the analysis draw upon interviews with relevant senior policy-makers and on analysis of relevant documents and media coverage.

Introduction

There is a considerable body of research literature (e.g. Nichols and Berliner 2007; Stobart 2008; Taubman 2009; Darling-Hammond 2010) demonstrating the perverse effects of high stakes testing upon teachers' pedagogical practices and upon students (Jones et al. 1999). We use the term 'perverse', following its use in that literature and by our research interviewees. Both usages refer to the anti-educational effects which result when performance measures become targets for systems and schools. However, we do not mean to imply that these effects are simply an aberration in new accountability regimes; rather, we see them as almost the 'new norm'. Contemporary regimes of accountability and testing in Australian schooling and their effects on and within educational systems are the concerns of this paper.

Specifically, we focus on the usage of national literacy and numeracy testing (National Assessment Program – Literacy and Numeracy, or NAPLAN) as a performance measure for State education systems. Federal 'reward funding' is currently being allocated based on systemic NAPLAN performance in relation to targets agreed in a bilateral fashion between the federal government and the States and Territories. The use of NAPLAN for this purpose facilitates comparative analysis of systemic performance and thus offers some potential to affect the 'reputational capital' (Brown and Scase 1997) of the different jurisdictions. As one of our interviewees observed, 'States ... guard very jealously their reputation and I would say that we were unfairly subject to a high level of reputational damage'. Our focus is on the effects of this form of accountability on three State education systems, where we will document some perverse outcomes of States setting and attempting to achieve performance targets and in so doing seeking to manage their 'reputational capital'.

In a sense, we are looking at the impact of what one of our research interviewees described as 'catalyst data', which is being used for accountability purposes on and across the various educational jurisdictions within Australia's federal system. 'Catalyst data' were described by one interviewee as data that encourage various stakeholders to ask questions about performance in the delivery of government services and, by implication, to make changes based on answers to these questions: 'We'll show you what's happened in terms of the data and it's a catalyst for you ... people like governments, the media, the community, academics, to ask the question: Why? Why is this so? What happened?' A catalyst is commonly understood to be a substance that facilitates a chemical reaction between other compounds, while remaining unchanged by this reaction. There is an obvious analogy here with the way in which high stakes testing data facilitate systemic effects in schooling, particularly through comparisons and 'reactions' between systems. However, catalysis also refers more broadly to processes of dissolution. In our use of the term 'catalyst data', we want to echo both the technical and broader senses of the term. Performance data have catalyzed media and subsequent systemic reactions, but in the context of Australia's federal system, such data are also contributing to a partial dissolution of the authority of State and Territory education systems, by constituting a national space of measurement, comparison and the associated allocation of funding.

While Australian education systems provide the cases for this paper, we see this commensurate space of comparative measurement produced through national testing as analogous to that which has been constituted by international testing schemes (Lingard and Rawolle 2011). These also encourage the intensification of testing within national and provincial educational systems. While our focus is on the systemic effects of a high stakes testing regime in Australian schooling, the research reported here has broader salience, as many nations around the globe have introduced national testing programs associated with particular accountability, funding and improvement regimes (e.g. *Race to the Top* under Obama in the USA) with effects on educational systems. This paper focuses on the effects of high stakes testing and the audit culture on policy-makers and politicians within and across education jurisdictions, using Australia's federal system as an example.

In Australia's federal political structure, schooling is the Constitutional responsibility of States and Territories. However, since the 1970s, there has been increased and systematized federal involvement in schooling, and since the 1980s, this has been linked to human capital arguments about the centrality of education and skills to the competitiveness and productivity of the Australian economy. When the Rudd Labor government was elected in 2007, it sought to strengthen and rework federalism, increasing the hand of the federal government vis-à-vis the provincial governments, including in schooling. This has been achieved through an Intergovernmental Agreement ratified by the States and Territories, which sets out a schedule for the distribution of federal monies based on the achievement of targets and performance measures for policy delivery. We would note here that the usage of 'national' in Australian politics, and this is very much the case in schooling, is a signifier of an attempt to gain policy consensus across federal, State and Territory governments, when a federal government is pursuing a particular agenda. In a sense, the introduction of NAPLAN can be seen at one level as a policy attempt to constitute a national system of schooling through national testing partially tied to performance funding. The current development of a national curriculum is another element here, as is the range of National Partnerships that the federal government has created to drive improvement in schooling.[1]

We provide a two-part case study of policy developments in response to the national reform agenda in education and outcomes on NAPLAN.[2] The first unit of analysis is the relationship between the federal government and three States (Victoria, New South Wales and Queensland) in negotiating performance targets linked to reward payments for improved literacy and numeracy outcomes. At the heart of this unit of analysis is the interface between the Council of Australian Governments (COAG) Reform Council, the three State systems of schooling and the federal Department of Education, Employment and Workplace Relations. The COAG Reform Council was created to monitor the pace of achievement of a range of national policies. We document some of the perverse effects that have resulted from tying federal funding, and very public media reporting, to systemic achievement in NAPLAN testing. The second unit of analysis is the Queensland system and the ramifications of perceived poor State performance on the 2008 NAPLAN tests. This resulted in the commissioning of the Masters Review of Queensland primary schooling, subsequent intensification of audit regimes (e.g. introduction of Teaching and Learning Audits of all Queensland government schools) and the creation of State-wide targets for improvement on NAPLAN. In this case, we focus on the work of one education region in Queensland and interviews conducted there to show the effects of both national and State pressures for improvement. Overall, this unit of analysis demonstrates how national testing and audit regimes have become high stakes for State education systems, in the first instance by demonstrating effects across systems, while in the second, demonstrating effects within the organizational structure of one system.

Our analysis draws on approximately thirty research interviews with (a) senior and relevant policy-makers in State and federal systems and in relevant statutory authorities at State and federal levels, (b) personnel in international organizations, including the Organisation for Economic Cooperation and Development (OECD) and the International Association for the Evaluation of Educational Achievement (IEA) and (c) researchers and academics involved in debates about national and international testing agendas. Out of concern to ensure anonymity, we have not named interviewees or their positions.

In the following section of this paper, we briefly review the audit and accountability literatures and set the broad context of their place in education system reforms, beginning with a focus on the emergent global education policy field that is being constituted through international comparative testing. We then provide a descriptive account of Australian developments, which constitute a specific case of a more general policy development in schooling systems around the world. The two units of analysis dealing with the impact of NAPLAN testing as high stakes for systems are then outlined. This paper concludes by drawing out implications of the systemic effects described for thinking about similar developments in other national educational contexts.

Theoretical framework and contextualizing the cases

Theoretical framework

The macro political setting of both cases is the meta-policy of neo-liberalism and related state restructurings (i.e. the new public management), as they work their ways out in educational policies within nations. However, a central point here is that these policies and state restructures, the so-called governance turn, have become globalized policy discourses associated with and advanced by international organizations such as the OECD. They are also linked to and are expressions of globalization in the period after the Cold War. There is now research arguing that as part of these developments, we are seeing the emergence of a globalized education policy field, using Bourdieu's concept of fields (Lingard and Rawolle 2011), and that this field is being constituted through a 'globalizing empiricism' (Torrance 2006). International measures of the comparative performance of schooling systems (e.g. the OECD's Program for International Student Assessment [PISA] and Educational Indicators and the IEA's Trends in International Mathematics and Science Studies [TIMSS] and Progress in International Reading Literacy Studies) are creating this global field as a commensurate space of measurement. Indeed, one of our international interviewees explained that through the expansion of the global coverage of PISA, the OECD aims 'to have the broadest possible picture of the global talent pool'.

Sassen (2007) has argued that globalization can be seen as the creation of a global infrastructure that facilitates the flows associated with the multiple circuits of the global economy. We see the creation of a global space of measurement of the comparative performance of national schooling systems as an important component part of this global infrastructure. National testing in Australia, and comparisons of individual school performance against 60 statistically similar schools facilitated by the federal government's My School website, is likewise helping to constitute a national system of schooling through its technical infrastructure. Grek et al. (2009) and Lawn and Grek (2012) have argued similarly about the use of policy as numbers to create a European educational policy space and have documented the interweaving of these supranational and national policy developments. The development of NAPLAN in Australia is also part of a globalized education policy discourse that argues that standards can only be driven up by such testing (Stobart 2008). Furthermore, the development of national high stakes testing around the globe is driven by and complements international testing programs and comparisons. One interviewee explained, in relation to the different functions of PISA and NAPLAN, that 'you need to have those perspectives: a perspective that looks inward (NAPLAN) and one that looks outward (PISA)'.[3] This interviewee added that internal measures only register national improvement or decline and, therefore, comparative international measures are necessary to benchmark this performance and provide a broader comparative indication of improvement or decline.

Related to these developments have been a number of other phenomena, including the rise of talk about evidence-based (and evidence-informed) policy (Head 2008; Wiseman 2010), policy as numbers (Rose 1999; Ozga 2009; Lingard 2011) and new forms of state accountability, as part of what Power (1997) has called the 'audit explosion'. Indeed, Power (1997, 44) sees the hollowing out of the state associated with new public management – its steering at a distance approach – as actually generating 'a demand for audit and other forms of evaluation and inspection to fill the hole'; he refers to this as a new form of the 'regulatory state' (52).

An interesting literature has also emerged on educational accountability, stretching from the critical and theoretical (e.g. Ranson 2003, 2012; Ravitch 2010; Suspitsyna 2010; Webb 2011) to the philosophical (e.g. Biesta 2004; Harvey 2010) and the more normative and policy pragmatic (e.g. Sahlberg 2010). Suspitsyna (2010) sees accountability mechanisms in education as technologies of governance, which *pace* Foucault have governmentality effects through ensuring that policy-makers and principals and teachers in schools become self-governing. This position has been outlined in some detail by Rose (1999) in his account of neo-liberal governance and the self-capitalizing and self-responsibilising individual. Webb (2011) argues that at the broader societal level we are transiting from what Foucault called a 'disciplinary society' towards what Deleuze described as 'control societies', with the latter evident in the reality of ongoing incessant measurement and assessment. These numbers also provide a way for the state to manage risk, an aspect of what Thrift (2005) sees as late capitalism becoming a project of knowing itself, with data being central to this self-knowledge.

In line with Webb (2011), we understand testing, audit and accountability regimes as mechanisms that operate according to the logic of 'control societies' (Deleuze 1995), enabling the continuous assessment of students, teachers and schools and giving rise to feedback loops through which education systems are continually modulated in response to test results and their public representations (cf. Lyotard 1984).[4] In each of our units of analysis, we attend to the practices through which data are constituted and represented and acknowledge how data assist in making the nation legible for governing (Scott 1998). As part of this process, statistical and scientific practices that inform and underpin high-stakes testing regimes are translated into representations that are conveyed by different media (e.g. graphs, news stories, political narratives and reports). One interviewee described how 'an optics problem' arises where graphical representation of data renders opaque crucial decisions relating to its collection and analysis. Interestingly, Rose (1999) observes that single numbers in policy accounts do political work in hiding the technologies that have gone into their construction. As with single policy numbers, and following Latour (1999), the representation of testing results can be understood to involve a series of translations that simplify the phenomenon being tested (e.g. students' literacy skills). This involves a process of reduction to generate standardized and comparable representations with an amplified capacity to have an effect as fact or evidence. As Porter (1995, 29) has noted, 'There is a strong incentive to prefer precise and standardizable measures to highly accurate ones'. For example, the Australian My School website represents school performance on NAPLAN testing using colour coding to indicate whether results for particular cohorts are better, worse or comparable with statistically similar cohorts. A complex technical process for determining levels of achievement, full of ambivalent analytical decisions, is ultimately represented in terms of 'green' for good and 'red' for bad. Through the high profile media reporting of NAPLAN results, this process of translation, and attendant 'optics problems', contributes to an affective politics (Massumi 2002; Thrift 2007), which manifests, for example, as moral panics in relation to declining literacy and numeracy standards or a 'nervousness' amongst senior policy-makers and politicians (see Massumi 2005; Sellar 2012).

In this paper, we are particularly interested in the ways that representations and readings of NAPLAN data give rise to feelings of anxiousness and nervousness amongst policy-makers in response to media and political pressures for their system to be 'seen' as improving and achieving at a high standard in comparison with other systems. Testing becomes high stakes for systems in part through this modulation of affectively registered pressure on policy-makers. We also suggest that a similar phenomenon is evident in national (and provincial) comparative performance on international measures such as PISA, TIMSS and PIRLS; for example, the various PISA 'shocks' that have occurred in a number of national systems (e.g. Ertl 2006; Takayama 2008). High stakes testing is thus linked to an affective politics through which the work of educational governance is increasingly operationalized within education systems in control societies. This is one vector of governmentality and the self-governing of policy-makers, school leaders and teachers.

Contextualizing the case

As noted above, Australia has a federal political structure. Section 51 of the Constitution outlines the powers of the federal government and those not listed are regarded as residual powers of the States and Territories. Schooling is one such residual power. During the Second World War, the federal government took over income tax raising powers from the States, resulting in the high degree of vertical fiscal imbalance in Australian federalism; that is, the federal government has the bulk of the revenue, while the States have the responsibility for the delivery of large and expensive public policy domains such as schooling, health and policing. This has often led to funding/compliance trade-offs between the federal government and the States. Since the centralist policies of the Whitlam federal Labor government (1972–1975), the peak moment of progressive Keynesianism in Australia, all public policy domains have had a complex mix of federal and State monies, involvements and policies, with the nomenclature of 'national' often signifying a policy domain in which agreements have been achieved between federal and State governments. Since its formation in 1992, the COAG (consisting of Prime Minister, State Premiers and Territory Chief Ministers, and the President of the Australian Local Government Association) has been the primary forum for managing intergovernmental relations and national policy reform. Since the 1930s, there have been intergovernmental councils in most policy domains that cut across federal and State jurisdictions. The Standing Council on School Education and Early Childhood (SCSEEC), the current intergovernmental council for education, was established in 2012 out of previous councils.

The significance of COAG has waxed and waned since its creation, but it took on a reinvigorated role after the election of the federal Rudd Labor government in

2007 (Carroll and Head 2010). As one senior policy-maker at the national level noted in an interview: 'I think the standout for Rudd is that he actually went to an election on these issues' and '… he won the election in November [2007] and held his first COAG in December. It was just astonishing. Then he held four a year for the next two years. Then he fell off the wagon'. During the 2007 election campaign, Rudd argued that cooperative federalism was important, as was the advancement of a range of national policy reforms, to ensure the global competitiveness and increased productivity of the Australian economy and to avoid blame shifting between the States and the federal government. At that time, the pursuit of cooperative federalism was aided by the fact that there were Labor governments in all States and Territories, a situation that has subsequently changed with non-Labor governments now in Western Australia, Victoria, New South Wales and Queensland. From 2009, a new *Intergovernmental Agreement on Federal Financial Relations* (IAFFR) took effect, with the aim of reducing the plethora of specific purpose payments (Section 96 grants) to the States through consolidation of these payments into single larger payments. This gave the States more policy autonomy, but also audit pressures associated with accountability frameworks negotiated with the federal government. The COAG Reform Council is the statutory authority with responsibilities for assessment and reporting of State performance in relation to the IAFFR.

Also pivotal to Rudd's 2007 election campaign was his commitment to a so-called 'Education Revolution' to be implemented through a range of national policies in schooling, including a National Curriculum, national testing (NAPLAN), a new transparency and accountability agenda evident in the creation of the My School website, and the establishment of a new statutory authority to oversee these national developments: the Australian Curriculum, Assessment and Reporting Authority (ACARA). The Australian Institute of Teaching and School Leadership (AITSL) has also been created to establish national standards and promote excellence in the teaching profession. As part of the broader IAFFR, a National Education Agreement was signed in schooling, outlining national outcomes, targets and performance indicators to which the States and Territories were party. The States also entered into National Partnership Agreements with the federal government in respect of specific schooling projects in three areas: Literacy and Numeracy, Teacher Quality and Low Socio-economic Status School Communities. These National Partnerships included both facilitation payments to fund reform and reward payments, paid when targets set for improvement are met. In schooling, NAPLAN is a key central performance indicator for the National Agreement and is the primary data-set for the establishment of reward targets for the National Partnership for Literacy and Numeracy. Our two units of analysis relate to this particular National Partnership.

Unit of analysis 1: systemic effects of federal funding based on NAPLAN performance

On 19 April 2011 *The Age*, Victoria's daily broadsheet newspaper, announced that the 'State flunks its own literacy, numeracy tests' and described how Victoria's schools had 'overwhelmingly failed' to make progress toward 2010 targets for improving literacy and numeracy in schools. While the headline implied that Victorian schools were underperforming, the article itself conceded that Victoria had set 'ambitious reward targets' and that its 'failure' did not mean that it had performed poorly in comparison with other States. However, the headlines ultimately had the greatest impact on public perception. As one interviewee from the Victorian education department explained:

> I think the fact that in the end we performed much the same as all the other higher performing jurisdictions, but it didn't present that way, that we didn't get funding because we had a more difficult reward framework. Yet all you see in the headlines is that we did badly and others did well, it's a lot of reputational damage, so a lot of nervousness I think in preparing for this year.

At issue here are the processes through which targets were set and progress assessed in relation to the National Partnership for Literacy and Numeracy. While a core theme in the 'Education Revolution' has been to increase transparency and accountability, the negotiation of reward funding frameworks for this National Partnership was not a transparent process for systems. Another interviewee in the Victorian education department explained,

> It was all secret. There was no transparency around what Victoria was negotiating with the Commonwealth and what other jurisdictions were negotiating. You had no idea of whether what you were putting forward was in any way comparable with anyone else.

This had important implications for setting targets and for the reporting and comparison of outcomes.

The opacity of framework negotiations appears reasonable given the intent of the National Partnership was that frameworks negotiated by each jurisdiction would *not* be comparable. While the National Education Agreement explicitly specifies national outcomes against which State and Territory governments are assessed and compared based on their performance, the National Partnerships are bilateral agreements and 'the diverse reform strategies being implemented in each State and Territory are not intended to support a comparative analysis of performance' (COAG Reform Council 2011, xiv). However, upon release of the COAG Reform Council assessments in 2011, systemic performance was compared in reductive and simplistic media accounts, subsequently raising the stakes for systems in terms of protecting their reputations. The key issues raised by interviewees in relation to this reporting of the National Partnership process included the different levels of 'ambition' reflected in the targets set by each jurisdiction; the diverse nature of targets across jurisdictions; and disparities in the baseline data against which achievement was measured. We address each of these issues here.

Under the terms of the National Partnership Agreement for Literacy and Numeracy, each jurisdiction was required to develop an Implementation Plan that formed the basis for bilateral negotiation of their reward funding framework with the federal Government. This included setting targets in relation to four mandated measures of NAPLAN performance and negotiating unique local targets for improvement in other areas.[5] In this unit of analysis, we focus specifically on the first measure, which was of students at or above the national minimum standard for reading and/or numeracy. While there was flexibility for each system to set reward frameworks that reflected their particular circumstances and broad objectives, the National Partnership specified that targets needed to be ambitious and the Australian

Council for Educational Research (ACER) was commissioned to assess this level of ambition. Notably, ACER considered that Victoria's proposed targets were not sufficiently ambitious and encouraged revision: 'ACER, in fact, said our targets were not ambitious enough and we needed to push them up, which we did. Everybody signed these off and, of course, bingo, we didn't achieve'.

Achievement in relation to the four mandated measures of NAPLAN performance was assessed for a set of schools nominated by each jurisdiction, with States and Territories putting forward quite different sample sizes (see Table 1). States and Territories also negotiated the specific data that would be used to measure their achievement. For example, Victoria opted for each year level (3, 5, 7 and 9) and area (literacy and numeracy) to be assessed in relation to each of the four measures (32 targets in total). In contrast, New South Wales opted to aggregate Year 3 and 5 results, across both literacy and numeracy, for a single assessment in relation to each of the four measures (four targets in total). Queensland negotiated a total of 16 targets. Table 1 provides an overview of the reward frameworks negotiated by each of these systems.

Tables 2–4 illustrate, in relation to the first mandated measure against which targets were set, the different structures of the targets, the different baseline data-sets, and the results and assessments. An assessment of 'A' was awarded where performance equaled or exceeded targets; a 'B' was awarded where performance exceeded the baseline but did not reach the target; and a 'C' was awarded when performance was at or below the baseline (COAG Reform Council 2011, 9).

Victoria's nomination of 32 targets and a large sample of schools reflected a perception within the system that it had strong capacities in data gathering and performance measurement, and this was manifest as an intent to enter into the spirit of the federal Government's transparency agenda and to lead by example in the National Partnership negotiations: '[T]here was a sense that we should do this properly, not play the game, not game the system first up'. In contrast, the aggregated groups nominated for measurement by New South Wales, and the fewer resulting targets, were perceived to obfuscate performance rather than render it transparent. One interviewee wryly noted that 'more aggregation leaves more flexibility for achievement'. For example, it is not possible to determine exactly which aspect of literacy or numeracy across Years 3 and 5 contributed to the small increases achieved in New South Wales, or indeed if declines in some areas were masked by relatively substantial gains in other areas.

Different jurisdictions were also measured against different baselines: 'The original establishment of the rewards framework was done on the basis of one year of NAPLAN data ... Nobody really understood how NAPLAN was going to behave, what it would show'. New South Wales and Queensland used 2008 NAPLAN data as a baseline; however, Victoria used the 2009 data-set. There was significant improvement nationally between 2008 and 2009, raising the possibility of an equating error between the two data-sets: 'that equating was not right, therefore everyone improves. So this ended up with, so with the COAG report saying Victoria are not getting funding ... it really had nothing to do whatsoever with improvement really'. Arguably, the 2009 data-set provided an artificially inflated baseline against which Victorian achievement in 2010 was then compared. This made further improvement difficult: 'the higher you are up the scale of performance the less it [NAPLAN performance] moves. It's a "ceilinged" instrument'. Aside from differences in the bilateral negotiations of targets by each system, the measurement of

Table 1. 2010 reward frameworks, New South Wales, Victoria and Queensland (reproduced from COAG Reform Council 2011, 99).

Participating schols/students	Assessed students and baseline year	Target groups	Target calculation
NSW – 4 targets for mandated measures			
147 schools	Measures 1–3: 12 442	Years 3 and 5 literacy *or* numeracy	Measures 1,2 and 4% decrease in proportions at or below, or below. Measure 3: scale point improvement
43 825 students 4% of NSW students	Measure 4: 1098 Baseline: 2008	Targets are aggregations of year levels and domains	
Victoria – 32 targets for mandated measures			
492 schools	Measure 1–3: 15 742	Years 3, 5, 7 and 9	Measures 1–4% improvement in scores based on 2009 gap between participating students and all Victorian students
184 506 students 22% of Vic. students	Measure 4: 335 Baseline: 2009	Literacy *and* numeracy	
Queensland –16 targets for mandated measures			
279 schools	Measure 1–3: 12 745 Measure 4: 1 388	Years 3 and 5 Literacy and numeracy	Measure 1–4% improvement on a projected decline, based on historical trend
17% of Qld. students	Baseline: 2008		

Table 2. Mandated measure 1: New South Wales, targets and performance (reproduced from COAG Reform Council 2011, 19).

Target group	Baseline 2008	Target 2010	Result 2010	Assessment	Participation
Target calculation: a decrease of 50% of the proportion of students below the national minimum standard (equivalent to an increase of 0.6% points in the proportion of students at or above the national standard)					
Year 3 and Year 5 reading and numeracy	88.5%	89.1%	90.5%	A	98.9% (+0.2 ppts)

Table 3. Mandated measure 1: Victoria, targets and performance (reproduced from COAG Reform Council 2011, 27).

Target group	Baseline 2009	Target 2010	Result 2010	Assessment	Participation
Target calculation: An improvement in the proportion of students at or above the national minimum standard equivalent to a decrease of 25% of the 2009 gap between students in participating schools and all schools					
Year 3 reading	92.3%	92.8%	91.5%	C	91.9% (−1.7 ppts)
Year 5 reading	89.2%	90.20%	88.3%	C	93.1% (−0.6 ppts)
Year 7 reading	91.4%	92.23%	92.9%	A	93.2% (−0.3 ppts)
Year 9 reading	87.6%	88.95%	86.9%	C	87.5% (−0.9 ppts)
Year 3 numeracy	90.2%	91.10%	92.3%	A	91.5% (−1.5 ppts)
Year 5 numeracy	92.8%	93.50%	92.3%	C	93.0% (0.0 ppts)
Year 7 numeracy	93.7%	94.25%	94.1%	B 72.7%	92.8% (−0.4 ppts)
Year 9 numeracy	94.2%	94.70%	90.9%	C	87.7% (−0.7 ppts)

Table 4. Mandated measure 1: Queensland, targets and performance (reproduced from COAG Reform Council 2011, 35).

Target group	Baseline 2008	Target 2010	Result 2010	Assessment	Participation
Target calculation: An improvement of 50% on trends observed from historical testing in the proportion of students at or above the nation minimum standard					
Year 3 reading	82.1%	81.5%	88.9%	A	95.2% (−2.5 ppts)
Year 5 reading	78.0%	77.6%	81.2%	A	96.0% (−1.8 ppts)
Year 3 numeracy	86.0%	85.9%	91.1%	A	95.0% (−1.9 ppts)
Year 5 numeracy	85.1%	84.0%	88.4%	A	95.5% (−1.8 ppts)

achievement against different baselines introduced a fundamental incommensurability that was largely elided in media reporting and in subsequent perceptions of comparative systemic performance.

Ultimately, Victoria's performance was variable in relation to its 32 targets and it received 5 As, 10 Bs and 17 Cs. New South Wales received 3 As and a B for progress made in relation to its four targets. Queensland's achievement exceeded each of the targets it set and the COAG Reform Council granted them an assessment of straight As. There were problems with this reporting of outcomes using A–C ratings, as described by one interviewee involved in the assessment process:

> [W]hen we say Queensland got all As and Victoria got mainly Cs, anybody who picked a report up like that would say gee, Queensland is way better than Victoria and Victoria must be terrible and that isn't the case because they're not comparative.

While the detailed performance reporting produced by the COAG Reform Council clearly specifies important differences in the reward funding frameworks negotiated by each jurisdiction, and the differences in data-sets and measures, the A–C reporting enabled simplistic and comparative media reporting that had damaging effects for the spirit of the COAG reform agenda and the reputation of jurisdictions such as Victoria. This has had implications for the ways in which States and Territories will engage with the process in the future:

> It's that 'gotcha' thing and then we, it's almost like then you lose the jurisdictions …
> and this is what the [Intergovernmental Agreement] … is, it is meant to improve performance. It's meant to improve and if there is too much focus on the 'gotcha', which there is in the media, then what we find in our relationships with jurisdictions, which are incredibly important, is they go undercover and then they'll argue the toss about every small … every point and they'll totally not, it's not the spirit that you're trying to look for. You can really understand from their point of view.

Media reports of these assessments have encouraged systems to become more cynical and to focus on the comparative representation of performance over and above substantive improvement. For example, one interviewee from the New South Wales system told us that in relation to comparative data:

> We all use results as it suits us, and it was of concern to New South Wales when we noticed our relative decline in performance, that Western Australia was suddenly up there above us. All we could come up with was sampling error. We did talk to ACER to really interrogate their processes and it was revealed that yes, they didn't actually include remote schools in the sample.

The high stakes of NAPLAN for systems has intensified debate over technical issues, including the application of political pressure to influence decision-making about testing methodologies and analysis. This is linked with efforts to massage results in order to preserve or improve public perception.

'Gaming' the intended spirit of the reforms – that is, the setting and pursuit of ambitious targets for improvement – has been a significant perverse effect of this process. One interviewee explained that 'as soon as you attach [performance measures] to rewards you create perverse incentives'. For example, differences in the nature of the targets set by each jurisdiction were substantial. For each of the mandated measures, Victoria set targets to reduce the gap between students in nominated schools and all students in the system by 25% (see Table 3). In contrast, Queensland set targets to reduce the rate of decline in performance (2006–2009), halving the gap between the baseline data and the projected decline in performance by 2010 (see Table 4). These targets were considered to be less ambitious than Victoria's, with one interviewee from another jurisdiction describing them as 'going backwards targets'. Another interviewee suggested that the targets set by Queensland reflected a breakdown of the mutual responsibility that State and federal governments shared for ensuring the integrity of the process:

> [A]lthough you could say gee, look at what Queensland did, in some regards I would put very much the responsibility back on the Commonwealth. It was the Common-wealth Department that agreed that Queensland could have these targets. Queensland didn't just say we've got them. … [I]f you want to have a reform agenda well, you have to put the weight on accountability very much to make it effective. Then the weight goes very much in this instance I would suggest also on the Commonwealth's role.

While Queensland set targets that ultimately served its interests in terms of how its performance was assessed and reported, this distortion of the process was sanctioned by the federal government through its bilateral negotiation. The fact that Queensland benefited in terms of funding and public perception has led bureaucrats in other systems to believe that the National Partnership process will be more explicitly 'gamed' in the future. One interviewee argued that, for systems such as Victoria, 'there will be a different dynamic and they will be much more hardnosed and much more cynical about playing the game'. Another interviewee observed that now the process is perceived to be 'definitely a game. It's a serious one because if Victoria doesn't meet these targets … we miss a lot of funding'.

This analysis highlights a number of important issues. Firstly, media reporting of systemic NAPLAN performance is placing pressure on policy-makers in systems. In this way, NAPLAN has become high stakes for systems and not just for the students sitting the tests, or the teachers and schools increasingly held responsible for their performance. These high stakes are manifest in the nervousness of policy-makers, felt in anticipation of upcoming rounds of testing, and in new political pressures to address performance 'crises'. In response to this media and political pressure, and the significant funding tied to outcomes, 'gaming' the National Partnerships is a rational and attractive option for States and Territories. In the next case, we examine in greater depth how system-wide performance 'crises' have translated into an intensification of audit and accountability within State systems.

Unit of analysis 2: systemic effects of poor NAPLAN performance in Queensland

Queensland performed comparatively poorly in the 2008 NAPLAN data that was used as a baseline for the National Partnerships reward funding. This caused a political furore in the State, with huge media coverage by the *Courier-Mail*, the Queensland daily newspaper, and also by radio and television. There was also extensive national media coverage documenting State system performances and Queensland's poor comparative performance. The immediate political response was for the then Premier, Anna Bligh, to appoint in December 2008 Professor Geoff Masters, CEO of ACER, to review the literacy, numeracy and science performance of Queensland primary school students. Science performance was included because of the apparently poor performance of Queensland students in the 2007 TIMSS. This was 'catalyst' data and Premier's Bligh's central role can be seen as an attempt to protect the reputational capital of Queensland, which has branded itself as the 'Smart State' (see Adie 2008), a signifier of a move away from the old 'Deep North' anti-intellectual construction of the State. Masters provided 'Preliminary Advice' to the Premier on 25 January 2009 and the final report, *A Shared Challenge Improving Literacy, Numeracy and Science Learning in Queensland Primary Schools* (hereafter the *Masters Report*) was released in April 2009 (Masters 2009a, 2009b).

In the Preliminary Advice, one can see the political imperative and its temporality driving the need to quickly improve Queensland's test results on NAPLAN. For example, Recommendation four states:

> That last year's NAPLAN assessment materials – including test booklets, administration manual, marking guides, and details of the performances of last year's cohort on each test question – be made available for all Year 3, 5 and 7 teachers at the start of the 2009 school year for use in establishing students' current levels of literacy and numeracy development and to assist in identifying learning needs. (Masters 2009a, 5)

This is the use of NAPLAN materials as a 'classroom resource' and the text suggested that, 'These materials also may provide students with some useful test taking experience' (Masters 2009a, 6). This is one common result of high stakes testing, a focus on improving test literacy and teaching to the test. To be fair, though, in both the Preliminary Advice and in the *Masters Report,* there were recommendations for longer term changes that reflected the temporalities associated with real and deeper educational change. The Preliminary Advice recommended that the State government set a target so that 'Queensland primary school students were performing at the level of students in the highest performing states in literacy, numeracy and science within the next three years'. Importantly, in the context of negotiating the State's National Partnership reward framework, this recommendation is for comparative improvement.

Here, we see a clear expression of the tight temporality of a political imperative and one with the added legitimacy of an expert review. This political imperative was obvious at the Premier's launch of the *Masters Report*, when in response to questions and discussion about why Queensland had done poorly on the 2008 NAPLAN, she explained that all of that evidence and associated explanations might well be true, but that there was a political urgency for her to do something, particularly in response to huge and negative media coverage, which was suggesting a problem with Queensland schools.[6] The Premier noted that in this context she had a political problem and had to act, thus commissioning the Masters review – a good exemplification of the 'mediatization' of education policy (Lingard and Rawolle 2004).

Structural reforms have also followed from the State's poor NAPLAN performance in 2008. Thus from 2015, Year 7 will be moved into secondary schooling in Queensland, bringing schooling structures into line with those in both Victoria and New South Wales, while the introduction of a new Preparatory year also will help align the ages of Queensland students with those in other States. This would seem to be an acknowledgement by the Premier that there were structural explanations for the 2008 performance. The government's commitment to the implementation of all Recommendations in the *Masters Report* also seems to suggest a commitment to broader change beyond the immediate enhancement of Queensland's comparative NAPLAN performance. What we see here, perhaps, is a mix of political tactics aimed at short-term test-score improvement, as well as longer term strategies.

These political tactics have had multiple effects, when placed in the context of the national reform agenda and the use of NAPLAN for allocating National Partnership reward funding. There have been perverse and gaming effects in the context of the Queensland system and schools having quickly to improve Queensland's NAPLAN performance to meet the time frame of the political agenda. NAPLAN thus became high stakes for the system in Queensland with effects rippling down the line to regions and to schools. The impact of this catalyst data was very clear in the account provided by an interviewee at the federal level:

> I felt the interesting thing about Premier Bligh's response is that she did it on the basis of the 2008 NAPLAN ... across Australia everybody knew that Queensland looked very different from States. I think Queensland would like to see itself close to and in comparison with States such as Victoria and New South Wales ... She brought in Professor Geoff Masters and did a review ... We can't say the Review had these results. But what we can say in 2010 ... is Queensland has improved. I know from a lower base, but better than other comparable institutions and governments. So you'd have to say something went on.

Later, this same interviewee commented:

> ... if you get the data right ... NAPLAN data is right, in the sense that it is extremely robust ... and the thing about it is you don't just do it once ... So it's not like you can say okay, let's just ride it out. The catalyst data says if you don't respond, it's not going away and furthermore it could even get worse over time if you don't act to do something now. So I think that's the weight of public accountability – with good data, it works, it's the benefit that it is there every year. It's against agreed and accepted data and good comparators and benchmarks or targets.

We can see here the political pressure on State systems and, in the Queensland instance, the taking up of this pressure by the Premier to improve Queensland's NAPLAN performance very quickly. The remainder of this analysis will draw on interview data to show the effects in a Regional Office and its respective region of the Queensland Department of Education. It shows some of the perverse effects of NAPLAN becoming high stakes for the system, including immediate structural effects such as the creation of positions in Head Office and in the Region to handle political pressure from the Premier's office. For example, an Assistant Director-General School Performance has been created to handle school data, especially NAPLAN. At the Regional Office, where we did research interviews, there is also a Principal Advisor School Performance position, or 'our data guru' as one interview put it.

One specific development to flow from the implementation of the *Masters Report* was the creation of the Queensland Education Department's Teaching and Learning Audit instrument developed by ACER, the implementation of which is now overseen by the Assistant Director-General School Performance.[7] Teaching and Learning Audits were conducted in each Queensland school in 2010 and will continue to be conducted every four years, with any new principal also having an audit conducted in their school. One interviewee at the Regional Office called this audit a 'sort of fallout' of the *Masters Report*. In the Foreword to the audit document, the Director General stated:

> In keeping with the plan (Department of Education and Training's 2009–2013 Strategic Plan) Education Queensland has developed a new and comprehensive strategy to improve student performance ... The strategy encompasses extensive audit requirements for state schools in the area of teaching and learning with a teaching and learning audit being conducted in every Queensland state school in 2010.

The Teaching and Learning Audit consists of eight elements.[8] Schools are ranked against each of these eight elements on a four point scale from Outstanding to Low. An interviewee in the Regional Office noted the strengths of the Audits: '... it's really focused people on a Teaching and Learning agenda'. In this particular Regional Office, research had been conducted on the correlations between a school's score on the Audit and their performance on NAPLAN. One interviewee explained that '... we don't always see an alignment do we between audit and achievement' (an observation directed towards the Regional Director). This person also noted that they had only really found correlations between certain of the audit elements: '... our initial feeling is that Two, Five and Seven are the elements that make a big difference here' in relation to performance measures such as NAPLAN; 'the bang for the buck will come out of these three we think'.[9]

Several of the interviewees made the point that if schools scored poorly on one of the other elements and were pressured to improve on that by the system, this would not necessarily improve their NAPLAN scores. As the data person in the Regional Office stated:

> ... you get your Teaching and Learning Audit and you've got two lows, so you feel this pressure that you've got to improve those two lows, you don't want to have a low, you want to move them, where in fact working on those two lows may have absolutely no effect on student achievement.

Here we can see potential goal displacement. Improved Audit scores become a target with potentially limited impact on NAPLAN, if the focus is not on elements which the Regional Office research had shown were correlated with test performance. This is interesting in an age of evidence-based or informed policy. The Audit purports to have been derived from international research evidence, but there is limited systemic research about its effects in respect of impact for improving NAPLAN performance. It seems that this region was the only one conducting research into the usefulness of the Audit instrument for its stated purposes. As one interviewee noted, 'So the system has not done any correlation of whether what you see in a Teaching and Learning Audit reflects in student achievement'.

The Regional Office interviewees also spoke of the State-wide performance targets set in response to the 2008 performance data, as well as in relation to the National Partnership reward framework.[10] Interestingly though, there was no mention of these national processes and pressures by those in the Regional Office. The pressure was seen to be a State one generated by the Premier's involvement, but as we have suggested the Premier's concerns were linked to the State's reputational capital and to the national reform agenda. One interviewee in the Regional Office commented:

I don't know if you're aware but in reaction to where Queensland performed in terms of NAPLAN 2008 the State set some State targets, which they anticipated would get us to a point where we'd improve and they were three percent each year ... It's a State wide target not a school'.

This was a statewide improvement of three per cent across the board in NAPLAN, irrespective of how schools performed on the 2008 tests. One interviewee in the Regional office commented in relation to this, 'an improvement in every part of NAPLAN – the silly percentage'. The same interviewee went on to note how the Region had decided to target two aspects of NAPLAN, reading and literacy, along with the target that 'a hundred per cent of eligible kids will be above the National Minimum Standards'. She continued that they then set local targets for different schools instead of blanket improvements target for all domains and all schools of three per cent: 'You set a local target for improving the upper two bands with an emphasis again on reading and numeracy, but where reading and numeracy's ok, you could actually look at the other domains as well'. Another interviewee heavily involved in data analysis observed, 'to have a global target is ridiculous'. The interviewees, though, also said this discrepancy between political targets set at State level, and Regional nuancing of these targets, caused some trauma for school principals. What came through very clearly in the interviews was the need for more complex and nuanced target setting for individual schools on the basis of data, a very different approach to that of the political pressure for rapid and almost immediate improvement that led to blanket State-wide improvement targets.

There was also much commentary on the limited statistical literacy of those leading schools and the need for a 'data team in school leadership': 'they actually don't understand target setting and stretching'; 'they really struggle with targets' (see Alegounarias 2011). This Regional person also stated that, 'sometimes like with all targets they go for the things that are easy to measure you know, as you would expect ... That's why spelling is a favourite for people, you know I can say how many more words I got right this week'. These are some of the perverse effects the literature has noted when targets are set in relation to high stakes testing (Stobart 2008). There was also commentary about the ambition of target setting by middle class schools and an observation that statistically similar school measures published on the federal government's My School website had made the Region aware of this lack of ambition. There was also comment on the conversion of targets to numbers of students at a given school and class level that must improve. This conversion to specific numbers at year levels 'meant far more to them' than targets. An interviewee at the federal level had made this exact point to us about the local impact of national accountability around NAPLAN: 'Have they (principals) ever said I have to lift 10 kids from there to there in national testing? They would never have done this without this [national accountability through NAPLAN]. So you need the architecture at every level'. Here, we see the triage effects in classrooms (Gillborn and Youdell 2000) and the focus on those close to achieving the required standards (Lipman 2004) that result from target setting. This Region was running Masters Classes to improve the statistical literacy of school leaders, as well as a coaching program. The use of data as central technologies of governance was also reflected in the utilization of school data-sets in interviews for the appointment of new school principals:

Data sets are a big deal, and they expect them to be able to speak cogently about the data in terms of how to utilise it … tell you what the implications of that data are in terms of: what I need to work on, where the priorities are, why I make these choices.

The Region was aware of these issues and was attempting to nuance them in research-based and educational ways, but all within a framework that had taken as given the agenda to improve test performance. To be fair, the Region was also committed to trying to improve educational outcomes for all students, in both the underperforming middle class schools and in disadvantaged schools. However, improved performance for one school necessarily means declining performance for another on the 'Statistically Similar Schools' measures, thus strengthening the ongoing fetish for improving test results redolent of Deleuze's depiction of control societies.

This unit of analysis has illustrated how reward funding tied to State improvement on NAPLAN, along with the politicization of NAPLAN performance through the close involvement of the Premier, have had considerable effects within the Queensland system. We see increased accountability surveillance through the Teaching and Learning Audits and their potential for goal displacement with improved Audit scores becoming the focus of school reform. This pressure has been strengthened somewhat with the *Courier-Mail* (28–29 January 2012) publishing a League Table of all schools' scores on the elements of the Teaching and Learning Audit. We also see the disjuncture between the temporalities of political demands to improve Queensland's NAPLAN performance and those required for real educational change, as well as the perverse effects of target setting at the State level. This analysis also clearly demonstrates the potential triage effects of target setting and the affective affordances associated with improved NAPLAN performances on personnel in the Regional Office. This is then deflected down the line to principals and teachers.

Conclusion

In the context of the contemporary national education reform agenda in Australian schooling, pursued through agreements between the federal government and the States and Territories, national literacy and numeracy testing data have become a potent form of 'catalyst data'. Introducing the education indicators in OECD's influential *Education at a Glance* report for 2011, current Secretary-General Angel Gurria has drawn attention to the role of these indicators as 'catalyst[s] for change':

At one level, indicators are no more than a metric for gauging progress towards goals. *Yet increasingly, they are performing a more influential role* [italics added]. Indicators can prompt change by raising national concern over weak educational outcomes compared to international benchmarks; sometimes, they can even encourage stronger countries to consolidate their positions. (OECD 2011, 9)

Such data and indicators now prompt politicians, policy-makers, the media, the schooling sector, and the public more broadly, to ask about how schools and systems are performing and what needs to be done to improve that performance. However, while they are being collected and reported in the name of transparency, accountability and improvement, the analyses presented in this paper demonstrate the wide scope for perverse incentives and effects to arise when funding and reputational capitals are tied to performance measures and comparisons. Drawing on an observation from a senior federal policy-maker and the analyses provided here, we define catalyst data as data and indicators that pressure politicians, policy-makers and systems to respond to comparative measures of performance and which have real and multiple effects beyond such measurement.

The first unit of analysis illustrates how NAPLAN has become high stakes for systems through reputational damage caused by the perception of poor performance. This process is analogous to the 'shocks' to national systems that have arisen from PISA. In contrast to talk about evidence-based policy, the pressure and nervousness felt by policy-makers and politicians in response to NAPLAN outcomes are more immediately motivated by concerns to improve or maintain the reputation of schools and systems and to secure funding, rather than the intended objective of improving literacy and numeracy outcomes in schools. In both cases, we have documented the affective dimension of responses to these pressures. Given the anomalies in the 2010 process for negotiating National Partnerships reward frameworks and assessing performance, it is understandable that systems would be inclined to massage the bilateral negotiation of targets to ensure achievability over ambition and to employ measures that obfuscate performance rather than making it transparent. This case provides clear examples of the fabrication encouraged in regimes of performativity (Ball 2003).

The second unit of analysis demonstrates that NAPLAN data also have the capacity to catalyse more substantial reactions, in the form of systemic reviews and structural changes. However, in Queensland, these have been accompanied by, or have spurred, an intensification of audit and accountability within the system with perverse flow-on effects such as goal displacement, teaching to the test and the naturalization of data as the most sensible medium for thinking about teaching and learning. While NAPLAN catalyst data have an undeniable capacity to produce reactions, these can permeate through systems in ways that are difficult to predict or control from the locus of the original policy agenda.

Finally, the analysis proffered demonstrates how comparative testing data in Australian schooling are helping to create commensurate spaces of measurement through new testing, assessment and funding infrastructures. These are facilitating an associated catalysis – in the sense of dissolution – of the autonomy and authority of State education systems towards a national system of schooling, despite federalism (Lingard 2010). Agencies that collect, analyse and report comparative data – in this case the federal Government and it statutory authorities – inherit a degree of control over the educational agendas of systems that are subject to comparison. The capacity to catalyse a reaction through the reporting of these performance data is also a capacity to dissolve, at least in part, the boundaries that have divided up the educational authorities being assessed, thereby constituting new fields of measurement and governance and an emergent national system of schooling. Of course, the Australian States and Territories jealously guard their responsibility for education and do not readily cede this authority; however, the increasingly hegemonic logic of policy as numbers is creating conditions in which the catalytic effects of performance data, and associated perverse effects, are becoming increasingly intense within education systems.

Acknowledgements

The research upon which this paper is based has been developed from an Australian Research Council (ARC) funded Discovery Project (DP1094850), *Schooling the Nation in an Age of Globalisation: National Curriculum, Accountabilities and their Effects.* We wish to thank all of the research participants for their generous contribution to the study on which this paper is based, and the two referees for their very useful comments.

Notes

1. The national curriculum in Australia works to establish a national system in an ideological way and through homogenizing the knowledge considered important across the nation. NAPLAN works to constitute a national system in a different more technical manner, through constituting the nation as a commensurate space of measurement in respect of school performance and through the creation of the category of 'statistically similar schools' across the nation. NAPLAN also helps constitute a national system through its implications for some federal funding of schooling, thus constituting a national system through funding/compliance trade-offs.

2. In Yin's (2009) terms, this is a single-case study with two embedded units of analysis. The case is the current national reform agenda in Australian schooling, specifically the effects of NAPLAN. The first embedded unit of analysis is Australian education federalism and relationships between federal and State/Territory governments in relation to schooling. The second embedded unit of analysis is the Queensland school system. It is also significant in relation to this point that the OECD has conducted a review of evaluation and assessment in Australian schools (Santiago et al. 2011). This review is also important in respect of the point about the complementarity between national and international testing.

3. It is also significant in relation to this point that the OECD has conducted a review of evaluation and assessment in Australian schools (Santiago et al. 2011). This review is also important in respect of the point about the complementarity between national and international testing.

4. Deleuze's (1995) brief comments in relation to education in 'Postscript on control societies' are prescient in their attention to the rise of performance pay for teachers, continuous assessment and the reconstitution of education as a business.

5. Jurisdictions were required to set targets for improvement in relation to four mandated areas: (1) Students at or above the national minimum standard (All students) (Reading/Numeracy); (2) Students above the national minimum standard (All students) (Reading/Numeracy); (3) Mean scale score (All students) (Reading/Numeracy); and (4) Students at or above the national minimum standard (Indigenous students) (Reading/Numeracy) (COAG Reform Council 2011).

6. These explanations include that students in any given year level in Queensland schools are a year younger than most in other States; a large Indigenous population across the State, including many remote Indigenous communities; the dispersed demographic structure of Queensland; high levels of poverty, including rural poverty; and Year 7 is located in Queensland primary schools, whereas in Victoria and New South Wales it is located in secondary school.

7. We note here the growing influence of ACER, a not for profit research organisation, as the most utilized source of data collection and analysis in Australian education, a point made to us in many interviews. ACER is self-funded, so has interests in generating further work from reviews and the like. The increasing involvement of 'edu-businesses' (e.g. Pearson) in the testing and accountability agendas of governments is also a point that needs to be made (see Ball 2012). Pearson now has interests in both national and international testing, such as NAPLAN and PISA respectively.

8. The eight areas that comprise the Teaching and Learning audit are: An Explicit Improvement Agenda, Analysis and Discussion of Data, A Culture that Promotes Learning, Targeted Use of School Resources, An Expert Teaching Team, Systemic Curriculum Delivery, Differentiated Classroom Learning and Effective Teaching Practice.

9. These audit data were collected from schools' representations of what they were doing, rather than from actual classroom observations of teacher practices. The latter would be necessary to really be able to comment on the varying impact of elements of the Teaching and Learning Audit.

10. While Queensland 'gamed' the target setting with COAG, as demonstrated in the first unit of analysis, the system was opposed to such low target setting and gaming within the state, as indicated by the setting of a state-wide improvement target of 3%.

References

Adie, L. 2008. The hegemonic positioning of 'Smart State' policy. *Journal of Education Policy* 23, no. 3: 251–64.

Alegounarias, T. 2011. Weighing and distributing the good of schooling. Paper presented at the Australian College of Educators National Conference, July 14, in Sydney, Australia.

Ball, S. 2003. The teacher's soul and the terrors of performativity. *Journal of Education Policy* 18, no. 2: 215–28.

Ball, S. 2012. *Global Education Inc: New policy networks and the neo-liberal imaginary.* London: Routledge.

Biesta, G. 2004. Education, accountability, and the ethical demand: Can the democratic potential of accountability be regained? *Educational Theory* 54, no. 3: 233–50.

Brown, P., and R. Scase. 1997. Universities and employers: Rhetoric and reality. In *The postmodern university? Contested visions of higher education in society*, ed. Anthony Smith and Frank Webster, 85–98. London: SRHE and Open University Press.

Carroll, P., and B. Head. 2010. Comparing the second and third waves of regulatory reform in Australia. Paper presented at the Australian Political Studies Association Conference 2009, September 28–30, in Sydney, Australia.

COAG Reform Council. 2011. *Education 2010: Comparing performance across Australia.* Sydney: COAG Reform Council.

Darling-Hammond, L. 2010. *The flat world and education: How America's commitment to equity will determine our future.* New York, NY: Teachers College Press.

Deleuze, G. 1995. *Negotiations.* New York, NY: Columbia University Press.

Ertl, H. 2006. Educational standards and the changing discourse on education: The reception and consequences of the PISA study in Germany. *Oxford Review of Education* 32, no. 5: 619–34.

Gillborn, D., and D. Youdell. 2000. *Rationing education: Policy, practice, reform, and equity.* Buckingham: Open University Press.

Grek, S., M. Lawn, B. Lingard, J. Ozga, R. Rinnie, C. Segerholm, and H. Simola. 2009. National policy brokering and the construction of the European Education Space in England, Sweden, Finland and Scotland. *Comparative Education* 45, no. 1: 5–21.

Harvey, C. 2010. Making hollow men. *Educational Theory* 60, no. 2: 189–201.

Head, B. 2008. Three lenses of evidence-based policy. *Australian Journal of Public Administration* 67, no. 1: 1–11.

Jones, M.G., B.D. Jones, B. Hardin, L. Chapman, T. Yarbrough, and M. Davis. 1999. Impact of high-stakes testing on teachers and students in North Carolina. *Phi Delta Kappan* 81, no. 3: 199–203.

Latour, B. 1999. *Pandora's hope: Essays on the reality of science studies.* Cambridge, MA: Harvard University Press.

Lawn, M., and S. Grek. 2012. *Europeanising education: Governing a new policy space.* Oxford: Symposium.

Lingard, B. 2010. Policy borrowing, policy learning: Testing times in Australian schools. *Critical Studies in Education* 51, no. 2: 129–47.

Lingard, B. 2011. Policy as numbers: Ac/counting for educational research. *The Australian Educational Researcher* 38, no. 4: 355–82.

Lingard, B., and S. Rawolle. 2004. Mediatizing educational policy: The journalistic field, science policy, and cross-field effects. *Journal of Education Policy* 19, no. 3: 353–72.

Lingard, B., and S. Rawolle. 2011. New scalar politics: Implications for education policy. *Comparative Education: An International Journal of Comparative Studies* 47, no. 4: 489–502.

Lipman, P. 2004. *High stakes education: Inequality, globalization and urban school reform.* New York, NY: RoutledgeFalmer.

Lyotard, J.-F. 1984. *The postmodern condition: A report on Knowledge.* Minneapolis, MN: University of Minnesota Press.

Massumi, B. 2002. *Parables for the virtual: Movement, affect, sensation.* Durham, NC: Duke University Press.

Massumi, B. 2005. Fear (The spectrum said). *Positions* 13, no. 1: 31–48.

Masters, G.N. 2009a. *Improving literacy, numeracy and science learning in Queensland primary schools, preliminary advice.* Melbourne: Australian Council for Educational Research.

Masters, G.N. 2009b. *Improving literacy, numeracy and science learning in Queensland primary schools.* Melbourne: Australian Council for Educational Research.

Nichols, S., and D. Berliner. 2007. *Collateral damage: How high stakes testing corrupts America's schools.* Cambridge, MA: Harvard Education Press.

OECD 2011. *Education at a glance 2011: OECD Indicators.* Paris: OECD.

Ozga, J. 2009. Governing education through data in England: From regulation to self-evaluation. *Journal of Education Policy* 24, no. 2: 149–62.

Porter, T. 1995. *Trust in numbers: The pursuit of objectivity in science and public life.* Princeton, NJ: Princeton University Press.

Power, M. 1997. *The audit society: Rituals of verification.* Oxford: Oxford University Press.

Ranson, S. 2003. Public accountability in the age of neo-liberal governance. *Journal of Education Policy* 18, no. 5: 459–80.

Ranson, S. 2012. Schools and civil society: Corporate or community governance. *Critical Studies in Education* 53, no. 1: 29–45.

Ravitch, D. 2010. *The death and life of the great American school system: How testing and choice are undermining education.* New York, NY: Basic Books.

Rose, N. 1999. *Powers of freedom.* Cambridge: Cambridge University Press.

Sahlberg, P. 2010. Rethinking accountability in a knowledge society. *Journal of Educational Change* 11, no. 1: 45–61.

Santiago, P., G. Donaldson, J. Herman, and C. Shewbridge. 2011. *OECD reviews of evaluation and assessment in education: Australia.* Paris: OECD.

Sassen, S. 2007. *Sociology of globalization.* New York, NY: W.W. Norton.

Scott, J.C. 1998. *Seeing like a state: How certain schemes to improve the human condition have failed.* New Haven, CT: Yale University Press.

Sellar, S. 2012. Fear and friendship: Potential politics in education. Paper presented at the 2012 Crossroads in Cultural Studies conference, July 2–6, in Paris, France.

Stobart, G. 2008. *Testing times: The uses and abuses of assessment.* London: Routledge.

Suspitsyna, T. 2010. Accountability in American education as a rhetoric and a technology of governmentality. *Journal of Education Policy* 25, no. 5: 567–86.

Takayama, K. 2008. The politics of international league tables: PISA in Japan's achievement crisis debate. *Comparative Education* 44, no. 4: 387–407.

Taubman, P. 2009. *Teaching by numbers.* New York, NY: Routledge.

Thrift, N. 2005. *Knowing capitalism.* London: Sage.

Thrift, N. 2007. *Non-representational theory: Space, politics and affect.* London: Routledge.

Torrance, H. 2006. Globalizing empiricism: What, if anything, can be learned from international comparisons of educational achievement. In *Education, globalization and social change*, ed. Hugh Lauder, Phillip Brown, Jo-Anne Dillabough, and A.H. Halsey, 824–34. Oxford: Oxford University Press.

Webb, P.T. 2011. The evolution of accountability. *Journal of Education Policy* 26, no. 6: 735–56.

Wiseman, A. 2010. The uses of evidence for educational policymaking: Global contexts and international trends. In *What counts as evidence and equity? Review of research in education*, Vol. 34, ed. Allan Luke, Judith Green, and Gregory J. Kelly, 1–24. New York, NY: AERA, Sage.

Yin, R. 2009. *Case study research: Design and methods*. 4th ed. Thousand Oaks, CA: Sage.

Untangling the global-distant-local knot: the politics of national academic achievement testing in Japan

Keita Takayama

School of Education, University of New England, Armidale, Australia

This study examines one of the most notable manifestations of Japanese education's incorporation into the global education restructuring movement: the 2007 reintroduction of national academic achievement testing (*zenkoku gakuryoku gakushuu joukyou chousa*). In so doing, I aim to untangle the complex intermingling of national and global pressures as the new mode of test-based governance became embedded in the Japanese education policy context. The study situates the discussion of global policy convergence in a close analysis of the Japanese history of political struggles over national academic testing and the domestic power dynamics at the time of the policy implementation. Particular focus is placed on the role of the Ministry of Education and other key political figures that facilitated, blocked, and mediated the globally circulated governance model and thus struggled over the particular configuration of the national assessment. In conclusion, I locate the findings in the wider literature on the complex link between global policy convergence and national particularities in education policy studies, and in so doing tease out the insights for articulating the role of 'engaged' policy scholarship in the increasingly globalized politics of education reform.

Global convergence and national divergences

The introduction of standard assessments and output-based accountability has become a global phenomenon in education policy, particularly among the advanced industrial nations. The emerging policy regime combines centralization measures in educational outputs through standardized curriculum and assessment, centralized goal setting, and the publication of performance indicators with decentralization in educational processes (e.g. day-to-day management and curricular work in schools). While decentralization measures supposedly 'free' schools from bureaucratic regulations and promote their autonomy and innovation, centralization measures hold them accountable for their outputs. This is what is referred to as 'simultaneously loose and tight' or 'controlled decontrol' in management literature (Ball 2008, 48). The odd combination of centralization and decentralization forms a new mode of governance in public sectors including education designed to 'steer from a distance,' as opposed to 'the use of traditional bureaucracies and administrative systems to deliver or micro-manage policy systems' (Ball 2008, 41).

Standardized academic testing is the central component of this new mode of educational governance. Government agencies enforce a standardized national curriculum and assessment, while deregulating various mandates to increase the flexibility and diversity in service provision. In exchange for this 'freedom,' individual schools and local boards of education are held accountable for their students' test outcomes. Days are gone when testing was a means to select students for further education. It now constitutes the core element of the New Public Management regime wherein performance indicators generated from standardized assessments are used to govern local school boards and individual schools and teachers 'from a distance' (Ball 2008). The central government now defines schools as 'learning organizations' that are expected to use the test results as part of their continuous self-evaluation cycle of *planning* (determining goals and methods of reaching them), *doing* (implementing the plan), *checking* (evaluating the results), and *acting* (taking appropriate action for improvement), or the so called planning, doing, checking, and acting (PDCA) cycle (e.g. MEXT 2006c; NSW Department of Education and Training 2009). This accountability regime, characterized by the shift 'from regulation to self-assessment' (Ozga 2009, 149), was initially implemented in a few selective nations such as England and the USA and then has been promoted as the 'global reform model' via networks of policy professionals and international organizations (Ball 2008; Kamens and McNeely 2010).

The sign of policy convergence to this global governance model is unequivocally visible in recent Japanese education reform. Just as in many advanced industrial nations where the New Public Management theory has guided state restructuring, the Japanese national government has made a marked shift from 'government' to 'governance' from the late 1990s onwards. Once powerful ministries such as the Ministry of Finance and the Ministry of Internal Affairs and Communications came to espouse the New Public Management logic as the guiding reform principle, they pressured the Ministry of Education, Culture, Sports, and Science and Technology (MEXT) to undertake similar reform in education (Nitta 2008; Rappleye 2012). A series of MEXT policy documents released from the mid-2000s onward stress the critical importance of implementing the PDCA cycle in its education system and the national academic assessment (MEXT 2005a, 2005b, 2006c). Commenting on the MEXT's (2005a) landmark report *Redesigning Compulsory Education in a New Era*, which epitomized the Ministry's structural reform plan implemented thereafter, Willis and Rappleye (2011) describe it as 'so convergent on global policy trends that it could have emerged from virtually any context worldwide' (25).

Driving the global convergence of education policy among advanced industrial nations is their incorporation into the system of global capitalism (Ball 2008; Dale 2000a, 2000b). As Cox (Dale 2000b) rightly argues, in the intensified global economic competition, states 'no longer serve as the buffers between external economic forces and the domestic economy'; instead each state now 'actively adopts domestic economies to the exigencies of the global economy' (100). Under the competitive state regime, therefore, the contradictory tension inherent in liberal-democratic and capitalist societies between demands for capital accumulation and those for democratic legitimacy collapses as the former is fully integrated as the key strategy to achieve the latter, thus resulting in the current 'economization' of education policy (Dale 2000a, 2000b; Lingard 2010). The introduction of national standardized testing and the new managerial logic is part of this larger state restructuring in response to the globalized economic circumstance; continuous evidence-based reviews of state educational services are supposed to help achieve the smaller and yet more effective state apparatus in securing high academic standards and economic productivity in a knowledge economy.

While recognizing the remarkably similar structural changes in state apparatus around the world and the global convergence of education policy as their corollary, however, it is important to stress that the particularities of the nation-state continue to manifest as the global governance model becomes increasingly incorporated into different national education systems. This is because various domestic policy actors facilitate, block, and mediate the 'importation' of the globally circulated model within the historically and institutionally formed policy conditions that are specific to each nation-state. The task for policy scholars is then to strike 'a subtle balance between what may be common across states, and be related back to processes of globalisation, and what needs to be understood in terms of the particularities of the nation-state' (Ball 2008, 31). As Ball (2008, 30) stresses, national policies are 'the product of a nexus of influences and interdependences, resulting in (...) the intermingling of global, distant, and local logics.' Here, Ball directs us to the emerging task for policy scholars in the era of globalization, that is, to untangle the intermingling of global, distant, and local logics in the configuration of given education policies, though, needless to say, a degree of caution must be exercised not to reify these spatial and temporal categories.

This untangling work necessitates a fully contextualized analysis of the political dynamics and actors which complicate the process of global policy 'diffusion.' Unfortunately, such a careful description and understanding of domestic complexities that constantly interact with the globalized policy discourse has been rather underemphasized in the macro-sociological discussion of globalization in education. Furthermore, theoretically driven accounts of 'globalized education policy field' grow out of the particular policy context of 'global reference nations' (e.g. England and the USA) wherein most of such theorists reside. Hence, they must be carefully tested and nuanced through a rigorous investigation of the material condition and the process in other parts of the world wherein the global, the national, and the local intersect with each other to such an extent that the distinction might collapse. As I will maintain in the conclusion section, this focus on understanding the processes of domestic-global infusion is critical not only for a better understanding of the policy diffusion process itself, but more importantly for making education policy scholarship more politically engaged, or 'critical' (Apple 2006).

Drawing on the critical insights and perspectives thus far explored, I examine one of the most notable manifestations of Japanese education's incorporation into the global education restructuring movement: the 2007 introduction of national academic achievement testing (*zenkoku gakuryoku gakushuu joukyou chousa*).[1] In so doing, I aim to disentangle the complex global-distant-local knot as the new mode of test-based governance became embedded in the Japanese education policy context. More specifically, I situate the discussion of global policy convergence in a close analysis of the Japanese history of political struggles over national academic testing and the domestic power dynamics at the time of the policy implementation. Hence, I examine the roles of policy actors who facilitated, blocked, and mediated the globally circulated governance model against the historically and institutionally constituted parameter within which such actors struggled over the specific configuration of the 2007 national testing.

One particular policy actor that the study focuses on is the MEXT, which has historically played a dominant role in Japan's centrally organized education system. Though the recent political shift towards decentralization has, to some extent, diminished its central regulatory power in certain administrative areas (Ogawa 2010) and the increasing economization of education policy has undermined the MEXT's control over the policy-making process (Rappleye 2012), I argue that the Ministry remains as the key player in the politics of Japanese education reform. Nitta (2008), Ogiwara (2002), and Takayama's (2008a, 2008b) recent studies support my view, demonstrating that the Ministry has been able to mitigate the increasing decentralizing and quasi-market reform pressures that could potentially undermine its administrative prerogatives. Building on these studies, I highlight how the Ministry selectively recontextualized the globally circulated governance model not only to meet, albeit partially, contradictory political demands from outside but also to safeguard and even advance its own interests.[2] I conclude this study by situating the findings in the wider literature on the complex link between global policy convergence and national particularities and in so doing tease out the insights for articulating the role of 'engaged' policy scholarship in the increasingly globalized politics of education reform.

Domestic political struggles over national academic testing

National academic assessment has a highly contentious history in Japan. The point of political struggle has been over whether the assessment should be mandatory for students of given grades across the nation or sampling based. In 1956, the Ministry of Education (later known as MEXT) introduced a sampling-based national academic assessment for 4–5% of the eligible primary, junior high, and high school students (Tozawa 2009). The assessment was implemented against a background of considerable disparity in educational resources and outcomes between urban and rural areas in the immediate postwar time. The Ministry needed to address the lack of equal educational opportunity across the nation and intended to use the data to justify its centralized distribution of educational funding and the preferential allocation of resources to disadvantaged rural schools (Kariya 2009a).

The national academic assessment became highly politicized, however, when the Ministry decided to introduce a mandatory assessment for junior high school students (Year 8 and 9) in 1961, alongside its sampling-based assessment for primary and high school students. The mandatory testing was more comprehensive in subject areas, covering the five core subjects of English, Japanese (reading and literacy), mathematics, science, and social studies, than the previous sample-based testing which assessed students in two subjects at a time (Tozawa 2009). The Japan Teachers Union (JTU) saw this shift as part of the ruling conservative Liberal Democratic Party (LDP)'s so called 'reverse course' (*gyaku kousu*) spanning from the late 1950s onward. During this period, the LDP, after the nation's independence from the Allied occupation in 1952, attempted to 'reverse' what it saw as the exceedingly decentralized and liberal reform 'imposed' by the US-led occupation. The LDP politicians perceived the demilitarization, democratization, and decentralization of education introduced during the occupation as eroding the nation's moral and spiritual basis. The postwar conservative politics in Japanese education thereafter came to locate as its core political agenda the 'normalization' (*seijouka*) of the 'exceedingly' liberal education, which was typically translated in the demands for the elimination of JTU teachers who would supposedly indoctrinate children into leftist ideology, the explicitly nationalistic teaching and moral education, the central regulation of school curricular and administration, and competition-inducing policies (Schoppa 1991). The 1961 introduction of mandatory national testing partly reflected this conservative political agenda, designed to strengthen the Ministry's central control over the decentralized schooling system at the time for economic and nationalistic ends (Nakajima 2007).

The JTU was vehemently opposed to the mandatory national testing, engaging in series of anti-testing campaigns across the nation. The resulting disruption caused by JTU's 'militant teachers' (Duke 1973) forced the Ministry to change the mandatory testing to 20% sampling in 1965 and then terminate all the sampling-based assessments by 1966 (Tozawa 2009). As a result of the national campaign, 61 JTU members were arrested and around 2000 members received administrative punishments in the forms of dismissals (20), suspensions (63), pay cuts (652), and reprimands (1189) (JTU 1989). The JTU legally challenged these decisions, eventually leading to historic verdicts from three lower courts questioning the legality of the compulsory national assessment (Tozawa 2009).[3] This was a major upset for the Ministry, a factor partly explaining its reluctance to reintroduce a compulsory national testing until 2007.

The mid-1990s marked the end of the intense political contestation between the Left (JTU, Japan Socialist Party, Japan Communist Party) and the Right (MEXT and LDP), symbolized by the 1995 agreement of collaboration between the Union and the Ministry. This historic turning point was certainly a factor explaining the 2007 reintroduction of the mandatory national assessment for the first time in 43 years (Chiyosaki 2005).[4] However, the residual memory of the past – the common association of national mandatory testing with the Ministry's subordination of education to the nation's political and economic necessities, the resultant excessive competition among schools and prefectures, and the chaos and disruptions in schools – was constantly invoked by progressive scholars and the liberal media in the lead-up to the test implementation, with many reiterating the lower court verdicts that deemed the testing unconstitutional (see *Asahi News* 2007; Chiyosaki 2005; Fujita 2005, 2009b; JTU 2007; *Mainichi News* 2009a, 2009b; Nakajima 2007; Oki 2009; Ono 2007; Shimizu 2009). The challenge for those who pursued the reintroduction of national testing was, therefore, to disarticulate it from its 'negative inheritance' (*funo isan*) (Kariya 2004).

Strange bedfellows

The reintroduction of mandatory national assessment gained political momentum in the early 2000s when nationalist politicians, such as Prime Ministers Junichirou Koizumi (2001–2006) and Shinzou Abe (2006–2007), seized the power in the ruling LDP in the context of rising economic disparity and prolonged recession. The conservative political discourse typically constructed the economic and social 'crises' as moral issues, highlighting the critical role of schools as the nation's social, cultural, economic foundations (see Nakanishi 2005). The proposed solution to the 'crisis' was to improve morality and work ethic among children, teachers, and parents. Fused with the psycho-behavioral discourse popularized in education at the time (see Ozawa 2002), this individualizing (de-socializing) discourse identified the causes of various school-related problems (bullying, violence, absenteeism, and declining motivation for learning) in the personal domains of children, teachers, and parents, hence constructing them as deficit subjects, the focus of direct policy intervention.

To such nationalist and social conservative reformers, the reintroduction of mandatory national testing was a continuation of their 'normalization' effort, a strategy to break with the liberal education reform 'imposed' by the US occupation and further extended by the MEXT and the JTU via the 2002 *yutori* (low pressure, constructivist) curricular reform (see Nakanishi 2005). In the immediate aftermath of the data release of the Programme for International Student Assessment 2003 (PISA 2003 shock), which registered Japanese 15-year-old students' ranking drop in some of the tested areas (see Takayama 2008a), the outspoken nationalist MEXT Minister Nakayama (2004) under the Koizumi Administration announced his intent to introduce various national assessments, not only on children's academic achievement, but on their health and athleticism. He perceived these assessments as a strategy to generate 'healthy competition' among schools and municipalities, which he argued had been belittled in the postwar 'liberal' Japanese education. Abe, Nakayama, and other like-minded nationalist politicians and intellectuals viewed the British education reform under Margaret Thatcher as the model and considered the reintroduction of national testing as a way to eliminate JTU teachers and discipline children and teachers through competition and curricular control (see Rappleye 2012; Takayama and Apple 2008).[5] To this end, they demanded that the testing be compulsory for all eligible children, as opposed to sample-based testing.

This social conservative rationale for the national assessment went side by side with the economic rationalist demands for budget cuts, financial and administrative devolution, expanded school choice, and market competition. Powerful business associations (e.g. *nippon keidanren* and *keizai douyuukai*) made a series of education reform proposals in the 2000s, stressing the importance of school choice, competition, decentralization, and standardized assessment (Keidanren 2004, 2005, 2007; Keizai douyuukai 2004, 2005). The same pressure also came from those parts of the central government that were closely associated with business and industry such as the Ministry of Finance, the Ministry of International Trade and Industry, and the Ministry of Internal Affairs and Communications, as well as various special committees created by the Prime Minister Koizumi in his effort to pursue 'structural reform without sanctuary' (e.g. Council for the Promotion of Regulatory Reform, Council on Economic and Fiscal Policy, and Council for Decentralization Reform) (Ono 2007, 2009). Fully embracing public choice theory, they proposed a national academic test in combination with other decentralizing, quasi-market, and competition-inducing measures (e.g. performance-based funding allocations, school vouchers, and corporate-run, for-profit schools) that 'place consumers of educational services (children and parents) as the leading actors in education reform' (Council for Decentralization Reform 2004, 1). In their mind, the MEXT was 'socialistic,' preoccupied with 'excessive egalitarianism,' and had promoted a 'soft' (child-centered) approach to teaching that had eroded the nation's economic competitiveness (Sakakibara 2001). They recognized national academic testing as the key to inducing market competition in education and by implication to boosting the nation's economic productivity and competitiveness. To this end, the national assessment must be mandatory to all schools across the nation, and the school-by-school results be published to inform consumer choices (Ono 2007, 2009).

While social conservatives and economic rationalists were similar in their demands for a mandatory assessment and academic competition, albeit for slightly different reasons, they disagreed over other education policy areas. In the curricula area, for instance, while social conservatives demanded more focus on academic basics, disciplines, and patriotic teaching, some economic rationalists preferred curricular emphasis on problem-solving, communication skills, and logical thinking, rejected nationalistic teaching, and by and large endorsed the constructivist curricular orientation of the 2002 *yutori* reform (see Keidanren 2004). In the area of educational administration, while social conservative reformers demanded stricter central control in all aspects of school operation, economic rationalist reformers criticized the MEXT for not sufficiently implementing its decentralization policy and consequently hindering schools' creative, innovative entrepreneurship (Keidanren 2004, 2005; Keizai douyuukai 2005; Kitashiro 2005). As many Japanese observers point out, these converging and yet contradictory conservative political forces have driven a series of educational reforms since the 2000s (see Fujita 2005; Hirota 2009).

The challenge for the MEXT was somehow to address these two conflicting political pressures, while at the same time safeguarding and even advancing its own prerogatives. To the MEXT's bureaucratic conservativism, both the explicitly nationalistic agenda proposed by social conservatives and the quasi-market reform plans by economic rationalists were too radical and divisive, most likely to bring the MEXT into an unwanted ideological minefield. Hence, the MEXT needed to mitigate these extreme reforms. As I will describe below, it was the introduction of mandatory national testing (as opposed to sample-based testing), the highly regulated disclosure of test results (prohibition on the publication of school-by-school and city by city average test scores), and output-based management plans (the PDCA cycle) that the MEXT recognized as the solution to this political conundrum. To achieve this sensitive political balancing act, however, the Ministry had to make a series of strategic moves to generate the widest possible political support for national academic testing, most importantly to disconnect it from its 'negative inheritance.'

MEXT's strategic moves

The LDP Prime Ministers from the late 1990s onwards aggressively pursued a series of administrative, financial, and political structural reforms to address the astronomical state deficit and to respond to capital's demands for the small and efficient state. In this process, the Organization for Economic Cooperation and Development's (OECD) publication *Governance in Transition: Public Management Reforms in OECD Countries* (1995) guided the Japanese state restructuring process thereafter (Nitta 2008). Drawing heavily on the New Public Management logic, the report proposed the new mode of governance marked by strategic planning, cost efficiency, human resource allocation, competition and choice, performance management, and accountability (Ball 2008; Rizvi and Lingard 2006). Japanese business associations (e.g. Keizai douyuukai 2004, 2005) called for the same governance reform, which was soon articulated in Prime Minister's Office (2006) policy statements, wherein the critical role of the PDCA cycle was highlighted to achieve the small but effective state. Given the relatively weak standing of the MEXT vis-à-vis the aforementioned other powerful ministries (Rappleye 2012), the MEXT had no choice but to accept the shift towards the new managerialist, output-based governance, though, as I shall demonstrate, this external pressure was mitigated through the MEXT's struggle to secure and expand its own interests.

The Ministry was initially reluctant to accept the new managerial reform plan. However, as the 'crisis' in education deepened, particularly in the aftermath of the 'PISA 2003 shock,' the Ministry started recognizing strategic merits in the shift towards outcome-based management (Nitta 2008; Takayama 2008a, 2008b). The governance-at-a-distance regime allowed the MEXT to act as 'a neutral, detached broker,' whose roles are to set the benchmarks and collect and disseminate information about each school's performance. It enabled the central government to export its legitimacy crisis downward to individual schools and municipal and prefectural school boards (Whitty, Power, and Halpin 1998). This strategy was particularly critical when the MEXT's political legitimacy as the central educational administrator was seriously questioned in the midst of the national academic achievement 'crisis' and the mounting pressure for administrative and fiscal decentralization.

As the MEXT came under business communities' increasing pressure for privatization and marketization reform, it had came to see output management as a political trade-off, a strategy to preempt the introduction of more radical neoliberal measures that would have undermined the political legitimacy of its central administration (Nitta 2008). As the proponents of output-based governance maintain, the new mode of governance does not demolish the MEXT's central administrative role to the extent proposed by radical pro-market proponents (e.g. Sakakibara 2001), but simply shifts its locus of control from educational process to output, 'from direct to indirect control' (Tsutsumi and Hashimoto 1999, 29–30). More importantly, the new educational governance allows the Ministry to partially introduce the economic rationalists' quasi-market logic in that it promotes academic competition, performance-based accountability, and the closer alignment of education to the nation's economic goals. In so doing, the MEXT can safeguard its policies from such radical neoliberal proposals as public release of school-by-school test results, unregulated school choices, school vouchers, and for-profit schools (see Ono 2007, 2009). At the same time, the introduction of the mandatory national test partially addresses the social conservatives' demands for academic basics, competition, and centralized curricular control.

As expected, the nationalist MEXT Minister Nakayama, who announced his intent to introduce national testing in December 2004, and the MEXT bureaucrats provided different rationales for the introduction of the national academic achievement test. While Minister Nakayama followed the socially conservative and economic rationalist rationales for the national testing as detailed earlier (e.g. inducing 'healthy' competition and eliminating JTU teachers from schools), the MEXT justified it as a means to assure educational quality across the nation and hence to achieve equal educational opportunity. The Ministry also stressed that the testing was part of its new school self-evaluation plan, the PDCA cycle (MEXT 2005a, 2006c). Hence, the MEXT's 'official' rationale drew heavily on the new managerial discourse of quality assurance and evidence-based policy reviews, and the liberal democratic discourse of equal educational access, differentiating itself from the common articulation of national testing among economic rationalist and social conservative reformers as a tool for marketization and ideological control.

The 2007 reintroduction of the mandatory national testing, however, could have been a major political liability to the MEXT. When by 2005, approximately 50 prefectural and metropolitan boards of education had already introduced their standard-test-based assessments in response to the public outcry over the academic 'crisis,' the reintroduction of national testing could have been not only dismissed as redundant, but also criticized for countering the educational decentralization that the Ministry publicly endorsed at the time (Chiyosaki 2005). Furthermore, the initially estimated cost of the national assessment (60 billion yen) could have been rejected as wasteful when the Cabinet Office and other powerful ministries were aggressively pushing for fiscal and administrative downsizing and decentralization. On top of these concerns, progressive scholars and the liberal media continued to remind the public of the 'negative inheritance,' warning about the undesirable consequences of the testing on educational equality and quality.

Because of this highly sensitized policy context, the MEXT's initial proposal for the national assessment was modest. In 2000, one of the MEXT's councils proposed sampling-based testing designed to 'assess the implementation of the National Study Course and to improve its standards' (Tozawa 2009, 45). However, it was the manufactured 'crisis' in December 2004 that drastically changed the policy context surrounding national testing. Minister Nakayama's exaggerated recognition of academic 'crisis' at the time of the 'PISA 2003 shock' powerfully legitimized his proposal for a nationally coherent approach to academic assessments (Takayama 2008a). The subsequent nationalist Abe Administration (2006–2007) acted on Nakayama's call for the reintroduction of mandatory testing. Drawing on a highly biased study on the 'success' of the English education reform where standard national testing supposedly played a key role in the 'English miracle' (Takayama and Apple 2008), the government proposed national testing as the key strategy for its 'educational regeneration' (*kyouiku saisei*) campaign (Kariya 2009b).

Sensing this dramatic shift in the political situation surrounding national testing, the MEXT decided to make the testing mandatory to all eligible public school students across the nation, despite its lack of initial interest in pursuing this potentially contentious option (Ono 2007). The Ministry made this decision, rejecting the contrary recommendations from the testing experts whom the Ministry had appointed to deliberate over the testing design, many of whom expressed concerns about the undesirable consequences of mandatory testing and instead proposed testing to sample 5–10% of eligible students (see Kariya 2009b). Kariya (2009b) speculates that the MEXT attempted to gain political trade-off from the mandatory testing to win the Abe Administration's support for other education policy measures that the MEXT was pursuing at the time, but were highly contested by the Ministry of Finance (e.g. the introduction of reduced class size in elementary schools). However, it must be stressed that the Ministry also came to recognize its own interests in the mandatory testing; the test results could be integrated as part of the PDCA, which the Ministry implemented earlier (MEXT 2006c) as a new school self-assessment scheme (Matsushita 2007; Nakajima 2007).

The MEXT's political decision for the contentious mandatory testing, however, forced the Ministry to dissociate the proposed national testing from its 'negative inheritance.' It was externalization – the use of 'foreign examples' and 'international consensus' to deterritorialize domestically contested policies (Steiner-Khamsi 2000) – to which the MEXT resorted to disarticulate the national testing from the past negativities. The widely accepted image of the OECD and the PISA as 'international,' 'independent,' and 'scientific' was particularly useful for the Ministry in order to repackage the contested national mandatory testing. With the triennial PISA data release generating considerable media frenzy over the ranking rise and fall of Japanese 15-year-old students, the MEXT had come to see the OECD and PISA as powerful resources for deterritorializing its contentious policies. The Ministry articulated the 2007 national assessment plan with the PISA's assessment orientation, situating it in the OECD's terminologies of 'key competency' and 'knowledge-based society' (see Central Council of Education 2009; MEXT 2006a, 2010c). Furthermore, as I will discuss shortly, the Ministry closely modeled Part B (application) of the national assessment after the 'PISA-type problems,' wherein students are to apply knowledge in real-life situations. These externalization strategies enabled the Ministry to remove the testing from the past imagery and repackage it in the future tense as a new quality/equity assurance measure and a strategy to prepare students for the emerging 'knowledge economy.' These political struggles thus far explored have shaped the very configuration of the testing itself, the topic to which I shall now turn.

Japanese inflection of the global model

Introduced in 2007 under the LDP rule, the national academic achievement test (*zenkoku gakuryoku gakushuu joukyou chousa*) assesses year 6 and 9 students in mathematics and literacy, to which science has been added from 2012 onwards. Though the schools' participation in the test was not legally binding and thus 'voluntary,' 98.95% of public primary and junior high schools (approximately 3.33 million students in total) participated in the first year (MEXT 2007) and the participation rate remained constant till the test was altered in 2010 to sample eligible students.[6] This fact attests to the MEXT's continuing regulatory power over the whole education system, despite the series of decentralization measures implemented from the late 1990s (Ogawa 2010). In 2011, the catastrophic earthquake that had affected the northeastern part of Japan forced the Ministry to cancel the nation-wide administration of the testing and leave the implementation up to each prefecture's discretion. The fact that only 11 out of 47 prefectures chose to administer the test when the participation in the testing was made optional (*Mainichi News* 2011) indicates the lack of genuine interest among prefectures in the national assessment and its coercive nature.

In fact, whether or not the test should be mandatory or sampling-based continues to be contested since its 2007 implementation. For the first three years, the assessment was mandatory for all the eligible public school students across the nation. However, the test shifted to sample 30 % of the students in 2010, once the Democratic Party of Japan (DPJ) gained political power in 2008 and pursued cost-cutting measures. Echoing many critics of the test (*Asahi News* 2007; *Mainichi News* 2009a, 2009b; Fujita 2009b; Kariya 2004, 2009b; Oki 2009; Shimizu 2009), DPJ reasoned that testing 30% of eligible students should provide data necessary to monitor the national academic trends. However, the testing is scheduled to be made mandatory once again in 2013, due partly to the continuing demands from social conservative and economic rationalist reformers and the Ministry's interests in linking the mandatory testing with individual schools' PDCA cycles.

Another point of political contestation was over the publication of test results. While pro-market proponents demanded the full public disclosure of school-by-school and town-by-town test results, with which parents could exercise school choice (see Ono 2009), progressive critics warned that this would cause excessive competition among prefectures, municipalities, and schools, as had happened 40 some years ago (Shimizu 2009). Liberal and left-leaning newspapers joined this chorus of concerns (see *Asahi News* 2007; Chiyosaki 2005; *Mainichi News* 2009a, 2009b), successfully making the pro-market proponents' demand for full disclosure look too radical and divisive. As a result, the MEXT demanded prefectural and municipal governments not publish city-by-city or school-by-school data (MEXT 2005a, 3; 2006a, 11). After the media reported that some prefectural governments had published town-by-town test results in the name of 'public accountability,' the Ministry made public its 'displeasure' (Hoshi 2008, 166) and sent out an official reminder to prefectural and municipal boards of school about its regulation on the data release (*Asahi News* 2008; MEXT 2008). However, the Ministry's directive has no legal basis (Tozawa 2010) and the Ministry officials have probably been aware of this fact all along (Kariya 2009b). In fact, local citizens demanding the disclosure of their neighbor schools' scores won lower court cases against the local board of education, which refused to release the data. Despite its legally shaky ground, the MEXT persisted with its cautionary stance on the public release of the localized test data, partly in an effort to disconnect the national assessment from its negative past. The highly regulated release of test results distinguishes the Japanese national testing from similar national testing in other advanced industrial nations (e.g. Australia, England, and United States), where school-by-school average test scores are released for public viewing (see Lingard 2010).

Furthermore, the very content of the national assessment itself demonstrates a clear sign of Japanese inflection of the global policy model. It is divided into two types of assessment, one for academic achievement and the other for learning conditions (*gakushuu joukyou*). The scholastic achievement test is further broken down into Parts A and B. While Part A tests children's basic knowledge (*chishiki*), which strictly follows the MEXT's national Course of Study, Part B goes beyond the Course of Study and tests their ability to apply knowledge (*katsu you*) in real-life situations (MEXT 2006a). This division reflects the dual emphasis in the MEXT curricular policy from the late 1990s. On the one hand, the former addresses the conservative criticism of the so called *yutori* (low pressure, constructivist) curricular reform and the demands for academic basics.[7] On the other hand, Part B continues with the MEXT's new curricular focus on integrated learning, problem-solving, and knowledge application influenced by the OECD's PISA curricular model (Fujita 2005, 2009b; Shimizu 2009; Tozawa 2010). As discussed earlier, the close linkage of the national testing with the OECD's PISA served to deterritorialize the contested national testing.

The second component of the national assessment consists of a set of extensive survey questions about 'learning conditions' for participating students and school administrators to fill out. For instance, year 6 students are to answer 77 multiple choice questions and statements about their lifestyles and study habits, such as 'I eat breakfast everyday,' 'How many hours do you play TV games per day?,' 'How many hours do you use the Internet per day?,' 'How many hours do you study over weekends?,' 'Do you do chores at home?,' 'I participate in local community events,' and 'When running into neighbors, and I usually greet them' (MEXT 2010a). The MEXT conducts a statistical analysis to identify the correlation between students' test scores and these 'learning condition' factors.

Problematically, these surveys exclude questions related to children's social class (e.g. questions about their parents' educational and income levels) (Mimizuka 2007; Shimizu 2009).[8] Hence, they perpetuate a reductive causal association between particular 'deficit' lifestyle and moral characteristics of students and their test scores, despite that the correlations are spurious at best (Kariya 2009b, 159). The MEXT-affiliated Central Council of Education (CCE 2009, 14), for instance, draws on the results of the previous national assessments and stresses that 'children who do homework at home, talk to family about events at school, eat breakfast daily, check items to bring before coming to school, and follow school rules' and 'who like reading and want to become sensitive to other's feelings' tend to score higher (see also MEXT 2006b; NIER 2010). The MEXT uses such reductive explanations to justify the schools' moralizing role in promoting to children and their families 'proper' lifestyle, study habits, and moral lessons. Hence, the surveys powerfully produce an individualizing school reform discourse wherein addressing student's moral and lifestyle 'problems' are constructed as the 'solution' for academic improvement, shaping how schools and local boards of education should conceive of strategies for improving student achievement (see MEXT 2006b).[9] Needless to say, this lack of attention to students' socioeconomic status contrasts with PISA's explicit acknowledgment of it as one of the key variables. The MEXT's selectivity in its appropriation of PISA-related policy ideas is obvious, given that, as discussed earlier, the Part B section of the Japanese assessment heavily draws on PISA questions.

Likewise, the survey questions for school administrators seek detailed information about teaching staff, children, and school facilities and schools' strategic plans for academic improvement. The survey for primary school administrators, for instance, contains 93 statements and questions, including: 'We earmarked hours for group reading time (e.g. morning reading time),' 'Did you provide children with supplementary learning on Saturdays?,' 'We teach children how to use books and the Internet for research purposes,' 'We encourage children to greet both at school and community,' 'We used the results of the 2009 national testing to improve teaching,' 'How often does your school hold meetings and administer surveys to receive guardians' opinions and requests?,' and 'How often do you (the principal) observe classroom teaching at your school?' (MEXT 2010b). The MEXT correlates these survey results with the test outcomes and reports back to participating schools and municipal and prefectural boards of schools. Individual schools are required to integrate the results as part of their PDCA cycles and engage continuously in the 'evidence-based' self-assessment/improvement work.

The survey component adds a new dimension to the regulative function of standardized testing identified by a large body of studies in other national contexts. Not only narrowing school curriculum and pedagogies, particularly in low performing schools (Lingard 2010), the Japanese national testing, coupled with the survey questions, generates powerful normative pressure to the subordinate organizations (prefectural and municipal boards of education and individual schools).[10] In the context of the highly centralized and hierarchical administrative structure, the survey questions are not simply designed to assess what factors contribute to academic performance in schools, as the MEXT's policy rationale might suggest, but more importantly pressure them to adopt strategies prescribed in the statements and questions, thus rendering them the de facto policy. The MEXT further reinforces its centralizing power through the PDCA cycle 'from a distance,' by requiring individual schools and school boards to publicize their improvement plans and performance reviews on the basis of the data drawn from the national academic assessment (MEXT 2006c). Hence, the standardized academic testing, combined with the extensive surveys and the PDCA cycle, enables the MEXT to maintain its centralizing authority over schools' day-to-day pedagogic work without necessarily resorting to its conventional top-down, bureaucratic reform measures, which would have been criticized by pro-market/decentralization proponents.

This intrusive state intervention in the schooling process defeats the core logic of the new governance reform proposed by the OECD and the MEXT itself. In the logic of New Public Management, national testing, along with the PDCA cycle, is supposed to hold service providers accountable for their performance in terms of the externally defined benchmarks, while increasing their autonomy over day-to-day operations and promoting ground-up initiatives. In this logic, the key to successful reform is the creativity and innovation of those 'on the ground' (teachers and schools), as opposed to the conventional MEXT-driven, top-down reform through legislative changes (Keizai douyuukai 2005, 1–2; Kitashiro 2005). To some extent, such decentralizing measures have been implemented in Japanese education from the late 1990s onwards, as seen in the introduction of measures designed to increase school principals' authority, the financial and administrative autonomy of prefectural and municipal boards of education, and teachers' pedagogic autonomy (as in the newly introduced Integrated Study Hours and in the redefinition of the National Course of Study as 'minimum essential') (Ogawa 2010). However, these decentralization reforms were effectively mitigated by the particular inflection of the new managerial logic. As it was inserted into the conservative political context of the time and Japan's highly centralized educational system, it became a new recentralizing measure. Contrary to the logic of 'local empowerment' well articulated in many of the MEXT policy documents (e.g. MEXT 2005a), the 2007 national assessment powerfully prescribes to schools what they ought to undertake in specific details.

Towards 'engaged' policy scholarship

By closely examining the domestic politics, power dynamics, and key actors within the institutional and historical context surrounding national testing in Japan, this study has demonstrated the particular inflection of the globally circulated model of educational governance. More specifically, focusing on the role of the MEXT, I have identified various strategic moves that the Ministry pursued and how they shaped the specific configuration of the national testing. While the conflicting political demands clearly influenced the specific design of the testing, the Ministry was not simply a passive political mediator, either. The Ministry came to recognize the standard test-based accountability not only to appease, albeit partially, radical pro-market reformers and social conservative reformers simultaneously, but also to export its legitimacy crisis downward. Furthermore, coupling the academic testing with the extensive surveys and the PDCA cycle scheme, the Ministry managed to configure the testing in a way to maintain its centralizing authority over the slowly but steadily decentralized educational system. The Ministry undertook all these tasks, while articulating the testing to the globalized policy discourse of the OECD and the PISA and thus effectively disarticulating it from its 'negative inheritance.'

Education systems around the world are increasingly 'governed by numbers' drawn from both national and such international standardized testing as PISA (Grek 2009; Lingard 2010; Ozga 2009). The Japanese case of national assessment has not only shown how the production of measurable goals and standardized assessments by the OECD and the national government dictates the recent Japanese education reform, but also how they intersect with each other. The

Japanese national testing is closely linked to PISA, not only in that its Part B was modeled after the PISA-type questions, but also in that the MEXT strategically forged the discursive link to disarticulate the testing from its undesirable legacies. At the same time, the MEXT's use of PISA as a model for its national testing was highly selective, as the Ministry deliberately excluded from the assessment design students' socioeconomic background, one of the central focuses of PISA. This domestic 'pull factor' is often ignored in the existing discussion of the global impact of the OECD's education policies (see, e.g. Ball 2008; Grek 2009; Lingard 2010; Rizvi and Lingard 2006).[11]

Furthermore, this study has illuminated the tensions and contradictions among those who pushed for the national academic assessment. The finding of this study confirms Apple's (2006) thesis that the direction of education reform is guided by the hegemonic alliance among multiple political interests, which are not necessarily in agreement over the specific details of the reform. Showing how the political alliance is formed through a series of strategic partnerships in the context of the US education, Apple identifies where gaps exist in the alliance and explores ways to pry them open for more egalitarian and socially justice policy interventions. Though Apple's work tends to understudy policy actors and the actual mechanism of policy-making, as well as somehow disconnecting US domestic politics from the globalized policy field, his attention to the nitty–gritty politics of education and his view of education reform as part of larger social movements are noteworthy, as these are often marginalized in the macro-sociological discussion of global convergence towards the economization of education and the dominance of New Public Management (see Ball 2008; Lingard 2010).

It is out of concern about such existing theoretical accounts of globalization in education that I chose to provide a fully contextualized discussion of the domestic politics over national testing in Japan and its intersection with the globalized policy field. It is important to remind us that the existing theoretical knowledge is 'local,' as opposed to 'universal,' in that it is generated out of the particular education policy contexts which such theorists – English-speaking scholars in a few nations – study and out of the particular epistemic location that they assume in the geopolitics of academic knowledge production. Hence, the 'universality' of such theory-driven scholarship must be constantly interrogated by 'rubbing' it against the rich description and understanding of heterogeneous policy contexts around the world with different institutional and historical legacies.

Furthermore, I chose to pursue a fully contextualized analysis of the domestic political dynamics and actors, because of its political implication. It not only helps us better understand the processes of global 'diffusion' of education policy, but more importantly make our education policy scholarship more engaged, or 'critical' (Apple 2006; Takayama 2012). While the recent theorization of the globalized policy context has generated new insights and helped us 'upscale' our analytical framework, its highly abstracted discussion, often disconnected from a careful analysis of domestic power struggles and the specific historical and institutional context of nation-states, might have removed policy scholarship from where the locus of political struggle remains, the national arena of policy-making. My study was a critique of this worrying trend. By demonstrating that the political 'consensus' on national testing builds on a loose alliance of multiple conflicting interests with multiple 'cracks,' it has indicated possibility for future interventions for more just and democratic policy redirections.

Acknowledgment

I would like to thank anonymous reviewers and the special issue editors for their helpful suggestions and Aaron Spooner for his editorial assistance.

Notes

1. The literal translation of the official title of the testing is 'national assessment for academic achievement and learning conditions.'
2. The level of policy autonomy that the MEXT enjoys might seem unusual to readers more familiar with the Westminster system. The detailed discussion of the MEXT's policy agency, to be explored in this study, hence must be understood in the particular adaptation of the Westminster governance in Japan wherein bureaucrats and ruling party backbenchers exercise considerably more influence over policy development than in, say, the UK (Iio 2007).
3. The two lower court verdicts in 1966 and 1968 ruled against the Ministry, arguing that the compulsory participation of schools in the national assessment violates the clause in the Fundamental Law of Education that prohibits the state's 'unlawful control' in education (*futouna shihai*) (Tozawa 2009). However, these lower court rulings were overturned in 1976 when the Supreme Court rejected them but concluded that MEXT could not force schools to participate in the test (*Asahi News 2007*).
4. The mandatory national academic assessment was implemented in 1961–1964. While the earlier assessment was for junior high school students, the 2007 assessment is for primary and junior high school students (Tozawa 2009).
5. Nakayama was forced to resign in September 2008 after his controversial comment that 'Japan Teachers Union is the cancer of Japanese education' and 'we should demolish it' (Fujita 2009a, 37). This is despite the fact that since 1976, the JTU has experienced consistent decline in the percentage of its members in the total public school teacher population. While in 1958, 86.3% of teachers belonged to the JTU, it is 26.6% in 2011 (MEXT 2011). Chiyosaki (2005) explains the declining influence of the Union is the key factor behind the largely undisputed reintroduction of the national assessment in 2007.
6. Inuyama city in Aichi Prefecture was the only municipality that did not participate in the test (*Asahi News* 2007). However, the city joined the test in 2009.
7. The 2002 *yutori* reform featured the constructivist curricular orientation (problem solving skills) and considerable reduction of teaching hours. Conservative critics criticized the policy for its 'soft' approach to teaching, warning that it would 'put the nation at risk' (Takayama 2007). In response to this criticism, then MEXT Minister Touyama announced a new policy keyword in 2002, *tashikana gakuryoku* (solid scholastic ability), to appease the growing concern about the policy's underemphasis on basic knowledge acquisition.
8. In December 2011, MEXT announced that the national assessment in 2013 would include questions pertaining to students' socioeconomic background to study its impact on their academic achievement (*Asahi News* 2011).
9. Such a reductive interpretation of the data has been widely popularized in the media (see Abe 2009; Hayama and Hirayama 2007).
10. In fact, the MEXT's centralized control has long been achieved through its nonformal communication channel, the use of 'guidance' (*shidou*), which is not legally binding but yet powerfully normative (Ogiwara 2002).
11. Recent studies focus on this domestic pull factor in understanding the international impact of the PISA. See, for instance, Rautalin and Alasuutari (2007, 2009) and Takayama (2010).

References

Abe, N. 2009. *atamaga iiko no seikatsu shuukan* [Lifestyle of smart children]. Tokyo: SoftBank Creative.

Apple, M.W. 2006. *Educating the 'right' way*. 2nd ed. New York, NY: Routledge.

Asahi News. 2007. daijoubu? gakuryoku chousa [Is everything going to be all right? The academic testing], April 21, 3.

Asahi News. 2008. zenkoku gakuryoku chousa rainendo mo deeta kouhyou jishuku motomeru [National academic testing data not to be disclosed next year, MEXT requests]. http://www.asahi.com/national/update/1215/TKY200812150216.html.

Asahi News. 2011. Gakuryoku chousa de kakei haaku e [Economic status examined through national testing]. http://www.asahi.com/national/update/1228/TKY201112280772.html.

Ball, S.J. 2008. *The education debate*. Bristol: The Policy Press.

Central Council of Education. 2009. *youchien, shougakkou, koutougakkou oyobi tokubetsu shien gakkou no gakushuu shidou youryou tou no kaizen nit suite (toushin)* [Recommendation for the improvement of the National Study Course for kindergarten, primary, secondary, and special schools]. Tokyo: MEXT.

Chiyosaki, S. 2005. zenkoku issei gakuryoku tesuto, 40 nen buri fukkatsu 'naze'. *Mainichi News*, September 3, 3.

Council for Decentralization Reform. 2004. monbukagakushou no gimukyouiku kaikaku ni kansuru kinkyuu teigen [Urgent proposal for MEXT's reform of the compulsory education]. http://www.kisei-kaikaku.go.jp/minutes/meeting/2004/08/meeting04_08_01.pdf.

Dale, R. 2000a. Globalization and education: Demonstrating a common world educational culture or locating a globally structured educational agenda? *Educational Theory* 50, no. 4: 427–48.

Dale, R. 2000b. Globalization: A new world for comparative education? In *Discourse formation in comparative education*, ed. J. Schriewer, 87–109. Frankfurt: Peter Lang.

Duke, B. 1973. *Japan's militant teachers: A history of the left-wing teachers' movement*. Honolulu, HI: University of Hawaii Press.

Fujita, H. 2005. *Gimukyouiku wo toinaosu* [Rethinking compulsory education]. Tokyo: Chikuma shobou.

Fujita, H. 2009a. Yugai muekina zenkoku gakuryoku tesuto [Harmful without a merit, national standard testing]. *Sekai* 786: 232–40.

Fujita, H. 2009b. Whither Japanese schooling? In *Challenges to Japanese education*, ed. J.A. Gordon, H. Fujita, T. Kariya, and G. LeTendre, 17–53. New York, NY: Teachers College Press.

Grek, S. 2009. Governing by numbers: The PISA effect in Europe. *Journal of Education Policy* 24, no. 1: 23–37.

Hayama, K., and T. Hirayama. 2007. gakuryoku nihonichi akita no himitsu [Secrets of Japan's number one academic performer, Akita]. *Asahi News*, December 19, 29.

Hirota, T. 2009. *kakusa, chitsujofuan to kyouiku* [Disparity, order anxiety, and education]. Tokyo: Sera shobou.

Hoshi, T. 2008. Hashimoto chiji no kyouiku kainyu ga maneku funo supairaru [Negative spiral caused by Governor Hoshimoto's education reform]. *Sekai* 12: 162–72.

Iio, J. 2007. *Nihon no touchi kouzou* [Japanese governance structure]. Tokyo: Chuukou shinsho.

JTU. 1989. *nikkyouso 40 nenshi* [40 years history of Japan Teachers Union]. Tokyo: Roudou kyouiku sentaa.

JTU. 2007. zenkoku gakuryoku gakushuu joukyou chousa iwayuru zenkoku gakuryoku tesuto no kekka kouhyou ni tsuite [On the publication of the results of the so called national academic testing]. http://www.kyoiku-soken.org/blog/activity/userfiles/document/20071112.pdf.

Kamens, D.H., and C.L. McNeely. 2010. Globalization and the growth of international educational testing and national assessment. *Comparative Education Review* 54, no. 1: 5–25.

Kariya, T. 2004. mondai ya bunseki ni chihou no koe o [Need to reflect local voices in the test design and analysis]. *Asahi News*, December 18, 15.

Kariya, T. 2009a. *kyouiku to byoudou* [Education and equality]. Tokyo: Chuuou kouronsha.

Kariya, T. 2009b. *kyouikusaisei no meisou* [Strayed educational regeneration]. Tokyo: Chukuma shobou.

Keidanren. 2004. 21 seiki o ikinuku jisedai ikusei no tameno teigen [Proposal for the next generation who survive in the 21st century]. http://www.keidanren.or.jp/japanese/policy/2004/031/honbun.html#part2.

Keidanren. 2005. *waga kuni no kihon mondai o kangaeru* [A thought on fundamental problems in our nation]. http://www.keidanren.or.jp/japanese/policy/2005/002/honbun.pdf.

Keidanren. 2007. kisei kaikaku no igi to kongo no jyuutenbunya kadai [Importance of deregulation reform and the areas and issues of pressing importance]. http://www.keidanren.or.jp/japanese/policy/2007/038.html.

Keizai douyuukai. 2004. kihon houshin 2004 ni mukete no iken [An opinion on the 2004 basic principle]. http://www.doyukai.or.jp/policyproposals/articles/2004/pdf/040528_02.pdf.

Keizai douyuukai. 2005. kyouiku no 'genbaryoku' no kyouka ni mukete [Towards strengthening education's local capacities]. http://www.doyukai.or.jp/policyproposals/articles/2004/pdf/040528_02.pdf.

Kitashiro, R. 2005. Gakkougenba no jishusei sonchou [Respect for schools' spontaneity]. *Nikkei News*, April 11, 25.

Lingard, B. 2010. Policy borrowing, policy learning: Testing times in Australian schooling. *Critical Studies in Education* 51, no. 2: 129–47.

Mainichi News. 2009a. Shasetsu: gakuryoku tesuto motto yuukouna tedateo [Editorial: More effective strategies than national academic testing]. http://MainichiNews.jp/select/opinion/editorial/news/20090828k0000m070118000c.html.

Mainichi News. 2009b. gakuryoku tesuto: genba ni toroukan, seido no gimon mo [National academic test: Fatigued teachers and systemic problems]. http://MainichiNews.jp/select/wadai/news/20090828k0000m040101000c.html.

Mainichi News. 2011. zenkoku gakuryoku tesuto: 11 todoufuken ga mondaisasshi wo riyou [National academic testing: 11 prefectures used the test]. http://MainichiNews.jp/life/edu/scholartest/news/20111230ddm041100055000c.html.

Matsushita, K. 2007. kyouiku hyouka toshite no mondai [Issues (with the national testing) as an educational assessment]. *kyouiku* 57, no. 8: 41–8.

MEXT. 2005a. *gimukyouiku no kouzou kaikaku* [Restructuring of compulsory education]. Tokyo: MEXT. http://www.mext.go.jp/component/a_menu/education/detail/_icsFiles/afieldfile/2010/11/29/05102602.pdf.

MEXT. 2005b. PISA2003 no kekka o uketa kongo no torikumi. www.mext.go.jp/b_menu/shingi/chukyo/chukyo3/siryo/04122102/003/002.pdf.

MEXT. 2006a. *zenkoku teki na gakuryoku chousa no gutai teki na jisshi houhou tou ni tsuite* [On the implementation of the national academic assessment]. Tokyo: MEXT. http://www.mext.go.jp/b_menu/shingi/chousa/shotou/031/toushin/06042601/all.pdf.

MEXT. 2006b. 'hayane hayaoki asagohan' kokumin undou no suishin nit suite [Promotion for the people's movement for 'keeping early hours and proper breakfast']. http://www.mext.go.jp/a_menu/shougai/asagohan/index.htm.

MEXT. 2006c. *gakkou hyouka ni yoru PDCA saikuru* [School assessment through the PDCA cycle]. Tokyo: MEXT. http://www.mext.go.jp/component/a_menu/education/detail/_ics-Files/afieldfile/2010/04/07/1230736_2.pdf.

MEXT. 2007. heisei 19 nendo zenkoku gakuryoku gakushuu joukyou chousa no sanka gakkou suu tou ni tsuite [On the number of participating schools in the 2007 national academic assessment]. http://www.mext.go.jp/b_menu/houdou/19/04/07042415/001.pdf.

MEXT. 2008. Heisei 20 nedo zenkoku gakuryoku chousa no kekka no toriatsukai ni tsuite (tsuuchi) [On the handling of the 2008 national academic assessment]. http://www.mext.go.jp/a_menu/shotou/gakuryoku-chousa/zenkoku/08020512/001.htm.

MEXT. 2010a. *Shougakko daorokugakunen jidou shitsumon yoshi* [Survey questions for Year 6 students]. Tokyo: MEXT. http://www.nier.go.jp/10chousa/10shitumonshi_shou_jidou.pdf.

MEXT. 2010b. *Shogakko gakko shitsumonshi* [Survey sheet for primary schools]. Tokyo: MEXT. http://www.nier.go.jp/10chousa/10shitumonshi_shou_gakkou.pdf.

MEXT. 2010c. *PISA 2009 no kadai o uketa kongo no torikumi* [New initiatives in response to the PISA 2009 challenges]. Tokyo: MEXT. http://www.mext.go.jp/component/a_menu/education/detail/_icsFiles/afieldfile/2010/12/07/1284443_07.pdf.

MEXT. 2011. *nikkyouso kanyuuritsu, shinsai kanyuuritsu no suii* [Changes of JTU's new entry rate and membership rate]. Tokyo: MEXT. http://www.mext.go.jp/a_menu/shotou/jinji/_icsFiles/afieldfile/2011/01/13/1301022_1_1.pdf.

Mimizuka, H. 2007. Determinants of children's academic achievements in primary education. *Kyouiku shakaigaku kenkyuu* 80: 23–38.

Nakanishi, T. ed. 2005. *Sacchaa kaikaku ni manabu* [Learning from Thatcher's reform]. Tokyo: PHP Shuppan.

Nakajima, T. 2007. kyouiku kihonhou kaiseigo no shinjiyuushugi kyouiku [Neoliberal education after the revision to the Fundamental Law of Education]. *kyouiku* 57, no. 8: 27–32.

Nakayama, N. 2004. kisoiau kimochi ga shuppatsu ten [Competitive spirit is the starting point]. *Asahi News*, December 18, 15.

NIER. 2010. heisei 22 nedo zenkoku gakuryoku gakushuu joukyou chousa, chousa kekka no pointo [2010 national academic achievement test, key findings]. http://www.nier.go.jp/10chousakekkahoukoku/10_point.pdf.

Nitta, K. 2008. *The politics of structural education reform*. New York, NY: Routledge.

NSW Department of Education and Training. 2009. *School self-evaluation support materials*. Bankstown: NSW Department of Education and Training. http://www.schools.nsw.edu.au/media/downloads/schoolsweb/learning/yr7_12assessments/npa/sse/ssesupportdoc.pdf.

Ogawa, M. 2010. *kyouiku kaikaku no yukue: kunikara chihou e* [The future of education reform: Shift from the state to municipal governments]. Tokyo: Chikuma shobō.

Ogiwara, K. 2002. On the content and form of Japanese education policy: Focusing on the changes from 1990's onwards. *Hokkaidou daigaku daigakuin kyouikugaku kenkyuuka kiyou* 85: 117–34.

Oki, N. 2009. Zenkoku gakuryoku tesuto wa muda de aru [National academic testing is a waste]. *Sekai* 11: 85–93.

Ono, M. 2007. gakkou kyouin hyouka to gakuryoku chousa no touseiteki sokumen [Controlling aspects of school teacher evaluation and academic testing]. *kyouiku* 57, no. 4: 31–8.

Ono, M. 2009. 'zenkoku gakuryoku, gakushuuchsusa' seisaku no keisei katei. *Bulletin of the Department of History and Philosophy of Education, Graduate School of Education, the University of Tokyo* 35: 9–21.

Ozawa, M. 2002. *kokoro no senmonka wa iranai* [Experts of mind are unnecessary]. Tokyo: Yousensha.

Ozga, J. 2009. Governing education through data in England: From regulation to self-evaluation. *Journal of Education Policy* 24, no. 2: 149–62.

Prime Minister's Office. 2006. *Keizai zaisei unei to kouzou kaikaku ni kansuru kihonhoushin 2006* [2006 Basic principal for economic management and structural reform]. Tokyo: Prime Minister's Office.

Rappleye, J. 2012. *Educational policy transfer in an era of globalization: History, spatiality, and comparison*. Frankfurt: Peter Lang.

Rautalin, M., and P. Alasuutari. 2007. The curse of success: The impact of the OECD's Programme for International Student Assessment on the discourses of the teaching profession in Finland. *European Educational Research Journal* 6, no. 4: 348–63.

Rautalin, M., and P. Alasuutari. 2009. The uses of the national PISA results by Finnish officials in central government. *Journal of Education Policy* 24, no. 5: 539–56.

Rizvi, F., and B. Lingard. 2006. Globalisation and the changing nature of the OECD's educational work. In *Education, globalisation and social change*, ed. H. Lauder, P. Brown, J. Billabough, and A.H. Halsey, 247–60. Oxford: Oxford University Press.

Sakakibara, E. 2001. 'Yutori kyouiku' de nihon metsubou [Yutori education will destroy Japan]. In *Kyouiku no ronten* [Debates in education], ed. Bungei shunju, 220–33. Tokyo: Bungei shunju.

Schoppa, L.J. 1991. *Education reform in Japan: A case of immobilist politics*. London: Routledge.

Shimizu, K. 2009. *zenkoku gakuryoku tesuto, sono kouzai o tou* [Pluses and minuses of the national achievement test]. Tokyo: iwanami shoten.

Steiner-Khamsi, G. 2000. Transferring education, displacing reforms. In *Discourse formation in comparative education*, ed. J. Schriewer, 155–87. New York, NY: Peter Lang.

Takayama, K. 2007. A nation at risk crosses the Pacific. *Comparative Education Review* 51, no. 4: 423–46.

Takayama, K. 2008a. The politics of international league tables: PISA in Japan's achievement crisis debate. *Comparative Education* 44, no. 4: 387–407.

Takayama, K. 2008b. Japan's Ministry of Education 'becoming the right': Neoliberal restructuring and the Ministry's struggles for political legitimacy. *Globalisation, Societies, and Education* 6, no. 2: 131–46.

Takayama, K. 2010. Politics of externalization in reflexive times: Reinventing Japanese education reform discourses through 'Finnish success'. *Comparative Education Review* 54, no. 1: 51–75.

Takayama, K. 2012. Bringing a political 'bite' to educational transfer studies. In *Policy borrowing and lending in education*, ed. G. Steiner-Khamsi and F. Waldow, 148–66. New York, NY: Routledge.

Takayama, K., and M.W. Apple. 2008. The cultural politics of borrowing: Japan, Britain, and the narrative of educational crisis. *British Journal of Sociology of Education* 29, no. 3: 289–301.

Tozawa, I. 2009. 'zenkoku gakuryoku chousa' o meguru giron [The debate over 'national academic testing']. *Refarensu* 5: 33–58.

Tozawa, I. 2010. Zenkoku gakuryoku chousa no minaoshi [Re-examination of national acadecmic assessment]. *Refarensu* 6: 49–72.

Tsutsumi, S., and D. Hashimoto. 1999. *Sentaku, sekinin, rentai no kyouiku kaikaku* [Education for choice, responsibility, and bonding]. Tokyo: Iwanami shoten.

Whitty, G., S. Power, and D. Halpin. 1998. *Devolution and choice in education*. Melbourne: ACER Press.

Willis, D., and J. Rappleye. 2011. Reimagining Japanese education in the global conversation. In *Reimagining Japanese education*, ed. D. Willis and J. Rappleye, 15–49. Oxford: Symposium Books.

Coloniality and a global testing regime in higher education: unpacking the OECD's AHELO initiative

Riyad A. Shahjahan

Higher, Adult, and Lifelong Education, Michigan State University, East Lansing, MI, USA

The Organization for Economic Cooperation and Development (OECD) is currently engaging in a worldwide feasibility study entitled International Assessment of Higher Education Learning Outcomes (AHELO). This feasibility study seeks to develop measures that would assess student learning outcomes that would be valid across different languages, cultures, and higher education institutions. Drawing on anticolonial perspectives, this article provides a critical policy analysis of the AHELO project. Based on a review of the AHELO texts, it presents two themes: (1) crisis and imperial logic in policy production and (2) Anglo-Eurocentrism as global designs and colonial relationships. It argues that, through AHELO, OECD is striving to construct a global space of equivalence for teaching and learning in higher education, and in so doing, perpetuates coloniality in global higher education. It concludes by noting some comparative observations between AHELO and Programme for International Student Achievement in terms of the increasing role of global knowledge for policy tools in educational policy.

Introduction

At a 2007 meeting held in Washington, DC, Organization for Economic Cooperation and Development (OECD) staff and experts acknowledged the 'considerable challenges' that lay ahead in developing, 'internationally comparative measures of higher education learning outcomes' (OECD 2007a, 2). These experts noted that there was 'no clear roadmap for overcoming these challenges and *some compared the situation with when Columbus set sail*' (Ibid., emphasis added). Is it merely coincidental that Columbus's journey came up at an OECD meeting? What does the use of this Columbus metaphor signify and suggest about colonial vestiges in contemporary educational policy? While on the one hand, Columbus' journey fueled the formation of global trade circuits, the European Renaissance, and the Western industrial revolution (Blaut 1993; Mignolo 1999, 2005), on the other, it instigated the pillage, rape, and exploitation of the colonized and their lands first in the Americas and then across the globe (Mignolo 2000; Smith 1999). As efforts to develop internationally comparative measures of learning outcomes 'set sail,' the OECD takes a steering role. This article considers the degree to which the OECD is an imperial agent in higher education policy today. I address this question by critically examining the role of the OECD in the production of a global testing regime in higher education currently underway – International Assessment of Higher Education Learning Outcomes (AHELO) initiative – from an 'anticolonial perspective' (see Shahjahan 2011).

I focus on the OECD for two reasons. First, over the past few decades, the OECD has become a major player in global higher education policy formation (Bassett and Maldonado-Maldonado 2009). It has acquired a brand identity and asserts 'soft power' among its member nations (and others) by constructing and disseminating knowledge about various higher education issues (e.g. documenting and forecasting trends, providing educational indicators, and supporting forums where stakeholders come together) (Shahjahan 2012). OECD here refers not to a self-contained entity, but rather to a vast network of policy circles and actors, including OECD staff, member countries, policy-makers, consultants, and researchers (Henry et al. 2001; Morgan 2009). Despite OECD's dissemination of a plethora of publications and reports on higher education globally, scant research exists on its influence on global higher education discourse (exceptions include Henry et al. 2001; King 2009; Martens, Rusconi, and Leuze 2007; Saarinen 2008; Shahjahan and Torres 2011). This article illuminates the role of OECD in the globalization of higher education policy about student learning outcomes.

Second, in recent years, we have witnessed a growing debate about global testing regimes and their impact on steering educational systems with great effects in K-12 schooling (Kamens and McNeely 2010; Rizvi and Lingard 2010). In particular, the OECD's Programme for International Student Achievement (PISA) has received significant attention (see Carvalho and Costa 2009; Corbett 2008; Grek 2009; Morgan 2009; Pereyra, Kotthoff, and Cowen 2011). This article extends this latter debate by offering a higher education standpoint; higher education institutions (HEIs) are vital players in the global knowledge economy and are the objects of various transnational policy tools and metrics (Luke 2011). Given the OECD's reputation with PISA in primary and secondary education, AHELO provides a comparative lens to understand the role of global 'knowledge for policy' (Carvalho and Costa 2009) tools in educational policy.

In this article, I argue that the OECD – in striving to construct a global space of equivalence (such as AHELO) – perpetuates coloniality. By coloniality, I refer to an imperial logic of domination that derives from colonial and imperial experiences (this concept is elaborated below). By using the term 'space of equivalence,' I denote a uniform space of measurement (Rizvi and Lingard 2010). I argue for the significance (or imperative) of developing an analytic understanding of coloniality in global educational policy because there is a scarcity of anticolonial theoretical perspectives in critical educational policy analysis (Rizvi and Lingard 2010), particularly in relation to globalization of higher education (see Rhee 2009; Sidhu 2006). The anticolonial perspective is salient because it brings to policy analysis the questions of Eurocentrism/Whiteness, colonial histories, the political economy, knowledge production, and power relations (see Appadurai 2001; Connell 2007; Shahjahan 2011; Smith 1999). For the most part, critical scholarship on higher education policy continues to ignore colonial experiences, and, thus, perpetuates Eurocentrism in policy analysis (Connell 2007; Pratt 1992).

I use the case of the AHELO project to illuminate how coloniality is perpetuated and reconstituted through global higher education policy. I briefly describe the purpose, components, and participants of the AHELO project. I then provide a critical policy analysis (CPA) of AHELO grounded in an anticolonial perspective. Based on my analysis of AHELO texts, I discuss two themes: (1) crisis and taming in the imperial logic of policy production and (2) Anglo-Eurocentrism as global designs and colonial relationships. I conclude by drawing some comparative observations between AHELO and PISA. My overall aim is to raise questions for readers instead of providing answers.

Overview of AHELO project

According to the OECD (2011a), AHELO is, 'the first international study of what students in higher education know and can do upon graduation' (2). Under the management and guidance of the Programme on Institutional Management in Higher Education (IMHE) of the OECD, the goal of AHELO is to create tests whose results are 'comparable internationally,' regardless of language, culture, or institution, and 'provide actual data on the quality of learning and its relevance to the labour market' (OECD 2010a, 5). AHELO measures various context-dependent learning outcomes at the institutional/departmental level and seeks to determine what factors influence them. The study itself consists of four areas of measurement focused on student and university performance (OECD 2010a, 2011a, 2011b, 2011c):

- *Generic skills assessment*: test questions designed to evaluate the skills that students in all fields should acquire during their postsecondary education (e.g. critical thinking, analytic reasoning, problem-solving, and written communication skills).
- *Discipline-specific skills assessment*: test questions designed to evaluate students' ability to extrapolate and apply what they have learned in particular disciplines to new contexts.
- *Contextual information*: 10-min questionnaires designed to link results from the generic and discipline-specific skills tests to institutional environment and student background.
- *'Value-added' measurement*: evaluation of the contribution of HEIs to student outcomes via raw scores of students (or the 'bottom line') and the incremental learning (or 'value-added') resulting from the quality of teaching at HEIs (i.e. the learning gained).

By May 2011, instruments had been created for the generic skills assessment and the two discipline-specific assessments in economics and engineering. Taking 90 min to complete, these instruments contain performance tasks (i.e. open-ended questions regarding realistic hypothetical situations) and multiple-choice questions (OECD 2011b).

As of March 2012, 17 countries are participating in the AHELO feasibility study: Abu Dhabi, Australia, Belgium, Canada, Colombia, Egypt, Finland, Italy, Japan, Korea, Kuwait, Mexico, the Netherlands, Norway, the Russian Federation, Slovak Republic, and the USA (OECD 2012a). Approximately, 150 HEIs (up to 10 HEIs within each country) will implement one or more of the assessment strands to determine the learning outcomes that best depict the quality of higher education worldwide (OECD 2010a, 2011b). AHELO will test around 30,000 undergraduates nearing the end of their first three- or four-year-degree (OECD 2011b). Participating countries have been divided among each strand, with nine countries conducting the generic skills assessment, seven countries assessing skills in economics, and seven countries assessing engineering skills (OECD 2011b). The feasibility study focuses on the disciplines of economics and engineering because they are assumed to be similar across cultures. All countries will be assessed with the contextual strand (OECD 2010b). If the three AHELO assessment instruments can demonstrate the feasibility of assessing student learning outcomes globally and across HEIs, then the final phase of the study will be the development of a value-added measurement, or the contribution of HEIs to the learning outcomes irrespective of a student's background or abilities (OECD 2011a). The study will conclude at the end of 2012 and findings will be reviewed at a final conference to determine if a full-scale AHELO project is 'scientifically and practically possible' (OECD 2011b).

A team of governments, HEIs, non-governmental agencies, and international experts are administering AHELO through the IMHE Governing Board. Approximately, 300 individuals are working directly on the project and about 10,000 leaders, faculty, and students, and thousands of public stakeholders are part of this initiative (Coates 2011). In addition, the Australian Council for Educational Research (ACER) – a key player in the formation of PISA – led the development of the discipline-specific tests for AHELO following the European Tuning approach (a European curriculum template for professional training). The feasibility study is financially supported by participating countries as well as through contributions from the Lumina Foundation for Education (USA), Calouste Gulbenkian Foundation (Portugal), Riksbankens Jubileumsfund (Sweden), the Spencer Foundation (USA), the William and Flora Hewlett Foundation (USA), the Higher Education Founding Council (England), and the Higher Education Authority (Ireland) (OECD 2010a, 2011c).

Theoretical framework and methodology

This article draws on CPA and anticolonial theoretical perspectives[1] to examine publicly available relevant AHELO texts. I use the CPA perspective to engage and understand the concept of *policy* as not *only* texts or public rules/laws, but also as a process (Ball 2006; Ozga 2000; Rizvi and Lingard 2010), a vehicle through which policy messages and values are constructed, circulated, contested, or modified (Ozga 2000). These vehicles may include research studies, policy forums, consultations, agenda setting, implementation, and evaluation. Rather than viewing policy as static, CPA considers policy as a movement: policy ideas flow from one context to another, are contingent and ad hoc, and involve power relations (Ball 2006).

This article also employs Walter Mignolo's theory of 'coloniality' to make sense of AHELO (see Delgado and Romero 2000; Mignolo 2000, 2005). Coloniality[2] moves beyond notions of postcolonialism and refers to an enduring logic of domination, 'that enforces control, domination, and exploitation disguised in the language of salvation, progress … and being good for everyone,' which underpinned the logical structure of imperial powers (Mignolo 2005, 6). This language of salvation and progress is central in the justification of educational policy today (Shahjahan 2011) and Rizvi and Lingard (2010) suggest that policy is constructed with an underpinning logic that it is 'good for everyone.' This policy discourse masks or erases the ideological and power interests that shape it. A coloniality perspective helps us unpack the imperial logics that underlie and legitimate educational policy discourses.

'Coloniality' presumes that knowledge production analysis involves geopolitical analysis. Mignolo notes that, 'local histories are everywhere but that only some local histories are in a position of imagining and implementing global designs' (Mignolo in Delgado and Romero 2000, 8). In terms of policy analysis, this means that only certain local knowledge systems, always already derivatives of particular historical-material conditions (even backed by military power), have the social privilege to shape global policy tools and designs. The term 'knowledge system' refers to a systematic way of knowing derived from concepts, or values, and/or collective experiences, specific to and derived from a particular social–political–historical–philosophical context (which could include cultural knowledge, language, and embodied experiences). For instance, the language of knowledge economy that stemmed from a Canadian delegation paper at an OECD meeting in the mid-nineties went viral via a series of OECD and World Bank reports and is now pervasive in global higher education policy circles (Peters 2001). In contrast, Cuba's higher education templates (e.g. absence of internal market competition) and 'social policy of knowledge' have not seen similar diffusion (Naidoo 2011). Policy diffusion involves and follows material power relations and global actors.

A coloniality perspective foregrounds the *coloniality of power* and *colonial difference.* The former refers to a *particular set of power relations* that interconnect imperial labor exploitation (and/or land appropriation) and the control of finance, authority, knowledge, and subjectivity (Mignolo 2005). In terms of policy analysis, this means that power relations structure the context of policy production, implementation, and evaluation, and these power dynamics are related to the control of the economy, political authority, knowledge, and subjectivity. A global policy space like AHELO also represents a site of colonial difference. The colonial difference is a space 'where coloniality of power is enacted' and 'where *local* histories inventing and implementing global designs meet *local* histories, the space in which global designs have to be adapted, adopted, rejected, integrated, or ignored' (Mignolo 2000, viiii). With respect to policy analysis, this means policy spaces are dynamic loci of knowledge production, translation, and internalization, whereby certain local policy ideas – becoming part of global policy regimes – encounter, invade, interconnect, and mediate with other local policy realms. Thus, the policy arena sometimes involves imposition, sometimes instills a sense of inferiority in those locales that pursue global policies to elevate their status, and always involves power hierarchies. However, local contexts display agency in mediating or ignoring global designs.

Using a CPA framework and drawing on Mignolo's coloniality perspective, I critically examined publicly available AHELO texts such as OECD's AHELO website, promotional materials, and declassified documents available on the website. The latter includes AHELO working papers, meeting minutes, seminar presentations, progress reports, newsletters, and interviews with various stakeholders. These documents not only serve as a rich source of qualitative data for understanding policy process (Merriam 1998), but also highlight the OECD's intentional commitment to transparency about AHELO. I selected these documents based on their visibility and availability in the AHELO debates during May 2010–November

2011. These documents were critically analyzed, using deductive coding that responded to my research questions. As a result, my analysis focused on identifying critical samples of texts that explored the following: rationale and purpose of AHELO; the role of higher education; quality assurance; stakeholders involved; generic strand development; discipline specific strand development; and stakeholders' responses to AHELO throughout the policy cycle.

To unpack the discursive effects of AHELO promotional texts, I followed Fairclough's (2003) suggestion that textual analysis should involve a critical examination of texts for their: assumptions; implications; evaluation in texts; value assumptions; representation of social agents; and rhetorical and persuasive features. To this end, I focused on AHELO brochures, newsletters, and project updates as they represent the 'official face' of the AHELO initiative. I deductively and inductively coded these promotional documents by paying attention to the underlying value assumptions and focusing on their rhetorical and persuasive features. To uncover policy mechanisms, I coded the AHELO meeting minutes, newsletters, interviews with various stakeholders, and project updates, to categorize and make sense of the players, discourses, and decisions that were made at the ground level. Lastly, I used 'writing as a method of inquiry' (Richardson and St. Pierre 2005) to engage in a CPA of the coded data. In the following analytic sections, where possible, I draw parallels with PISA's development as a knowledge for policy tool.

Crisis and taming in the imperial logic of policy production

Since the sixteenth century, the imperial logic of modernity – and its attendant efforts to refine administration, order crisis, and eliminate inefficiency – has sought legitimation in salvation discourse, obscuring the pernicious consequences of colonialism such as pillage of land and exploitation of labor (Mignolo 2005; Smith 1999; Stewart-Harawira 2005). In this section, I suggest that a similar discourse of salvation operates to legitimate the OECD's efforts to optimize global higher education[3] in the midst of crisis or disorder. Specifically, I show that AHELO is represented as the means to salvation and a utopian higher education system, even as it ushers in a new imperial order anchored in a socially efficient neoliberal higher education system tied to the global labor market.

The discourse of crisis

The colonial discourses of crisis, disorder, and salvation are evident in the narratives of AHELO texts. Frequently foregrounding the growing global demand for higher education, fierce competition among HEIs, and the reign of university rankings, AHELO texts tell a story of higher education in crisis. For instance, a road map of AHELO states: 'Following decades of rapid expansion of higher education and its growing internationalisation, there is increasing recognition that greater attention should now be paid to its quality and relevance to ensure quality provision for all' (OECD 2010c, 4). Furthermore, an OECD promotional brochure states:

> Some 135 million students are enrolled in an estimated 17,000 higher education institutions (HEIs) worldwide, twice the number a decade ago. Almost three million of them join degree programmes outside their own countries. (OECD 2009, 3)

Drawing temporal comparisons and deploying hard numbers, the OECD heralds a new era of global higher education in need of urgent attention. Readers of AHELO literature are called upon to imagine global higher education's unprecedented (and currently uncontrolled) expansion, variety, significance, and mobility.

Further elaborating on the discourse of crisis, the OECD diffuses narratives of quality assurance, competition, and rankings in higher education. For instance, the OECD states: 'An unhealthy air of competition surrounds rankings. Universities change educational missions and cut programmes in a desperate effort to climb the ranks' (OECD 2009, 5). Furthermore, international rankings 'derived from inputs or research-driven outputs are distorting decision-making by individuals, institutions and governments' (OECD 2010c, 4). The OECD not only paints a crisis picture of global higher education, but also suggests the consequences suffered by students and administrators amid structural disorder:

> Faced with such diversity, a student hardly knows where to turn when choosing a university: Will I learn what I want to learn? Will my diploma prepare me for a career? Will it be recognised if I transfer to a different university or move to another country? University administrators are concerned too: Is our university up to standard? How can we improve? Do we really have to cut this degree programme because it doesn't contribute to securing us a higher place in the ranks? (OECD 2009, 5)

The OECD blames the pervasive confusion of higher education stakeholders on a lack of reliable sources of information;[4] a similar rhetoric of 'unreliable information' was utilized to justify the OECD's construction of PISA (Morgan 2009). Whereas the dominant narrative depicts and 'fixes' students as concerned about validity of credentials on the labor market, credential transferability, and learning objectives, administrators are, so the story goes, concerned with university standards, university decision-making through rankings, and improving quality. What is missing in these definitions of students and administrators are people who may not see HEIs as serving merely instrumental ends, but as pathways to self-development, meaning-making, and the production of active citizenry.

The discourse of salvation and utopia

According to the OECD, salvation for the global higher education system lies in global solutions centered on comparative assessment tools absent from the existing assessment toolkit: '[T]here are no tools available to compare the quality of teaching and learning in institutions on an international scale' (OECD 2011a, 2). PISA garnered credibility through the same logic of global quality assurance that OECD employs to legitimate AHELO (Morgan 2009). On the AHELO website (OECD 2012b), the OECD offers itself as the 'savior,' showcasing its competency as a reputable and quintessential global consultant. OECD appears well placed to establish a transnational higher education testing regime that will forge a global space of equivalence in higher education. The OECD further suggests that such an assessment tool offers salvation from the current chaotic state of higher education because it serves a diversity of stakeholders:

> For frontline higher education practitioners – from academics to institutional leaders – AHELO will provide valuable information on effective teaching strategies to enhance learning outcomes. Institutions will therefore be able to reduce drop-out rates, enable

more students to complete their degrees successfully irrespective of their personal background or characteristics, and hence contribute to fostering equity in our higher education systems ... Students, governments and employers also stand to benefit. AHELO will shed light on whether the considerable resources invested in higher education are being used effectively, and on the capacities of graduates to enter and succeed in the labour market. (OECD 2011a, 2)

Given that AHELO is in progress, the OECD also projects a future imaginary of global higher education that normalizes an evidence-based culture in higher education policy. For instance, in its AHELO Roadmap, the OECD argued that a successful AHELO will prove the possibilities of assessing student learning outcomes 'in an internationally comparable, efficient and scalable way' and introduce new methodological tools to higher education policy. Consequently, various stakeholders (who include policy-makers, institutional leaders, faculty, and students) will appreciate the assessment of student learning outcomes 'as an essential checkpoint in the educational process' (OECD 2010c, 5). Furthermore, AHELO will provide various institutions and policy-makers the tools to ensure a more socially efficient higher education system tied to the global labor market. Overall, AHELO is driven by a utopian imaginary that envisions a new world order where higher education policy-making is evidence-based, globally comparative, and employs rigorous checkpoints.

In their efforts to de-territorialize higher education policy via implementation of a transnational testing regime, AHELO narratives also re-territorialize the policy problem by carving an imperial frontier of crisis – higher education – for OECD, the new imperial agent, to 'save,' control, and manage (Tikly 2004). We might consider these promotional AHELO narratives as global spaces of equivalence that are fragile and contested entities. Given the socially constructed nature of this global test (wrought with technical difficulties), AHELO remains 'susceptible to contestation,' hence its feasibility and authority as a future policy tool (i.e. discursive power) remain incomplete (Morgan 2009, 202). Thus, AHELO requires constant legitimization by the OECD.

Colonial discourse and social engineering towards an imperial order

Coloniality applies taxonomies to order and know the world (Pratt 1992; Smith 1999). To this end, Chow (2002) noted, 'the imperialist agenda for transforming the world into observable and hence manageable units ... must be seen as inseparable from the historical conditions that repeatedly return the material benefits of such processes to European subjectivities' (2). AHELO's agenda is imperialist in two main ways. First, AHELO's emphasis on developing and testing learning outcomes rests on transforming the amorphous phenomena of teaching and learning into observable, manageable, and comparable units across institutions and nations. Second, AHELO represents a policy tool that brings material benefits to the OECD and its stakeholders[5] who occupy a privileged position in a neoliberal world order. The OECD's vested interest in the success of AHELO as a social scientific experiment is apparent:

... given uncertainties ... to the scientific and operational feasibility of such an assessment[,] the OECD needs to demonstrate that it is feasible to measure learning outcomes in valid and reliable ways across cultures, countries, languages and institutions before significant resources can be invested in the development of an AHELO as part of the regular OECD programme of work and budget. (OECD 2010c, 14)

The OECD carves, sustains, and justifies its role in higher educational policy through AHELO's success, even in its fragility as a contested knowledge for policy tool (Morgan 2009).

This knowledge for policy tool is also tied to neoliberal agendas that prioritize higher education's function to prepare 'future workers' to enhance national, corporate, and transnational productivity. Further, higher education systems must demonstrate their capacity to make adequate returns on investments (Rizvi and Lingard 2010, 78). In AHELO's 2010–2011 brochure, Barbara Ischinger, OECD Director of Education, points to the importance of measurement tools in this context:

> In this changing global economy, high quality tertiary education is essential and students need to obtain the right skills to ensure economic, scientific and social progress ... Tools are needed to measure students' knowledge and whether they are equipped, at the end of their tertiary education, with the skills needed for the emerging job market. (OECD 2010d, 2)

Elsewhere, I and others argue that global colonialism continues as a neoliberal agenda is advanced and as new imperial myths – such as the myth of salvation and utopia discussed here – are created to support the advancement of neoliberal economies (Mignolo 2003; Shahjahan 2011; Stewart-Harawira 2005).

The OECD deploys a particular colonial ideology that portrays AHELO comparative measures as a savoir from the barbarous disorder of higher education policy-making. In considering global higher education policy processes, however, we must ask: What kinds of knowledge are being validated and what kinds of knowledge are being displaced?

Anglo-Eurocentrism as global designs and colonial relationships

Modern epistemology perpetuated coloniality by delocalizing and detaching its concepts (e.g. rationality, logic, and epistemic virtues) from local histories and presenting them as applicable to everyone (Connell 2007; Mignolo 2005; Smith 1999). Therefore, situating knowledge and knowers in a local context is paramount in considering AHELO through a coloniality lens. Stanfield (1999) argues that global assessment tools are not value-free; often 'white supremacy norms and values' implicitly contribute to these 'measurement epistemologies, techniques, and interpretations' (421). These assessment tools normalize white Euro-American experiences as the baseline through which to compare and contrast people of color (Stanfield 1999). Where do AHELO's ideas of assessment of student learning outcomes come from? Whose frameworks are used to develop these assessment tools? What kinds of difference are being overlooked in the production of these global designs?

US academic hegemony in quality assurance and generic skills strand

The policy idea to foreground students' learning outcomes in higher education quality assurance stemmed from a recent movement in the US' accreditation community (Lewis 2009). This idea took center stage and was integrated into the OECD at a 2006 meeting of education ministers. Student learning assessment was a major concern in a 2006 report entitled *A Test of Leadership: Charting the Future of US Higher Education* by the Commission on the Future of Higher Education, appointed by US Secretary of Education Margaret Spellings. One of the key recommendations of the Spellings report was that HEIs should measure student learning through use of externally produced standardized assessments that are 'primarily intended to allow comparisons to be made between institutions' (Lewis 2009, 337). According to Lewis (2009), the 2006 Education Ministers' meeting echoed the US accreditation debate and suggested the need to develop better evidence of learning outcomes (338). In response to these debates, the OECD launched AHELO in 2008.

AHELO's generic skills strand derives its tools and templates from US local histories. The OECD awarded a $1.2 million contract to US Council for Aid to Education (CAE) to develop an international version of its Collegiate Learning Assessment (CLA) to test the generic skills strand (Lederman 2010). The introduction of CLA as part of AHELO is not a coincidence. Four of the 11 participants in the inaugural meeting in 2007 were from the USA, including the President of CAE. The introduction of CLA was solidified in AHELO in a second meeting of these experts. Jamil Salmi (from the World Bank), Marshall Smith (from the William and Flora Hewlett Foundation), Roger Benjamin (from the US Council for Aid in Education), and an expert from The Educational Testing Service (ETS) participated in both meetings (OECD 2007a, 2007b). Two years later, OECD justifies the use of CLA by arguing 'CLA assessments administered by US institutions show no marked difference between the performance of domestic and foreign students, suggesting that the CLA is easily adaptable to different cultural backgrounds' (OECD 2009, 8). There was no evidence given to support this claim.

The two performance tasks to be used in the generic strand – 'Catfish' and 'Lake to River'[6] – also originated in the USA (OECD 2010e). At the beginning of the generic strand New York meeting in 2009, teams discussed nine possible performance tasks that could be included in AHELO (OECD 2010f). At the meeting, a 'straw vote' was taken to determine degrees of agreement about the top candidates for inclusion; 'Catfish' and 'Lake-to-River' were the two favorites. 'Catfish' raised only minor issues of translation and all agreed there were no obstacles. 'Lake-to-River' raised the issue of student familiarity with lakes and rivers and led to a discussion of the universality of performance tasks. The issue was resolved by noting that, 'while higher education students *may not directly experience* lakes and rivers everyday, a higher education student *should be able to reason* about environment issues surrounding such a situation. Hence, Lake was unanimously selected as well' (Ibid., 5, emphasis added). The OECD also suggests that it views 'universality of tasks' not as 'commonality of local situations across countries,' but refers to the 'knowledge and experiences expected of most all college students across countries' (Ibid., 7). The local nature of these case study examples became apparent in the testing stages of generic strand development. While countries like Korea, Kuwait, and Norway had to go through preliminary tests, US counterparts did 'not require a site visit in translation and translation review since the Lake-to-River and Catfish performance tasks originated in the United States' (OECD 2010e, 9). Hence, these performance tasks are US templates normalized to be part of global designs that require 'others' to translate and internalize them. In short, the US experience becomes the 'baseline to design' this assessment instrument (Stanfield 1999, 421).

These above performance tasks also assume and internalize certain ideas related to the ways of knowing the world that is Eurocentric. The OECD does not see these performance tasks as an exposure problem, but a reasoning issue. To put it simply, reasoning supersedes embodied knowledge (experiential knowledge). Invoking Spivak (1999), views such as this represent the 'Eurocentric arrogance of conscience' (171), the simplistic assumption that these epistemologies are universal and any system of knowledge (e.g. environmental issues) can be accessed. Here, I raise concerns not only with where AHELO's generic strand derives its *content*, but also with the *terms* (underpinning epistemologies and values) by and in which knowledge is produced (Appadurai 2001; Connell 2007; Smith 1999). Grounded in US experiences and Eurocentric notions of knowledge, the AHELO project integrates particular local knowledge systems into a global design.

Discipline-specific strands

The impetus and templates for AHELO's discipline-specific strands derive mainly from European–American contexts. The drive for this strand grew out of the European higher education reform movement's efforts to address student mobility and standardization of credits and degrees through formulation of 'minimum competencies' in major academic disciplines (ETS 2006). AHELO adopted the Tuning project from Europe for the professions.

In the last year, the US-based ETS has led the development of the *Economics Framework* and *Assessment* (OECD 2011c). According to the OECD (2010g), ETS adopted Economics test items from two of the Economics tests that it has already developed – the GRE Subject Test in Economics and the Major Field Test in Economics (p. 24). The AHELO's Economics Expert Group reached consensus on a draft economics framework, based on the 'Tuning-AHELO Conceptual Framework of Expected and Desired Learning Outcomes in Economics' and the UK 'QAA subject Benchmark Statement for Economics 2007' (OECD 2011a). After the framework was developed, ETS staff audited the test items against it. According to the OECD (2011a, 6–7):

> There was a lot of uncertainty on the feasibility of getting academics from different countries to agree on what to measure in the disciplines, and to agree on an assessment instrument ... One of the remarkable findings of the feasibility study to date is that it has in fact been easier than anyone thought to get economics experts to agree on what an AHELO should cover and measure. The reason for this is that AHELO goes above content-knowledge and rather focuses on the 'language' of economics.

The language of triumph and relief is apparent in this narrative. The OECD instrumentalizes this 'triumph' to herald the usefulness of AHELO as focused 'on above content' knowledge similar to its PISA counterpart.

On the other hand, the *Engineering Framework* and *Assessment* are being developed by a consortium of international organizations (IOs) led by the ACER and including Japan's National Institute for Educational Policy Research (NIER) and a European network of engineers (Eugene) managed by the University of

Florence in Italy (OECD 2011c). Interestingly, the test items for AHELO's Engineering strand are being translated and adopted from Japanese licensing exams for civil engineers (Coates 2011).

Given the translation and integration of Japanese test questions, some readers may disagree with the premise of my argument that AHELO is dominated by Euro-American knowledge systems. Though Japanese engineering licensing exams are a small part of the multiple-choice tests, the *framework* of this assessment strand still grows mainly out of the European Tuning project. Furthermore, the inclusion of Japanese items does not hinder my argument about coloniality. As its second largest funder, Japan continues to be a major player in the OECD (Woodward 2009) and certainly a stakeholder with strong interest in the 'neoliberal world order.' Therefore, AHELO's knowledge dependency runs parallel to OECD's economic dependency on these various national/regional contexts.

From a coloniality perspective, what this above trend suggests is that we need to consider the underlying geopolitical relations of power between parts of the world that manifest in the production of policy tools such as assessment strands. Furthermore, while AHELO borrows questions from Japanese tests, this does not necessarily entail the integration of Japanese knowledge systems (e.g. epistemologies from the Japanese socio-historical context). The values and epistemologies underpinning AHELO remain Euro-American, while the content of these assessment tools may be derivative of non-Euro-American contexts that play increasingly important roles in the neoliberal world order.

It is crucial to consider the values and categories used to represent the world in AHELO as they are the future benchmarks 'against which perceived changes are measured and represented' in teaching and learning in higher education (Dale and Robertson 2009, 114). Through construction of discipline specific strands that derive their philosophies and aims from Euro-American contexts, the OECD's AHELO project perpetuates coloniality.

Colonizer–colonized relationships in global higher education

The production and circulation of AHELO also enfolds colonizer–colonized relationships and foregrounds colonial difference. In the following discussion, I show how the Global South internalizes, adopts, and mediates Euro-American frameworks for their own systems, highlighting the underlying power relations in global policy transfers. 'Language' as a knowledge system has become the key-mediating tool. Here, 'language' refers not only to a medium of communication, but encompasses a way of knowing (e.g. system of representation) and a cultural carrier (Thiongo 1986). For instance, Korean stakeholders pointed out that 'word by word translation' of AHELO tests did not work, but instead suggested that, 'the translation of tests should focus more on general intent translation, as well the Korean language is more formal than English and translation should reflect this' (OECD 2010f, 8). Similarly, translating pilot tests in Kuwait into Arabic proved difficult and concerns were raised about the test's scoring rubric. Standard Arabic writing differs greatly from English writing. As Kuwait's National Project Manager (NPM) Imad Al-Atiqi writes:

> All documents needed multistep translation. The first step concentrated on accuracy to
> the English version but eventually was not in a style deemed to be suitable to students

and assessment staff. Thus linguistic adaptation took more effort than was originally planned. (OECD 2011d, 3)

The encounter between these various knowledge systems highlights the space of colonial difference. Localized Euro-American knowledge systems that invent and implement global designs meet with other *local* histories, which in turn adapt, modify, and reconcile these global designs into their policy tools. This raises the question: Why are Kuwaiti or Korean tools not translated into English for AHELO? Mignolo (2005) and Chakrabarty (2000) succinctly articulate my own concerns with academic cultural hegemony. Mignolo (2005, 9) notes:

> Europeans, in general, did not have to incorporate Indigenous languages and frameworks of knowledge into their own. For Indigenous people …, the situation was different. They had no choice but to incorporate European languages and frameworks of knowledge into their own.

Similarly, Chakrabarty (2000) notes with respect to historians, 'Third-world historians feel a need to refer to works in European history; historians of Europe do not feel any need to reciprocate' (28). In other words, the production of AHELO is anchored in and stages a colonizer–colonized relationship, whereby Euro-American local histories and knowledge systems are *subjects* of global designs, and the non-west act as mere *objects* of these global designs (see Connell 2007; Smith 1999).

However, 'colonized' countries are also complicit in perpetuating coloniality. Following a recent review of its higher education systems by the World Bank and OECD, Egypt discovered that it was ranked 65th out of 128 countries in the Global Competitiveness Index in 2007 (OECD 2011c, 5). This joint report recommended policy actions to bolster Egypt's competitiveness in the global knowledge-based economy. As a result, the Egyptian Government has decided to follow the West and participate in AHELO. As the Egyptian National Project manager of AHELO states:

> The dissatisfaction expressed in the abovementioned report conflicts with the great history of civilization of Egypt and its central global and regional role. Therefore, the Egyptian government has conducted extensive studies to analyze the situation, define the solutions and adopt reform projects. In this context, participation in the AHELO pilot study offers Egyptian Higher Education Institutions the opportunity to assess their graduates' outcomes on an international basis … [and] will help the institutions to enhance the quality of the services they provide as well as to achieve a global educational preparation. (OECD 2011c, 5)

Thus, Egypt was 'shamed' by these IOs into joining the global higher education market and signing on to AHELO. In the Egyptian example, we witness how IOs' recommendations can act as cultural invasions and tools of governmentality; colonized nation-states internalize global benchmarks and assessments and then self-regulate themselves in line with the West's agenda for global higher education (Naidoo 2011). Whereas the World Bank has the option to exercise hard power through its funding lever, the OECD can only enact soft powers of persuasion (e.g. by imposing national/international comparisons of performance) (Bassett and Maldonado-Maldonado 2009; Shahjahan 2012). The Egyptian stakeholder's narrative suggests that the colonized live an illusion that they are 'in the same social and cultural sphere as that of the metropolis' (Choi, cited in Rhee 2009, 63).

Mignolo's (2003) observation that epistemic dependency runs parallel to economic dependency is especially pertinent here (110).

Luke (2011) rightly asks: 'What are the substantive consequences of attempts to move educational innovation and educational science from one cultural context to another, from one nation to another, from one jurisdiction and system to another?' (367). According to Rhee (2009), AHELO 'silences the deeper issues of inequality and the hegemony of the Euro/American centric language, knowledge, and education' (77). While the Global North possesses the material privilege to shape global designs, countries in the Global South become mere 'objects' of these global designs (Connell 2007). Mignolo (2005) observes: 'the West is the only geo-historical location' that continues to have 'the privilege of possessing the dominant categories of thought from which and where the rest of the world can be described, classified, understood, and "improved"' (36, emphasis in original).

Conclusion

In this article, I have argued that even as OECD employs AHELO to construct a global space of equivalence of teaching and learning in higher education, it perpetuates coloniality on two fronts. First, the OECD mobilizes a colonial discursive landscape that suggests that global higher education is in a state of crisis that can be ordered and 'saved' by AHELO. This imperial rhetoric is underpinned by the social engineering of higher education towards a new neoliberal world order tied to the global labor market. Second, construction of AHELO's generic and discipline specific strands perpetuates coloniality by incorporating particular Euro-American templates and local experiences that are cast as universal and become part of global designs. These global designs come into contact with other local knowledge systems, which in turn adapt, translate, and mediate them, thereby representing a site of colonial difference. Finally, AHELO perpetuates coloniality vis-a-vis the colonizer–colonized relationships that are constructed when certain countries participate in AHELO – dance to the tune of IOs – to optimize their integration into the imperial global economy.

AHELO provides a comparative case to PISA, which began in 2000. (It is beyond the scope of this article to go into details about PISA here – please see: Carvalho and Costa 2009; Grek 2009; Morgan 2009). In fact, there are more similarities than differences between these two OECD policy tools. First, AHELO takes a similar approach to PISA in using test questions that focus on students' capacity to extrapolate from what they have learned and apply their competencies in novel contexts unfamiliar to them. Second, AHELO follows the PISA rationale for education, in viewing 'new knowledge and skills necessary for successful adaptation to a changing world a[s] continuously acquired throughout life' (OECD 2009, 8). Third, as in the case of AHELO, American influence was integral to the creation of PISA. Whereas the Clinton administration sought to equip youth with the right skills for the world of work (Morgan 2009), the current rationale focuses on student learning outcomes in higher education. Finally, AHELO and PISA share similar players: the ACER, the CAPSTAN Linguistic Quality Control Company in Belgium, Westat, ETS, and the NIER in Japan. However, there is one notable difference between PISA and AHELO. Unlike PISA, AHELO does not use nation-states or systems as their units of analysis for comparisons, instead focusing on institutions as units of analysis. As AHELO progresses, we can further analyze other points of convergence and divergence between these two OECD initiatives meant to act as 'edumometers' (thermometers of educational institutions and systems) around the world (Corbett 2008). Is there no utility in comparative data or global testing regimes? Some may argue that AHELO's primary objective is to carry quality education everywhere, to ensure equal participation in the global economy, and to improve student learning. Others may suggest that AHELO's strands, despite their origins in Euro-American contexts, indeed measure necessary skills in global contexts. In response, I suggest reflection on the following questions: Who determines that 'quality' is a problem? In whose terms and under which cultural assumptions is quality being defined? What power relations lie in the production of policy problems and their solutions (e.g. edumometers)?

As I have argued elsewhere, the notion of an evidence-based policy mechanism tied to global testing regimes such as PISA and AHELO is not new, but has been used throughout imperial histories to produce and discipline colonized labor (Shahjahan 2011). Furthermore, the notion of universal skills and equal participation in the global economy suggests that jobs are universally accessible and that the global economy is equitably structured. While comparative international data can be a valuable source of information for making local policies, this 'evidence' becomes problematic when indicators become the so-called 'objective' tools by which the performance of education systems or institutions are assessed. As this article argues, these assessment tools are underpinned by particular values and local knowledge systems that are universalized as global designs. These assessment tools are not objective or ahistorical criteria, but are usually products of instrumental values that tie higher education to a knowledge economy discourse (Dale 2005; Rizvi and Lingard 2010). I concur with scholars who argue that these comparative indicators are tied to market reform and the production of colonized labor, and perpetuate the global packaging of higher education (Barriga and Torres-Olave 2009; Robertson 2009). Rather than proliferate global testing regimes, we should instead invest our time and energy into addressing the glaring global systemic inequities that privilege some knowledge systems (language, curricula, and culture) over others (Stewart-Harawira 2005). The coloniality perspective allows us to grasp these systematic inequities by unpacking underlying colonial relations and foregrounding the intersections between knowledge, power, race, and the political economy (Connell 2007; Smith 1999).

Notes

1. It is beyond the scope of this article to fully flesh out what the anticolonial perspective entails. For details on this perspective, please see Shahjahan (2011).
2. I use the term coloniality deliberately. The term postcolonial has supplanted 'Third World' and designates the end of formal colonial administrations across the globe. Coloniality, on the other hand, encompasses a logical structure of colonial domination that remains with us today. Further, the term is more inclusive of the experiences of Latin America, a region that has been overlooked amid postcolonial studies' exclusive focus on British and French Empire (see Mignolo 2000, 2005).
3. When I refer to 'global higher education,' I am not suggesting a given, static system, but a system that is it still emerging. Marginson (2008) notes that the 'global dimension of higher education is in continuous formation, the map of positions is continually being reworked and novel positions are emerging' (313). The AHELO initiative will undoubtedly be an important change agent in global higher education.

4. One could raise the following questions: Has the OECD pursued an AHELO approach because global league tables of university research performance have already become quite established? Is this initiative another 'market choice' metric? According to AHELO texts, the answer to these questions would be mostly affirmative. AHELO texts identify major problems with 'research rankings' that ignore teaching and learning; the OECD presupposes an established global rankings system. Elsewhere, I (e.g. Shahjahan and Torres 2011) suggest that AHELO could be an attempt by the OECD to secure a market niche in higher education as part of the global accountability market (which includes the Times Higher Education global rankings and the EU's new U-Multirank scheme).

5. Here stakeholders refers not only to individuals in Euro-American circles, but also to non-Euro-American OECD member countries, consultants, think tanks, and agencies involved in this project, and non-member countries that buy into programs like AHELO (e.g. BRIC countries courted as partners).

6. At the end of this meeting, it was suggested that the following case studies will be introduced in testing. The Catfish task uses the following situation: 'A deformed catfish was recently discovered in a local lake. The mayor of the city asks you to review evidence (documents) that support or refute three alternative explanations for the appearance of a 3-eyed catfish. The "Lake-to-River" PT sets up the following situation: A county Board of Supervisors is considering the pros and cons of removing the county's dam. You have been asked to review a set of documents and recommend a course of action' (OECD 2010e, 6).

References

Appadurai, A., ed. 2001. *Globalization*. Durham, NC: Duke University Press.

Ball, S.J. 2006. *Education policy and social class: The selected works of Stephen J. Ball.* New York, NY: Routledge.

Barriga, A.D., and B. Torres-Olave. 2009. International organizations in Latin American higher education: Projects and contradictions in the post-world war II and post-Washington consensus era. In *International organizations and higher education policy: Thinking globally, acting locally?* ed. R. Bassett and A. Maldonado, 212–28. New York, NY: Routledge.

Bassett, R., and A. Maldonado-Maldonado. 2009. *International organizations and higher education policy: Thinking globally, acting locally.* New York, NY: Routledge.

Blaut, J. 1993. *The colonizer's model of the world: Geographical diffusionism and Eurocentric history.* New York, NY: Guilford Press.

Carvalho, L., and E. Costa. 2009. Production of OCDE's 'Programme for International Student Assessment' (PISA). Final report. Orientation 3 – WP 11, Project KNOWand-POL. http://www.knowandpol.eu/ (accessed March 20, 2011).

Chakrabarty, D. 2000. *Provincializing Europe: Postcolonial thought and historical difference.* Princeton, NJ: Princeton University Press.

Chow, R. 2002. *The protestant ethnic and the spirit of capitalism.* New York, NY: Columbia University Press.

Coates, H. 2011. AHELO feasibility study [PDF document]. http://www.acer.edu.au/documents/AHELOAU%20Hamish%20Coates%20Symposium%20Presentation.pdf (accessed February 20, 2012).

Connell, R. 2007. *Southern theory: The global dynamics of knowledge in social science.* Cambridge: Polity press.

Corbett, D. 2008. The Edumometer: The commodification of learning from Galton to the PISA. *Journal for Critical Education Policy Studies* 6, no. 1. http://www.jceps.com/?pageID=article&articleID=125.

Dale, R. 2005. Globalisation, knowledge economy and comparative education. *Comparative education* 41, no. 2: 117–49.

Dale, R., and S. Robertson. 2009. Capitalism, modernity, and the future of education in the new social contract. *Yearbook of the National Society for the Study of Education* 108, no. 2: 111–29.

Delgado, E., and R. Romero. 2000. Local histories and global designs: An interview with Walter Mignolo. *Discourse* 22, no. 3: 7–33.

Educational Testing Service (ETS). 2006. *A culture of evidence: Postsecondary assessment and learning outcomes*. Princeton, NJ: ETS.

Fairclough, N. 2003. *Analysing discourse: Textual analysis for social research*. New York, NY: Routledge.

Grek, S. 2009. Governing by numbers: The PISA 'effect' in Europe. *Journal of Education Policy* 24, no. 1: 23–37.

Henry, M., B. Lingard, F. Rizvi, and S. Taylor. 2001. *The OECD, globalization and education policy*. Oxford: Pergamon Press.

Kamens, D., and C. McNeely. 2010. Globalization and the growth of international educational testing and national assessment. *Comparative Education Review* 54, no. 1: 5–25.

King, R. 2009. *Governing universities globally: Organizations, regulation and ranking*. Cheltenham: Edward Elgar.

Lederman, D. 2010, January 28. Measuring student learning, globally. Inside higher education. http://www.insidehighered.com/news/2010/01/28/oecd.

Lewis, R. 2009. Quality assurance in higher education – its global future. In *To 2030: Volume 2 globalisation*, ed. Higher Education, 323–52. Paris: CERI.

Luke, A. 2011. Generalizing across borders: Policy and limits of educational science. *Educational Researcher* 40, no. 8: 367–77.

Marginson, S. 2008. Global field and global imagining: Bourdieu and worldwide higher education. *British Journal of Sociology of Education* 29, no. 3: 303–15.

Martens, K., A. Rusconi, and K. Leuze, eds. 2007. *New arenas of education governance: The impact of international organizations and markets on educational policy making*. New York, NY: Palgrave Macmillan.

Merriam, S. 1998. *Qualitative research and case study applications in education*. San Francisco, CA: Jossey-Bass.

Mignolo, W. 1999. *The darker side of the renaissance: Literacy, territoriality and colonization*. 2nd ed. Ann Arbor, MI: The University of Michigan Press.

Mignolo, W. 2000. *Local histories/global designs: Coloniality, subaltern knowledges and border thinking*. Princeton, NJ: Princeton University Press.

Mignolo, W. 2003. Globalization and the geopolitics of knowledge: The role of the humanities in the corporate university. *Nepantla: Views from South* 4, no. 1: 97–119.

Mignolo, W. 2005. *The idea of Latin America*. Malden, MA: Blackwell.

Morgan, C. 2009. *The OECD programme for international student assessment: Unraveling a knowledge network*. Saarbrucken: VDM Verlag Dr. Muller.

Naidoo, R. 2011. Rethinking development: Higher education and the new imperialism. In *Handbook of globalization and higher education*, ed. R. King, S. Marginson, and R. Naidoo, 40–58. Cheltenham: Edward Elgar.

OECD. 2007a. *Assessing higher education learning outcomes summary of first meeting of experts*. Paris: OECD. www.oecd.org/dataoecd/15/5/39117243.pdf (accessed May 16, 2010).

OECD. 2007b. *Assessing higher education learning outcomes summary of second meeting of experts*. Paris: OECD. www.oecd.org/edu/highereducationandadultlearning/39117295.pdf (accessed May 16, 2010).

OECD. 2009. *The OECD assessment of higher education learning outcomes (AHELO) brochure*. Paris: OECD. http://www.oecd.org/dataoecd/3/13/42803845.pdf (accessed May 16, 2010).

OECD. 2010a. *OECD feasibility study for the international assessment of higher education learning outcomes 2010–2011 brochure.* Paris: OECD. http://www.oecd.org/dataoecd/37/49/45755875.pdf (accessed May 19, 2010).

OECD. 2010b. *OECD: About IMHE.* Paris: OECD. http://www.oecd.org/dataoecd/28/41/46178955.pdf (accessed October 27, 2010).

OECD. 2010c. *Roadmap for the AHELO feasibility study – 3rd version.* Paris: IMHE. http://www.oecd.org/officialdocuments/displaydocumentpdf/?cote=EDU/IMHE/AHELO/GNE(2010)4&doclanguage=en (accessed April 23, 2010).

OECD. 2010d. *Group of national experts on the AHELO feasibility study: Progress report (abridged).* October 2010 meeting. http://www.oecd.org/officialdocuments/displaydocumentpdf?cote=EDU/IMHE/AHELO/GNE(2010)13/FINAL&doclanguage=en (accessed September 15, 2010).

OECD. 2010e. *Progress report on generic skills strand: March 2010 meeting.* Paris: OECD. http://www.oecd.org/officialdocuments/displaydocumentpdf/?cote=EDU/IMHE/AHELO/GNE(2010)2&doclanguage=en (accessed May 16, 2011).

OECD. 2010f. *Summary of progress: AHELO generic skills strand. October 2010 meeting.* http://www.oecd.org/officialdocuments/displaydocumentpdf/?cote=edu/imhe/ahelo/gne(2010)14&doclanguage=en (accessed May 17, 2011).

OECD. 2010g. *AHELO assessment design.* http://www.oecd.org/officialdocuments/displaydocumentpdf/?cote=edu/imhe/ahelo/gne(2010)17&doclanguage=en (accessed May 16, 2011).

OECD. 2011a. *AHELO project update – May 2011.* Paris: OECD. http://www.oecd.org/dataoecd/8/26/48088270.pdf (accessed November 20, 2011).

OECD. 2011b. *Testing student and university performance globally: OECD's AHELO.* http://www.oecd.org/document/22/0,3746,en_2649_35961291_40624662_1_1_1_1,00.html (accessed November 20, 2011).

OECD. 2011c. *AHELO newsletter – May 2011.* http://www.oecd.org/dataoecd/17/63/47932932.pdf (accessed November 20, 2011).

OECD. 2011d. *Progress report on the generic skills strand.* Paris: OECD. http://www.oecd.org/officialdocuments/displaydocumentpdf/?cote=edu/imhe/ahelo/gne(2011)3&doclanguage=en (accessed November 15, 2011).

OECD. 2012a. *Interim feasibility study report – executive summary.* http://www.oecd.org/officialdocuments/displaydocumentpdf/?cote=edu/imhe/ahelo/gne%282012%296&doclanguage=en (accessed April 20, 2012).

OECD. 2012b. *Testing student and university performance globally: OECD's AHELO.* http://www.oecd.org/document/22/0,3746,en_2649_39263238_40624662_1_1_1_1,00.html (accessed April 10, 2012).

Ozga, J. 2000. *Policy research in educational settings: Contested terrain.* Buckingham: Open University Press.

Pereyra, M., H. Kotthoff, and R. Cowen. 2011. *PISA under examination.* Rotterdam: Sense Publisher.

Peters, M. 2001. National education policy constructions of the 'knowledge economy': Towards a critique. *Journal of Educational Enquiry* 2, no. 1: 1–22.

Pratt, M.L. 1992. *Imperial eyes: Travel writing and transculturation.* London: Routledge.

Rhee, J. 2009. International education, the new imperialism, and technologies of the self: Branding the globally educated elite. *Multicultural Education Review* 1, no. 1: 55–82.

Richardson, L., and E.A. St. Pierre. 2005. Writing: A method of inquiry. In *The Sage handbook of qualitative research*, 3rd ed., ed. N. Denzin and Y. Lincoln, 959–78. Thousand Oaks, CA: Sage.

Rizvi, F., and B. Lingard. 2010. *Globalizing education policy.* New York, NY: Routledge.

Robertson, S. 2009. Market multilateralism, the World Bank, and the asymmetries of globalizing higher education: Toward a critical political economy analysis. In *International organizations and higher education policy: Thinking globally, acting locally?*, ed. R. Bassett and A. Maldonado, 113–31. New York, NY: Routledge.

Saarinen, T. 2008. Persuasive presuppositions in OECD and EU higher education policy documents. *Discourse Studies* 10, no. 3: 341–59.

Shahjahan, R.A. 2011. Decolonizing the evidence-based education and policy movement: Revealing the colonial vestiges in educational policy, research, and neoliberal reform. *Journal of Education Policy* 26, no. 2: 181–206.

Shahjahan, R.A. 2012. The roles of international organizations (IOs) in globalizing higher education policy. In *Higher education: Handbook of theory and research*, Vol. 27, ed. J. Smart and M. Paulsen, 369–407. Dordrecht: Springer.

Shahjahan, R.A., and L. Torres. 2011. Unpacking the PISA of higher education: OECD, higher education policy and the AHELO Initiative. Paper presented at the Annual Meeting of the American Education Research Association (AERA), April 10, in New Orleans, Louisiana.

Sidhu, R. 2006. *Universities and globalization: To market, to market.* Mahwah, NJ: Lawrence Erlbaum.

Smith, L. 1999. *Decolonizing methodologies: Research and indigenous peoples.* London: Zed Books.

Spivak, G.C. 1999. *A critique of postcolonial reason: Toward a history of the vanishing present.* Cambridge, MA: Harvard University Press.

Stanfield, J.H. 1999. Slipping through the front door: Relevant social sciences in the people of color century. *American Journal of Evaluation* 20, no. 3: 415–31.

Stewart-Harawira, M. 2005. *The new imperial order: Indigenous responses to globalization.* London: Zed Books.

Thiongo, N.W. 1986. *Decolonising the mind: The politics of language in African literature.* Oxford: James Currey.

Tikly, L. 2004. Education and the new imperialism. *Comparative Education* 40, no. 2: 173–98.

Woodward, R. 2009. *The Organization for Economic Co-operation and Development (OECD).* New York, NY: Routledge.

Expert moves: international comparative testing and the rise of expertocracy

Sotiria Grek

School of Social and Political Science, University of Edinburgh, Edinburgh, UK

Through a sociological analysis of the knowledge and actors that have become central to international assessments, the paper focuses on the processes that influence the production of shared narratives and agendas, adopting the position that their existence is not organic, but rather the product of undertakings that often fabricate and manage, rather than strive for 'real' consensus. The paper suggests that limiting the analysis to the role of travel and exchanges of experts and policy-makers in the making of policy is, in fact, the construction of an 'ideal-type' of an international policy-making world. Recent research on these encounters suggests that one needs to focus on actors' conflict and struggles, rather than processes of 'collective puzzling'. Using the concept of 'political work', as well as elements of Bourdieu's field theory, the paper shows the ways that international comparative testing in the field of education has not only offered policy-makers with much needed data to govern, but has in fact almost fused the realms of knowledge and policy; expertise and the selling of undisputed, universal policy solutions have now drifted into one single entity and function.

Introduction

International comparative testing and its results have become the lifeblood of education governance in Europe and globally. This paper is located in the field of the transnational governance of education and aims to offer an explanation of the work of governing through a sociological analysis of the knowledge and actors that have become central to it over the last decade.

In particular, national educational systems have been increasingly regulated externally through OECD and European Union (EU) performance measurement tools. These include a number of explicit regulatory mechanisms, which they either lead or support, such as the open method of coordination or the millennium development goals, as well as more 'implicit' governing technologies, such as large international comparative tests, which have had significant effects on the governing of European education systems and the governance of learning in Europe overall. This paper investigates the development of similar testing in the field of adult literacy. It regards these tests as critical, as their scope is progressively changing to blend learning with the societal and economistic goals of measuring – and hence improving – labour market outcomes. I am equally interested in the knowledge produced through the

157

'test', as well as a sociology of the actors that construct and mobilise it. In particular, in regard to the EU, which European Commission actors participate in these developments, why and with what effects? What is the role of experts in producing and pushing this agenda forward?

The paper takes advantage of this major, currently unfolding development to examine the tensions in 'hard' and 'soft' governing forms. 'Hard' governing forms could be described as the continuous production of data to foster competition, for example, target setting, performance management, benchmarks and indicators, while newer 'soft' governing forms, appear to be operating through attraction (Lawn and Grek 2012); in other words, drawing people in to take part in processes of mediation, brokering and 'translation', and embedding self-governance and steering at a distance though these processes and relations. Thus, I will focus on the processes of construction of international comparative testing more generally and especially in relation to adult skills, and examine the extent to, and means by which the 'political work' undertaken through them does not only represent a technocratic exercise in order to fabricate an improved measuring instrument, but also a political technology, which aims at securing consensus amongst participant actors and winning 'hearts and minds'. This, although not an officially declared mission, nevertheless is a recurrent theme of discussions not only in the field of international testing, but in other sites of international debate and decision-making as well (e.g. the EU2020 political agenda).

The paper builds on current ESRC-funded research entitled 'Transnational policy learning: a comparative study of OECD and EU education policy in constructing the skills and competencies agenda' (2010–2012) (RES-000-22-3429) and uses mainly qualitative data derived from observations, interviews and discourse analysis of policy materials. It is structured as follows: first, I give an overview of the global context within which international comparative testing has been emerging and continue by discussing the theoretical underpinnings of the research project the paper uses data from. I then move on to a discussion of three specific adult literacy studies, the International Adult Literacy Survey (IALS), the Adult Literacy and Life Skills Study (ALL) and the Definition and Selection of Competencies project (DeSeCo) and finish off with a critique of the scholarly literature which sees the policy learning that emerges from the development of international comparative assessment as merely a process of consensus building. Instead, I argue for the need to sociologically analyse knowledge and actors for the study of education governance in Europe today, by focusing not only on the common and collective processes of meaning-making, but crucially on those less known and hidden conflicts and struggles amongst actors in the policy field.

The global context

This analysis is built onto three significant premises. First, that the demands of governing at a distance have resulted in the development of a complex and ever-evolving system of global accountability based on the calculation of national performance through the devising and – in some 'deviant' cases the stringent – monitoring of performance data. Second, the economic crisis which began in 2008 and has recently culminated in events that threaten the very existence of the monetary and indeed the EU itself, appears to be directing governing efforts towards the construction of a new social contract between governments and populations, one that will not depend solely on the economy as an indicator of progress, but rather on more positive, 'soft' indicators such as learning and well-being. This, I would suggest is not simply a change of focus and political direction; rather, it constitutes a sustained effort to search and find legitimacy for the work of governing, at times when the latter has been increasingly disputed and even fought against in many European and world cities by 'indignant' citizens and especially the youth, whose future life chances education is meant to improve. Finally, the third premise builds on Massey's (2005) work on the limits of the geographical imagination of many scholars so far, who have put emphasis on the ways that the 'global' impacts on the 'national', but have failed to acknowledge the extent to which the national is critical, if not *the* critical element, in the formation of global policy agendas. Indeed, current research reinforces this argument, as it points towards the artificiality of 'levels' as distinct boundaries of political activity and instead emphasises the interdependency of actors and travelling ideas in the framing of problems and policy directions (Grek 2010).

Indeed, current efforts by the OECD, the United Nations, the World Bank and the European Commission aim to 'move beyond GDP' (Stiglitz, Sen, and Fitoussi 2009; EC 2010) and foster 'a global conversation' (Hall 2009) for the measurement of 'human progress'. According to the OECD, 'education [is] one of the key dimensions of progress' (Hall and Matthews 2008, 18). Further, education is often seen as instrumental to the development of attitudes and dispositions that will help counter 'megatrends', such as mistrust in national governments. International comparative testing appears then as much more than simply a statistical project; it has become part of consistent efforts to restore legitimacy and trust between populations and their governments. As Hall contends, 'building legitimacy requires potential users in the process, as well as technical experts. The most important role of indicator sets may be in framing the issues and defining the problems, rather than suggesting the solutions' (Hall 2009). The discursive construction of international comparative assessments is part and parcel of the larger and more challenging task not only to create a set of measurable objectives for national governments, but in fact envelop the discourse around 'trust in numbers' with *meaning*; for example, the call for indicators to become more meaningful and open to a far greater variety of stakeholders, who can appropriate and 'believe' in them, rather than simply calculate them, is at the heart not only of education governance, but wider European and global governance developments.

Indeed, the governance of international comparative testing reflects these values. Project boards usually work in conjunction with a large range of consortia of international partners and technical advisors (statisticians, media specialists and, interestingly, philanthropists); they also consult with a vast array of different actor groupings, such as academics, private companies, policy-makers, associates, country correspondents, regional working groups and others. Regular training courses are delivered as well as seminars, and regional, thematic and global conferences. All these initiatives suggest sustained efforts to include and create consensus with the greatest number of stakeholders possible. The aim of this paper is to examine how such consensus is achieved; through ethnographic study and sociological analysis of how these meetings are organised and run, it offers a closer view and understanding of the work of governing at the level of the transnational.

Theoretical frame and key intermediary concepts

In order to understand this emergent reality, one needs to start with a broad theoretical frame that might help think and analyse the relationship between the production of *knowledge and policy*, as well as examine current trends in that relationship. Ozga (2011) distinguishes 'post-bureaucratic' from conventional 'bureaucratic' regimes, by suggesting that each presupposes a specific kind of knowledge and a specific way of using it. While bureaucratic modes of government require 'established' bodies of knowledge to be translated into 'vertical' relations, post-bureaucratic modes of governance consist rather in attempting to turn actors' autonomy and reflexivity into means of governing. Therefore, instead of placing the state at the centre and consider the national as an autonomous entity (as subsidiarity rules might have defined it in the past), where knowledge is produced by few professionals and academics for the benefit of the 'nation', post-bureaucracy is rather polycentric, by being simultaneously international, transnational, subnational *and* national. As a result, it is made up by a multiplicity of actors taking part not only in the policy process but – crucially for the focus of this paper – in the production of knowledge. Under post-bureaucracy, 'knowledge is pluralistic; it is flexible, provisional and it is always policy- and future-oriented' (Ozga 2011). Above all, it is comparable and can travel fast; it derives its legitimacy not only from scientific knowledge, but also from know-how and experience (Grek and Ozga 2010).

Secondly, the notion of *comparison* is seen as crucial, as it is through processes of constant comparison that national contexts have increasingly shed their bounded logics, in favour of achieving a place in the global 'order' – even when the national appears as nationalistic at times, it is more often than not because of its relentless exposure to the global 'other'. In fact, these processes increasingly appear as less and less voluntary – comparison is all-encompassing and often quite heavy handed, as the example of the PISA study and its effects on the education system in the 'failing' Germany has shown (Grek 2009). This is what Freeman described as living in Galton's world, 'a world of international interdependence, of the continuous, reciprocal reproduction of global and local … a world of comparison'. In this sense, comparison can be seen as not simply informative or even reflective – in fact, it fabricates new realities and hence has become a mode of knowledge production in itself (Freeman 2011).

A considerable body of research has already focused on the work of international organisations (IOs) in the field of education (see, e.g. Henry et al. 2001; Lawn and Lingard 2002; Ozga and Lingard 2007; Lawn 2003; Pépin 2006; Martens 2007); however, this research does not examine the interaction between them. IOs are often seen as monolithic institutions, or actors with similar interests in a similar context, without attention to the complex set of realities that bring them together and apart over time. In addition, IOs are often also seen as internally stable – this means that divisions of authority, institutionalised norms, expectations and values are thought to be commonly shared by all actors within an IO. Nevertheless, 'most of the time, […] at least some of the actors within an IO will be seeking to change at least some of its institutions, whilst others will work to retain their stasis' (Jullien and Smith 2011, 4). The examination of *actor alliance formation and mobilisation* is hence vital in order to understand these relations – both upstream, i.e. the setting of rules and problem framing, as well as downstream, namely the application and maintenance of rules amongst the actors who are all engaged in competitive relationships (Jullien and Smith 2011).

Thus, one of the key intermediary concepts that has mobilised the research behind this paper is the notion of 'political work' (Smith 2009), as it is very rich at a number of analytical levels. First, when one studies political work, institutions themselves are not the objects of study per se; rather, the focus of the investigation is on the continual cycle of institutionalisation, deinstitutionalisation and reinstitutionalisation of ideas and values within the organisation in question. The study of policy instruments like adult skills testing, can become a particularly fruitful context for such an analysis, as one can examine 'political work' as those processes that engender the construction of new arguments and the activation of new alliances, in order to spark processes of problematisation and hence either the politicisation or technisation of the problem in question; subsequently, they either produce change or reproduce institutions, namely actors' rules, norms and expectations (Jullien and Smith 2011).

Thus and to conclude this section, the paper suggests that in order to analyse global education governance, one needs to bring together two important, interdependent aspects; first, an empirical sociological analysis of knowledge as communicated through the construction of international tests; and, second, a sociology of the trajectories and positions of European and national education actors and groups who take part in these projects and also 'make' the European education policy space, by being active mediators between the two. Of course, the scope of this paper can only be far more limited than that; thus, it focuses on the processes that influence the production of shared narratives and agendas, adopting the ontological position that their existence is not organic, but rather the product of undertakings that often fabricate and manage rather than reach 'real' consensus.

International comparative testing and the skills agenda

Skills and competencies have been central to the OECD's work, as its most high-profile international assessment, PISA, has suggested. PISA has had a high impact on curriculum reform in several European countries by pushing education systems in the direction of more 'can-do' dispositions towards education, rather than more traditional pedagogic approaches (Grek 2009). PISA also built the OECD's image as a technically competent and scientifically robust organisation for performing such comparative ranking and ordering of national performance (Ozga et al. 2011). In addition, as we will examine further on, the OECD's DeSeCo project (1997–2005) was a major effort to provide 'a sound conceptual framework to inform the identification of key competencies, to strengthen international assessments, and to help to define overarching goals for education systems and lifelong learning' (DeSeCo homepage, see http://www.deseco.admin.ch/). Finally, prior to the development of the Programme for the International Assessment of Adult Competencies (PIAAC), the OECD had already conducted two international adult skill surveys: the IALS (1994–1998) and the ALL (2002–2006). It is to these three studies that we will now turn, in order to examine their development and reporting as key in the construction of very specific and influential policy directions in education in Europe in the post-Lisbon era.

The development of international adult literacy studies: IALS, ALL and DeSeCo

The IALS was the first and largest international comparative study of its kind. Conducted from the early 1990s, it was an innovative study, as it was the first time ever that an international comparative dimension was added to the construction of a literacy survey instrument. Thus, it heralded a new era in the construction and evolution of international comparative studies, as for the first time ever it gave international testing a comparative dimension, where measurement against other countries' performance offered unprecedented visibility and thus exposure. As it was an original and new endeavour, slowly at the start but increasingly later on, IALS boosted confidence in the construction of measurement tools of this kind, increased their persuasive power in regard to their validity and transparency, and created substantial revenues to the research agencies administering them. Finally, and perhaps above all, it created a circle of like-minded individuals, a 'magistracy' of influence (Lawn and Lingard 2002), who found in these studies a platform for promoting the problematisation of specific issues, their institutionalisation through their exchanges and the setting up of the study, as well as their legitimation, in the form of advice to failing countries, once the results were published.

IALS started as a nine-country initiative in 1994 (Canada, France, Germany, Ireland, the Netherlands, Poland, Sweden, Switzerland and the USA); it grew further later on, as five additional countries joined in 1996 (Australia, Flemish Belgium, the UK, New Zealand and Northern Ireland) and, finally, nine other countries or regions joined the study in 1998 (Chile, the Czech Republic, Denmark, Finland, Hungary, Italy, Norway, Slovenia and the Italian-speaking region of Switzerland). By the time the study was complete, it had reached the impressive number of 23 participating countries. It was also the first time that such a study established a cycle of data collection, involving three rounds of testing, thereby managing to get more support and momentum as it went on, as well as improve its tools and techniques. The study was led by the OECD, in collaboration with the EU and UNESCO, and administered by Statistics Canada, the Educational Testing Service (ETS) and the National Centre for Education Statistics (NCES) – all North American agencies.

IALS examined literacy 'as a particular capacity [information-processing competency] and mode of behaviour' and assessed performance levels 'along a continuum' (OECD 2000, iii). Individuals from age 16 to 65 took part in the study, with nationally representative samples, in order to 'provide insights for policy makers responsible for the design of lifelong learning, and social and labour market policies' (OECD 2000, xiii). In other words, high levels of literacy were presented as the essential ingredient of a flourishing society, without which, according to the study, 'globalisation, technological change and organisational development' (OECD 2000, xiii) – the challenges of the twenty-first century – could not be met.

Apart from relating skills to increased earnings, IALS also managed to skilfully connect literacy (and thus the findings of the study) with a range of other outcomes, such as social capital, community engagement, voluntary participation, social cohesion, political participation of women, better health and wider social benefits. 'Health literacy', for example, was to become a new measure of the ability of individuals to lead healthier lives, with literacy being seen as a mediating factor in health disparities (Rudd, Colton, and Schacht 2000). Through the masterly build-up of such a discourse, IALS – again, for the first time – was transcending the boundaries of education research, as it claimed to show the 'complex relationships between human capital, economic outcomes and social benefits' (OECD 2000, 84). Thus, with literacy being turned into not only the sine qua non of workplace learning, but almost the sine qua non of living, IALS was slowly managing to shift education policy into the foreground of the governance of high-achieving, well-to-do societies in Europe and beyond.

Above all, according to the OECD, IALS established 'a new standard for providing a theoretical basis for its measurement framework' (2000, 87–8) – hence, a new logic. It also followed 'an advanced psychometric approach', moving the focus to psychometric testing, and thus opening up the field to significant commercial interests. Finally, claiming to have achieved 'unprecedented levels of reliability in scoring open-ended items across cultures and languages', the study boasted the decontextualisation of literacy (OECD 2000, 87–8). This was a new argument in the field of literacy studies, which was essentially sideling the New Literacy studies field; the latter proclaims that literacy has meaning only within its particular context of social practice and does not transfer unproblematically across contexts (Barton and Hamilton 1998). Indeed, the management of the study received a lot of criticism precisely because of the relative lack of literacy specialists involved in its design (Blum, Goldstein, and Guerin-Pace 2001, 226), some of whom were taking particular issue with the study's assumption that a valid common definition of literacy across cultures could be established (Street 1996; Hamilton and Barton 2000). In fact, some critics went as far as to argue that 'those involved in the IALS research are testers and technicians, committed to quantitative methodologies' (Hamilton and Barton 2000, 379). In a similar manner, Harvey Goldstein elsewhere argued that the technical complexity of studies such as IALS often acts as a well built and fixed barrier that protects their designers (usually technical experts), by shielding them away from the critical comments of subject specialists. In fact, Goldstein contends that this is 'fertile ground for the psychometrician to dominate the debate, invoking the high status generally associated with mathematical reasoning', as well as simultaneously attracting 'powerful commercial interests in the shape of largely US testing agencies as providers of sophisticated know-how' (Goldstein 1998, no page numbers). He continues:

> Subject matter specialists are involved in designing questions and tasks but thereafter they assume a much more passive role. If they are brave enough to suggest that some complexities have been overlooked then they may well be dismissed as having not properly understood the technicalities. (Goldstein 1998, np)

To conclude, IALS created fertile ground for the OECD to push its education policy agenda, through measurement and comparison that would 'provide empirically grounded interpretation upon which to inform policy decisions' (Kirsch 2001,1). As Irwin Kirsch, director of the Centre for Global Assessment at the ETS, suggested:

> … while the chief benefit of constructing and validating a framework for literacy is improved measurement, a number of other potential benefits are also evident. Namely:
> -A framework provides a *common language and a vehicle for discussing* the definition of the skill area;
> -Such a discussion allows us to build *consensus* around the framework and measurement goals;
> -An analysis of the kinds of knowledge and skills associated with successful performance provides an *empirical basis* for communicating a richer body of information to various constituencies. (Kirsch 2001, 2, my emphasis)

Finally, the study did what all such studies always do – it created the need for the design and delivery of yet another study of its kind. That was the ALL.

The processes that initiated the construction of ALL can merely be described as the mobilisation of a large number of experts, statisticians and national policy-makers in a series of meetings across Europe; of course, most of them were people already having been involved in IALS and thus already in broad agreement about the purposes and operationalization of the new study. Therefore, the first meeting of these actors, hosted by the Swedish Educational Authority (Skolverket), decided to build on IALS in order to create a survey that would look at foundational skills, such as prose literacy, document literacy, numeracy and problem-solving, as well as familiarity with and use of information and communication technologies. Statistics Canada suggested that the study be organised as a computer-based assessment of samples of workers derived from within firms in order to produce 'explicit statistical linkages … to isolate the impact of observed skill on economic productivity and indicators of firm success such as employment growth and profitability' (Murray, Owen, and McGaw 2005, 13). There was a decision to organise a second meeting of the group, at the University of Amsterdam, in order to discuss the possibility of such a study. However, the operational implications of fielding a computer-based assessment were insurmountable at the time. A third meeting, closer to the study's home this time at the NCER's headquarters in Washington DC, concluded 'on pragmatic grounds' (Murray, Owen, and McGaw 2005, 13) that the test would be undertaken using the humble paper and pencil, and that the sample would be drawn from households rather than the workplace.

As a result of the two meetings, a Project Advisory Group (PAG) was formed in order to work further in refining the transnational comparability of the measures for numeracy, problem-solving, teamwork and practical cognition. Two subsequent meetings of the international study team were hosted by the US National Center for Education Statistics in Washington in 1998, in order to work on more accurate measures for problem-solving, teamwork and computer literacy, resulting in new development teams being recruited and funded by Statistics Canada, NCES and the Governments of Sweden and Luxembourg. Additional meetings were held in the USA: first, a meeting of all development team leaders in Washington in January 1999 'to help integrate the different assessments and to provide expert feedback' (Murray, Owen, and McGaw 2005, 14); second, another meeting of the development team leaders was held in Princeton in August of the same year 'to review the frameworks' (Murray, Owen, and McGaw 2005, 14). Finally, a separate international team developed the background questionnaire for the study.

The sheer number of meetings organised merely to initiate the workings of these groups of experts is such that, analytically, one cannot but underline the significance and impact of meetings in the transfer of ideas at a global level. In fact, it was not simply necessity that pushed their organisation. Instead, meetings became a significant means of pushing the agenda forward, as:

> … success in this complex field depends not only on theoretical and empirical work, but also on a constant dialogue and exchange among the various specialists and stakeholders to assure that an iterative process takes place. (Murray, Owen, and McGaw 2005, 33)

Finally, a parallel development to the design and implementation of the ALL study was the development of another project focusing on defining and measuring competences – the DeSeCo: Theoretical and Conceptual Foundations project, launched in 1997. DeSeCo was primarily a theory-oriented study that would complement the work that was being done in a range of studies, designed either to be implemented in the near future, or taking place at the time. These assessments were TIMSS (the International Association for the Evaluation of Educational Achievement [IEA] study), IALS, ALL and PISA. More interestingly, DeSeCo, as well as theoretically backing the empirical work that these studies were undertaking, offered another crucial means of support to them, as it facilitated further exchanges and meetings between experts in the field. Indeed, the number and variety of stakeholders involved was wide, as the project brought together 'sociologists, economists, anthropologists, philosophers, psychologists, a historian, education researchers, statisticians, assessment specialists, policy-makers and policy analysts, unionists, employers and other stakeholders' (Murray, Clermost and Binkley 2005, 34), representing various sectors and national and international institutions. As with IALS, drawing on what the study claimed to be 'a common vision of society as a normative anchoring point', DeSeCo built a 'demand-oriented approach to competence', which 'designates a complex action system encompassing cognitive and non-cognitive components', in order to create today's 'flexible, adaptive, innovative, creative, self-directed, self-motivated and responsible ... learner, worker, citizen, family member, or consumer' (Murray, Owen, and McGaw 2005, 36).

To conclude this section, three crucial points have to be raised in relation to the history of the development of adult literacy studies in the 1990s and 2000s. Interestingly, all of them, as their designers themselves suggest, moved policy directions and thus policy-makers and nations 'towards a common, coherent international discourse on competence and skill development' (Murray, Owen, and McGaw 2005, 39). What they have also done – and they themselves proclaim – is create 'a bridge between student and adult competence assessments' (Murray, Owen, and McGaw 2005, 42), thus breaking down the boundaries between schooling and the rest of the lifecourse. This is important because after claiming to have achieved decontextualisation, these studies made for the first time a move towards the deinstitutionalisation of learning, and thus bringing lifelong learning to the fore of education governance – the late 1990s–early 2000s was the period when lifelong learning was becoming the sine qua non of all education policy reforms in Europe. Finally, international comparative testing, as with the studies described briefly above, appear to have created a decisive and undisputed starting point, on the basis of which all similar debate and work would now have to build on; re-inventing the wheel, apart from being time inefficient is also very costly. Finally, they established networks of experts in the field – a field which exceeds the limits of achieving educational success to the much larger and all-encompassing idea of reaching personal and societal 'well-being':

> It *is important to build future assessment on existing studies, expertise and knowledge, thus not to reinvent the wheel* ... DeSeCo and ALL have established networks of researchers that can contribute – from different perspectives – to continued research on key competencies and the educational, social, and economic factors that contribute to improve the education and training and to enhanced returns on investments in competencies in terms of personal, economic, and social well-being. (Murray, Owen, and McGaw 2005, 43; my emphasis)

Expectocracy moves and rules

The account of the development of the early adult literacy studies shows some of the reasons why international comparative testing became one of the prime instruments in the steering and exchange of governing knowledge in education in Europe today. The stories of IALS, ALL but similarly PISA and PIAAC as other research has shown (Grek 2009, 2012), have created the necessary preconditions for achieving policy understanding, travel, translation and thus, despite local idiosyncrasies and histories, policy consensus. Nonetheless, the narration of a story of meetings, and perhaps more importantly the narration of a story of dinners, drinks and research tourism, could potentially misguide towards the creation of a picture of genuine debate and the building of real friendships and collaborations. Indeed, in one of my earlier papers, I argued for the significance of 'learning by meeting' (Grek 2012) and, following Freeman's work on public policy learning, suggested that:

> ... increasingly members of this 'small community' like each other, they learn to work together, they call one another, and finally become friends. We trust to learn from friends, rather than strangers (Forrester 1999), especially when these friends provide us with the information we need. Friends are those that understand our situation and the values which inform our choices (Freeman 2008); they help us deliberate and offer persuasive arguments to be used in more hostile contexts. (Grek 2012, 56)

Nonetheless, more recent work on the development of the PIAAC study, reveals that the analysis above is perhaps closer to the construction of an 'ideal-type' of a policy-making world; on the contrary, a close examination of the production and exchange of knowledge and learning transnationally creates quite a different and more complicated picture, rather than the one described above. This is indeed a world of travel, exchange and collaboration, and certainly a place where new friendships can be built; nonetheless more often than not these exchanges take place in an increasingly competitive field, where most large international research organisations strive to secure the limited and diminishing funding available from national governments for the conduct of these studies. As a result, collaboration amongst them for the delivery of studies and the collection of education statistics is not a choice anymore, but rather a plain necessity. This is a fairly new development in the field of international comparative testing, the history of which, especially if one is to consider the two main organisations delivering such studies, the OECD and the IEA has not always been a rosy one – in fact, digging a bit deeper in the relationships between them and speaking with some of the key actors involved in both, one is soon confronted with a history of accusations for the stealing of methods and technical expertise for the delivery of international assessments. On the other hand, a closer examination of the relationship between the OECD and the European Commission Directorate General Education and Culture (DG EAC) is again one of strife and conflict – the ideological struggle between them, although lessened since the launch of the Lisbon Strategy, is still present with some of its staff, who see their own work at DG EAC as focused on the more social and democratic function of education, rather than its direct linking with economistic goals and outcomes. Returning to the IEA and OECD's 'undeclared war', the quotation below is enlightening:

> The main reason is that they are competitors and both in scientific and in financial terms it is getting more and more difficult to conduct these surveys. There was a message from member states to the OECD and the IEA – get together, sit down and

discuss it and do it. Now, 6 months later, we all come together and we ask what was the result of that meeting and the answer was that we didn't find a date. They don't work together because they don't like each other. (EC9)

Interviewees also describe internal conflict within IOs and their departments, for example within the OECD itself. The following quotation describes the conflict between CERI (the Centre for Educational Research and Innovation) and the Directorate of Education, similar to the kinds of processes Jullien and Smith (2011) describe when they discuss IOs as internally unstable institutions, rather than the opposite:

They live in different worlds – the same floor at the OECD but in different worlds. They don't like each other – one is more research-based, the other one more indicators and data, surveys. One is more reflection, the other one is more publicity, the charts – different traditions, the same director. (EC12)

Finally, another account which describes the conflict and competition for securing contracts for education research in Europe, comes from another interviewee, a key member of staff of one of the Commission's research agencies:

I think because the OECD is very much looking for member states' subsidies and grants and financial support for each separate research activity, they are also keen in showing that they do something unique and innovative in order to get such funding. And so then in a way they are in competition with us. An example is they did a recent policy review which is called 'Learning for Jobs' which basically deals with VET. And they didn't invite us to some national expert groups and so on that are in development – and they did very little use of our work because they wanted to do something that was different and specific so that they could sell it to the member states – this is my interpretation, of course. But I think that there is this kind of competition, differentiation between European institutions because we are in competition for funding. (EC3)

The quotations above come in stark contrast to descriptions of a field of actors who come together regularly and on equal terms to achieve consensus for the pushing of certain agendas. On the contrary, they highlight the need to also focus our attention and study on those meetings that *never* happen, as well as those actors who are consistently *not* invited to expert meetings. As the case of the New Literacy academics, who were regularly and persistently excluded from the production of the ALL study that we saw above, the quotations in this section direct us to an understanding of a field, which is more often than not riddled with internal and external competition for funding, especially in times of reducing national budgets in an era of austerity. Nonetheless, the emerging data make the whole picture even more interesting, especially given the supposed significance of the meeting for the development of shared understandings (Freeman 2011). Here is another European Commission actor:

We create an expert group, we do the same as the OECD, we ask member states to designate experts ... Actually member states are represented by different people who have different views around the same questions. Very often I would almost kill myself at the meetings because I would say, well that is what we've just decided with the member states yesterday. And the member states were sitting there, saying we've never heard of it. And we don't agree ... What you discover ... is that people don't know each other – they don't even know the others exist. They have never heard of them. They come from different institutions, different backgrounds, different interests, policies, objectives. The member states are not even aware of these contradictions. The result of it is that they don't have any influence. (EC10)

And he continues:

> ... I am not sure if it is in the interest of the OECD or the Commission to solve that problem – because these institutions will benefit from that – the more they contradict each other, the more the institutions decide .... And with OECD, surely it is the same. This is so obvious – that's what they do – OECD is Andreas. We always have a joke with Andreas – where he is brilliant, is to conclude. He is fantastic in this – conclusions! He is the conclusions expert – they are in before the meeting (laughs) ... It is very convenient. (EC10)

This paper intended to analyse and explain the significance of the expert travels and moves for the construction of a space of equivalence, where policy objectives can now be shared and where improvement of performance is achieved through constant comparison. At the same time, however, as its title tried to suggest as well, it also attempted to give another dimension to this emergent knowledge and policy world, where the 'expert moves' of IOs, such as OECD's impressive capacity to bring together and effectively steer debate towards predetermined decisions – like the very eloquently put quotation above suggests – has effectively become *the* reason why the OECD's influence has been key in the construction of the European education policy space. In other words, OECD's capacity has not only been its ability to 'move' experts around the world and bring them together around the same table, but also to then effectively steer and direct them towards its own prespecified agenda.

Discussion

A number of issues arise from the inquiry above – as this research and analysis of its findings are currently ongoing, one could only arrive at some preliminary conclusions. In the introductory sections of the paper, I suggested the significance of a combination of a sociological analysis of knowledge and actors in order to cast light on the workings and ways of education governance in Europe today. The concept of 'political work' is therefore a very useful one, as through an observation of the everyday, routine work as identified through the close observation of meetings and detailed analyses of the documents produced through them, one can perhaps appreciate the persistent and continuous labour required before consensus and decision-making can be achieved – in other words, both the necessary movement and travel of experts, but also all those expert OECD moves in order to arrive at conclusions 'together'.

I would suggest that if one was to highlight one key issue from this paper, that it would probably be the relationship between the production of knowledge and policy. In previous work, we suggested that if one wants to predict and understand why and where policy is moving towards, then one should be looking at the management of knowledge, rather than policy itself (Grek and Ozga 2010); this is largely confirmed from the description of the development of the early adult literacy studies above. Although there is a vast literature on the knowledge and policy continuum, I would contend that what we are confronted with here is a new governing reality altogether. What was discussed in this paper is not simply a case of knowledge *informing* policy; it is in fact fusion of the two realms in such a conscious and strategic manner that raises very interesting questions regarding the extent of the technicisation and depoliticisation of education problems or, for that matter, the problem of governing per se. In a way, the case of the international comparative assessment could potentially be viewed as 'prototypical': we could speculate that studying this example may help us understand a phenomenon of growing significance not only in the field of education governance, but in governing terms more generally: that is, the shift from previous accounts of 'knowledge *and* policy' or 'knowledge *in* policy' to almost a new reality where knowledge *is* policy – it *becomes* policy, since expertise and the selling of undisputed, universal policy solutions drift into one single entity and function.

Thus, drawing on Bourdieu, education governance appears as a field of actors who constantly negotiate and push their own agendas forward; according to Bourdieu (1993), the logic of positionality is what gives the notion of the 'field' meaning. In other words, the positions occupied by the different agents in the field, their advances and withdrawals, relate to their efforts for distinction within this field as an expression of their professional, educational or other interests. Meanwhile, the structure of the field is neither static, nor does it change in any systematic way. On the contrary, it is endlessly reformulated, according to the agents' struggles for recognition and improvement of their situation. Agents use the force of their capital, economic, social, cultural or in the case under examination, knowledge capital, to raise their game and advance their front. Nevertheless, it is the *relational* nature of these advances that gives the field its explanatory significance. In this sense, all expert new and old love affairs and wars I discussed earlier appear as not merely a parallel development or processes to be investigated separate from the policy field. On the contrary, it increasingly looks as if this *is* the policy field; it is where ideas move around and either become extinct or rule. This paper has argued that it is not only in the consensus or translations or shared meaning that we need to focus our attention and inquisitive potential on, but also and crucially in the competition and struggles amongst these actors.

References

Barton, D., and M. Hamilton. 1998. *Local literacies*. London: Routledge.

Blum, A., H. Goldstein, and F. Guerin-Pace. 2001. International Adult Literacy Survey (IALS): An analysis of international comparisons of adult literacy. *Assessment in Education: Principle, Policy and Practice* 8, no. 2: 225–246.

Bourdieu, P. 1993. *The field of cultural production*. Cambridge: Polity Press.

European Commission. 2010. Communication from the commission: Europe 2020 – a strategy for smart, sustainable and inclusive growth, COM (2010) 2020.

Forrester, J. 1999. *The deliberative practitioner: Encouraging participatory planning processes*. Cambridge, MA: MIT Press.

Freeman, R. 2008. Learning by meeting. *Critical Policy Analysis* 2, no. 1: 1–24.

Freeman, R. 2011. Comparison and performance. Draft Working Paper.

Goldstein, H. 1998. Models for reality: New approaches to the understanding of the educational process. Professorial lecture given at the Institute of Education, July 1, in London, UK. http://www.bristol.ac.uk/cmm/team/hg/models-for-reality.pdf (accessed 23 May, 2012).

Grek, S. 2009. Governing by numbers: The PISA effect in Europe'. *Journal of Education Policy* 24, no. 1: 23–37.

Grek, S. 2010. International organisations and the shared construction of policy 'problems': Problematisation and change in education governance in Europe. *European Educational Research Journal* 9, no. 3: 396–406.

Grek, S. 2012. The black box revisited: International comparative studies as tools in governing Europe. In *World yearbook of education 2012 – policy borrowing and lending*, ed. Gita Steiner-Khamsi and Florian Waldow, 41–61. London: Routledge.

Grek, S., and J. Ozga. 2010. Re-inventing public education: The new role of knowledge in education policy-making. *Public Policy and Administration* 25, no. 3: 271–288.

Hall, J. 2009. The global project measuring the progress of societies: A toolkit for practitioners. Presentation from the 3rd OECD World Forum, Busan. http://www.oecd.org/site/progresskorea/44117539.pdf.

Hall, J., and E. Matthews. 2008. The measurement of progress and the role of education. *European Journal of Education* 43, no. 1: 11–22.

Hamilton, M., and D. Barton. 2000. The international adult literacy survey: What does it really measure? *International Review of Education – Internationale Zeitschrift für Erziehungswissenschaft – Revue Internationale de l'Education* 46, no. 5: 377–389.

Henry, M., B. Lingard, F. Rizvi, and S. Taylor. 2001. *The OECD, globalization and education policy*. Oxford: Pergamon Press.

Jullien, B., and A. Smith 2011. Conceptualising the role of politics in the economy: Industries and their institutionalizations. *Review of International Political Economy*, 18, no. 3: 358.

Kirsch, I. 2001. The international adult literacy survey (IALS): Understanding what was measured. Research Report RR-01-25. Princeton, NJ: Educational Testing Service, Statistics and Research Division.

Lawn, M. 2003. The 'usefulness' of learning: The struggle over governance, meaning and the European education space. *Discourse: Studies in the Cultural Politics of Education* 24, no. 3: 325–336.

Lawn, M., and S. Grek. 2012. *Europeanising education: Governing a new policy space*. Oxford: Symposium.

Lawn, M., and B. Lingard. 2002. Constructing a European policy space in educational governance. The role of transnational policy actors. *European Educational Research Journal* 1, no. 2: 290–307.

Martens, K. 2007. How to become an influential actor: The 'comparative turn' in OECD education policy. In *Transformations of the state and global governance*, ed. K. Martens, A. Rusconi, and K. Lutz, 40–56. London: Routledge.

Massey, D.B. 2005. *For space*. London: Sage.

Murray, S., Y. Clermont, and M. Binkley. 2005. *Measuring adult literacy and life skills: New frameworks for assessment*, Catalogue no. 89-552-MIE, no. 13, Statistics Canada: Ottawa.

Murray, T.S., E. Owen, and B. McGaw. 2005. *Learning a living: First results of the adult literacy and life skills survey*. Ottawa: Statistics Canada and the Organization for Cooperation and Development.

OECD, Statistics Canada. 2000. *Literacy in the information age: Final report of the international adult literacy survey*. Paris: OECD and Ottawa.

Ozga, J. 2011. Bureaucracy, post-bureaucracy and the role of knowledge. Lecture at the Final FP6 'Knowledge and Policy' project conference, September 2011, in Brussels.

Ozga, J., P. Dahler-Larsen, C. Segerholm, and H. Simola, eds. 2011. *Fabricating quality in education: Data and governance in Europe*. London: Routledge.

Ozga, J., and B. Lingard. 2007. Globalisation, education policy and politics. In *The Routledge Falmer reader in education policy and politics*, ed. Bob. Lingard and Jenny. Ozga, 65–82. London: RoutledgeFalmer.

Pépin, L. 2006. *The history of European cooperation in education and training: Europe in the making – an example*. Luxembourg: Office for Official Publications of the European Communities.

Rudd R.E., T. Colton, and R. Schacht. 2000. *An overview of the medical and public health literature addressing literacy issues: An annotated bibliography.* National Center for the Study of Adult Learning and Literacy, January 2000. http://www.hsph.harvard.edu/health/literacy/literature.html.

Smith, A. 2009. *Studying the government of the EU: The promise of political sociology.* Edinburgh: Europa Institute Seminar Series, University of Edinburgh.

Stiglitz, J.E., A. Sen, and J.-P. Fitoussi. 2009. Report by the commission on the measurement of economic performance and social progress. http://www.stiglitz-sen-fitoussi.fr/en/index.htm (accessed 22 January, 2011).

Street, B. 1996. *Literacy, economy and society. Literacy across the curriculum* 12, no. 3: 8–15. Montreal: Centre for Literacy.

The OECD and global governance in education

Sam Sellar and Bob Lingard

School of Education, The University of Queensland, Brisbane, Australia

This review essay discusses the history, evolution and development of the Organisation for Economic Co-operation and Development (OECD) and traces the growing impact of its education work. The essay is in four main sections. The first discusses Carrol and Kellow's *The OECD: A Study of Organizational Adaptation* (Edward Elgar) and provides a brief historical account of the Organisation. The second section reviews Woodward's *The Organisation for Economic Co-operation and Development* (Routledge) and considers the different modes of governance employed by the OECD, particularly its exercise of soft power through peer review. The third section considers Tucker's edited book, *Surpassing Shanghai: An Agenda for American Education Built on the World's Leading Systems* (Harvard Education Press) and the effects that Shanghai-China's 2009 Programme for International Student Assessment (PISA) success has had on education policy debates in the USA and globally. The final section engages with Sahlberg's *Finnish Lessons: What Can the World Learn From Educational Change in Finland?* (Teachers College Press) and describes factors that have contributed to the high quality and equity of schooling in Finland. The review essay thus moves from an examination of the role and function of the OECD in general terms to more specific discussion of the recent impact of its PISA, which has drawn attention to particular school systems and has influenced education policy-making in both member and non-member countries. We conclude by providing a framework for understanding the epistemological and infrastructural governance functions of the OECD in education globally.

Introduction

In this review essay, we describe the history, evolution and development of the Organisation for Economic Co-operation and Development (OECD) and trace its role in global governance, drawing on Carroll and Kellow (2011) and Woodward (2009). Carroll and Kellow provide a detailed historical account of the changing global positioning and influence of the OECD in relation to political and economic developments over the past 50 years. Woodward provides a useful theoretical framework for understanding the role of the OECD in global governance today and its policy effects within its 34 member nations and also its non-member nations. While neither of these books deals in much detail with the role of the OECD in global educational governance and with the constitution of a global education policy field

(Lingard and Rawolle 2011), we will extrapolate to considerations of the OECD's education work in this respect.

This is complemented by our review of two additional books that, to varying extents, focus on the OECD's education work, particularly its data work, which we might see as 'policy as numbers' written global (Lingard 2011), through the annual publication of *Education at a Glance* indicators data, the Programme for International Student Assessment (PISA) and the development of other comparative international tests in education, such as the Programme for International Assessment of Adult Competencies. We firstly deal with Tucker's (2011) edited book, *Surpassing Shanghai*, which seeks to analyse and draw lessons from Shanghai's outstanding performance on PISA 2009. This success has helped to reconstitute global 'reference societies' for many national systems, as nations now 'look East' to borrow from other systems or at least use their superior performance on international tests such as PISA to push national reform agendas (Sellar and Lingard 2013a). We then review Sahlberg's (2011) *Finnish Lessons*, which documents 30 years of school system reform in Finland that have seen it become an outstanding performer on PISA since the first survey in 2000: the first PISA 'poster boy' before the recent success of Shanghai. There are many significant policy lessons in Sahlberg's book and they are not the lessons that nations and education politicians usually take from results on tests such as PISA.

We document and provide critique of these four books before, in the concluding section, using the powerful insights they provide to proffer a brief account and analysis of the changing nature of the OECD's education work and, drawing on Woodward, provide a framework for understanding the OECD's global governance role in education. In line with the argument of Henry et al. (2001), we accept that in today's globalised and globalising world the OECD has taken on more significant policy actor role, supplanting popular conceptions of it as merely a 'think tank' supporting the economic interests of rich nations. Since the 1990s, education work has grown as an area of importance within the OECD itself and the Organisation's role in education globally has also increased (Lingard and Sellar 2013a). Woodward (2009) argues that its mode of soft governance fits almost symbiotically with the contemporary political structure of feeling and perhaps serves as a model for other international organisations (IOs) in this respect. In our view, the OECD's work across recent years has been both a response to globalisation and an attempt to frame it in a particular way.

The OECD: an evolving intergovernmental organisation

Carroll and Kellow's (2011) *The OECD: A Study of Organizational Adaptation* is a current monograph that examines the history and organisation of the OECD as a whole. In this respect, it perhaps stands alone among literature on the Organisation and provides an indispensible reference text. The book draws on a combination of archival research and interviews with senior members of the OECD secretariat and a significant number of permanent delegates from member countries, past and present, to provide an insightful account of the Organisation's development and evolution in response to significant political and economic changes over the past five decades.

The first three chapters introduce the organisational structure and key processes of the OECD, outlining the complex structure of councils that oversee its work, the

Secretariat that supports much of this work and the committees through which member states influence the Organisation's multiple agendas. Carroll and Kellow (2011) emphasise that the intergovernmental structure of the Organisation, as opposed to a supranational structure like that of the United Nations, is the source of its distinctiveness among IOs and underpins its exertion of soft power through the creation of epistemic communities of policy analysts, bureaucrats and politicians within the Organisation and in member countries. This is perhaps most clearly illustrated in the peer review processes at the heart of the OECD's work and through which the performance of member governments in various policy areas is subject to critical examination.

The OECD was created in 1961 from the Organisation for European Economic Co-operation (OEEC), which was founded by the US in 1948 to oversee Marshall Plan reconstruction of post-war Europe and as a bulwark against Communism through its support of liberal democracy and market economics. Carroll and Kellow (2011) note how the peer review process was created in the OEEC to enable 'confrontation' regarding the usage of Marshall Plan aid by member nations; however, the picture that emerges of this process as it has developed within the OECD is one of the considered analysis and diplomatic consultation to provide public accounts of the performance of member governments. Peer reviews generally involve Secretariat staff consulting with the country being assessed and preparing a draft survey and final report. The relevant committee or other body then provides a forum for assessment and approves the published findings, seeking agreement from all members. This process provides a basis for policy learning and transfer. As Caroll and Kellow (2011, 34) explain, '[t]he key to the effectiveness of peer reviews lies not in any coercive sanctions for non-compliance but, rather, their hortatory nature'.

The subsequent four chapters of the book trace the evolution of the OECD from the 1960s to the present, examining key organisational developments by decade. The 1960s was a period of consolidation as the Organisation fashioned a new role for itself in global affairs. The aims of the OECD, detailed in article 1 of its convention, include the promotion of economic growth in member countries, contribution to the expansion of developing economies through aid and the expansion of world trade. These were clearly reflected in its early work, which extended from that of the OEEC and included the adoption of the Codes of Liberalisation in 1961 to free up trade, as well as the creation of important bodies to oversee development assistance and international economic coordination.

In many ways, the next chapter examining the changing role of the Organisation during the 1970s is at the centre of the book. The breakdown of the Bretton Woods system and the 1973 oil crisis led to the convention of the Group of seven finance ministers, signalling a lack of confidence in the OECD to address these new challenges. However, Carroll and Kellow (2011) show how the publication by the OECD of the McCracken report in 1974 made a significant contribution to the emergence of a new consensus about the need to shift from Keynesian to monetarist approaches in order to address stagflation. Further, the Secretary-General at the time, Emile van Lennep, was a vocal proponent of structural adjustment policies. Carroll and Kellow (2011, 69) note that the McCracken report provided a new analytical framework for the OECD's review work, and that 'the focus on structural adjustment had a pronounced ripple effect throughout the OECD' (71). A picture emerges of the OECD fashioning a more prominent role for itself in global governance, in response to economic crisis and the emergence of the G7, through its adoption and promotion of a new economic policy orthodoxy that began to permeate its epistemic communities. This promotion of market-oriented economic policy continued in its work during the 1980s.

The next major period of change for the Organisation was the 1990s and into the 2000s, following the end of the cold war. This presented a challenge to the Organisation's role in promoting a countervailing ideology in relation to Communism and changed the configuration of Eastern Europe. This period was marked by the accession of Eastern European countries, following the collapse of the Soviet Union, and also of Mexico and Korea, enlarging the membership of the Organisation and broadening its focus to the Asia-Pacific region. This can be seen as the beginning of a longer process of opening up that has culminated in further accessions (Chile, Estonia, Slovenia and Israel), as well as the development of the Organisation's 'enhanced engagement' programme to increase cooperation with major non-member economies such as Brazil, Russia, China, India, Indonesia and South Africa.

This period was also one of internal reform prompted by questions about lax standards of corporate governance within the Organisation itself and the need to establish its relevance in the context of globalisation. During the mid-1990s, the online information system (OLIS) was developed, providing an infrastructure for documents and statistical data to be communicated between the Secretariat, committees and member countries. Carroll and Kellow (2011) argue that:

> [i]t is doubtful ... that the OECD's work outputs could have increased in the way that they did in the later 1990s and into the twenty-first century ... without the advent of OLIS, email and the internet. In the case of the OECD, whose committees formed the core of a wide range of existing policy networks, their performance was enhanced, fortuitously, at just the right time. (101)

The OECD was well ahead of other IOs in terms of its use of this online infrastructure, which was particularly well suited to its organisational structure and to expediting work across its policy networks.

The final chapters of the book shift from the elaboration of this historical narrative to look across a number of different areas of the OECD's work, including policy transfer processes associated with the accession of member states, relationships between the OECD and other international and civil society organisations, and the emerging significance of the environment and health as areas of work for the Organisation.

The account provided for the campaign against the Multilateral Agreement on Investment (MAI), which Carroll and Kellow (2011) use to illustrate the changing approach taken by the OECD in its relationship to civil society organisations, is one particularly revealing aspect of this latter part of the book. The MAI was designed by the OECD as a convention to prevent member nations from discriminating against foreign investors. Opposition to the MAI intensified in the late 1990s, driven by activists who formed part of the growing anti-globalisation movement that came to international prominence with the 1999 World Trade Organisation (WTO) protests in Seattle. Carroll and Kellow characterise the MAI as a relatively benign instrument that simply required countries to treat foreign and domestic investors equally, and argue that the criticisms of activists, who felt the MAI would limit the sovereignty of governments in relation to global capital and was being negotiated under a shroud of secrecy, reflected their lack of engagement with publically available information about the work of the OECD. While bruising for the Organisation, Carroll and Kellow argue this campaign was not the primary reason for the collapse of the MAI, but did sharpen the attention of the Organisation to public relations, communications and engagement with non-government organisations (NGOs), prompting the development of conventions on corruption and corporate responsibility designed to mitigate, and be perceived as mitigating, the excesses of global capitalism.

This description of the MAI *contretemps* could be read as a bowdlerised account from the perspective of the OECD. However, it is interesting insofar as it challenges one popular view of the OECD as only a neoliberal think-tank clandestinely pursuing the interests of rich nations. While it may be the case that rich nations actively pursue their interests through the OECD, the book counter conspiratorial views of the Organisation and demonstrate the complex and often internally contested work of the OECD across its vast committee structure. Carroll and Kellow (2011) emphasise the resource-intensity of participating in this work, which effectively limits the engagement of many NGOs, even though participation may be open to them. Here, the OECD appears as a large technocratic machinery, which can be difficult to reform in ways that improve its efficiency and, to borrow from one of Carroll and Kellow's (2011) informants, could almost be used to bore participants into submission.

Notably, in terms of our argument here, Carroll and Kellow (2011) make only passing references to the education work of the OECD, noting its rising importance within the overall work of the Organisation since the 1990s, particularly with the increasing influence of PISA. Carroll and Kellow's excellent book instead provides a detailed account of developments in the core economic work of the Organisation during its 50-year history, in effect providing a narrative of post-Second World War global economic and political developments from the perspective of the OECD as, at different times, a leading actor or a bit player. The key moments in this narrative, in terms of understanding the contemporary role of the Organisation in global governance, include the emergence of a new economic orthodoxy in the 1970s that permeated the Organisation and its epistemic communities; the acceleration, from the mid-1990s, of the OECD's statistical and policy analysis work into policy domains such as health, the environment and education; and its increasing engagement with a broader group of member and non-member countries and economies in the context of globalisation.

The OECD's four modes of governance

Woodward's (2009) *The OECD* is one of the first full-length studies of the OECD, which is surprising, given that the OECD has been an important international player. Woodward's is a most useful book tracing the history of the OECD from its development in 1961 and its growth and evolution through the cold war and post-cold war eras. The book consists of six, quite short, yet important chapters, dealing with the OECD's origins and evolution, organisation and functioning, its role in global governance, current issues, reform and the future of the OECD. Woodward (5) suggests that the 'central contention of the book is that the OECD is a pivotal international organization because it sows the seeds of international consensus and cooperation that allow humankind to reap a greater capacity to manage our common affairs'.

The book is part of Thomas Weiss's edited Routledge Global Institutions series and in the Foreword, he suggests that the OECD has been a 'much under-appreciated player in global governance' (xiv). In this observation, he signifies the theoretical framework of global governance that Woodward uses to understand the functioning and effects of the OECD across the plethora of public policy issues in the 34 member nations and increasingly in non-member nations. It is the framework for understanding the OECD's role in global governance that we see as the important contribution of Woodward's book and which we will focus on here, as it provides a most useful way of understanding the role and functioning of the OECD in education policy.

Woodward outlines four overlapping dimensions of the OECD's role in global governance, namely, cognitive, normative, legal and palliative. He briefly deals with each in the introductory chapter before elaborating on them in Chapter 3. This is an important contribution to understanding the rescaling of contemporary politics and policy-making associated with the various dimensions of the move from government to governance (Rhodes 1997; Rosenau 2005). Similarly to Carroll and Kellow (2011), Woodward's thesis is that the OECD achieves policy effects through soft modes of governance, modes which we would suggest are conducive to the contemporary post-ideological world. This is because the OECD has few carrots and sticks to give effect to its policy preferences in member nations.

Cognitive governance, according to Woodward, functions through the agreed values held by member nations and is a distinctive mode of influence of the OECD, as it does not have to reconcile competing ideological positions across current and aspiring members. Commitment to liberal democracy, market economics and human rights are requirements for OECD membership. The second mode of OECD governance described by Woodward is normative governance, which picks up on and denotes the epistemological assumptions underpinning the OECD's policy work and its functioning as a 'laboratory of policy concepts' (7). Woodward (8) suggests that: 'Normative governance is the vaguest dimension of the OECD but it is argu- ably through challenging and changing the mindsets of the people involved that the Organization achieves its greatest influence'. This is the impact on national policy- makers from participation in OECD committees that affects their assumptive worlds and produces what we might see as a particular 'policy habitus' (Lingard, Rawolle, and Taylor 2005). What we see is an alignment across and creation of epistemic communities at OECD and national policy-making levels (Ball 2012). This is also linked to the important international comparative data role taken by the OECD.

The OECD is not a 'prolific legislator', according to Woodward (8), with other modes of governance being more important than legal ones in terms of its global impact. This is especially true in the policy domain of education. Additionally, enforcement of OECD legal agreements functions through 'surveillance and peer pressure', rather than through sanctions (8). Palliative governance is the final mode in Woodward's typology and refers to its role in greasing 'the wheels of global governance' (8). The OECD, Woodward argues, does this in a number of ways: through plugging gaps in global governance, interrogating emergent policy issues, its interdisciplinary approach to policy issues and its work in support of the WTO and Group of Eight (G8) nations.

In a sense, the founding *raison d'etre* for the OECD has become redundant since the end of the cold war and the emergent hegemony of neoliberalism and a global capitalist economy. In the final chapter, Woodward provides six arguments for why he believes the OECD will continue to be a significant player in global governance, despite this transition. Brief consideration of these arguments will provide additional understanding of the way the OECD works and the domains in which it works.

Woodward suggests firstly that the OECD has become important in the context of globalisation, read performatively as neoliberal market capitalism (Bourdieu 2003), which it helped to propagate. Secondly, he argues that the OECD is not beholden to any particular departments or policy domains within national governments, has a chameleon like character and is 'adept at carving out niches' (125) for itself across the various public policy domains; this is the organisational adaptation highlighted by Carroll and Kellow (2011). He also acknowledges that the OECD's institutional memory provides it with sure-footedness that other IOs, particularly emerging ones such as the Group of Twenty (G20), do not possess. A further strength ensuring its future is that it complements, rather than competes with other IOs. This is the filling of policy gaps argument linked to palliative global governance.

The OECD, as Woodward assiduously documents throughout, operates through soft power and largely through cognitive and normative governance. This *modus operandi* is perhaps the future for IOs and global governance. A final reason for Woodward's optimism regarding the future of the OECD is the clever pragmatism of the current Secretary-General, Angel Gurria. As Carroll and Kellow (2011) also show, Gurria has instituted negotiations for more accessions to OECD membership and also deepened engagement with non-member countries and civil society organisations. In the post-cold war era, Woodward suggests that it is the elasticity of the OECD's functions (in perpetual flux) and its felicitous capacity for multidisciplinary work across multiple public policy domains that ensure its ongoing significance.

We would add that a number of other features of the contemporary world contribute to the ongoing significance of the OECD. The first links to the mooted move from government to governance (Rhodes 1997; Rosenau 2005), which has manifested in a restructured state at national levels, functioning through a steering at a distance approach with much privatization of public functions and a rescaling of modes of governance. Comparison is now central to governance as it operates across multiple layers (Novoa and Yariv-Mashal 2003). The OECD has proselytised for these changes linked to the neoliberal globalisation of the economy and has enhanced importance in this context, especially in education. The steering at a distance mode of governance associated with the restructured state at national level and new public management has witnessed a more significant use of data in policy processes (Ozga 2009; Lingard 2011). The OECD has strengthened its hand as a centre of technical expertise, data collection and data analysis, at a time when data have become central to the new governance at both global and national level. The 'global eye' and 'national eye', in Novoa and Yariv-Mashal's (2003) terms, now govern together and make the globe legible for such governing. There has also been the rise of a post-ideological politics: politics as managing the quotidian in an incrementalist way, which sees numbers and data as central to new modes of governance, both within and across nations.

This book provides a very good introduction to an under-researched IO. Its particular strength in our view is its significant contribution to understanding the global governance functions of the OECD. As such, it offers an excellent complement to Caroll and Kellow's historical narrative. While the book notes the increasing significance of the OECD's education policy work – it suggests it has overtaken United Nations Educational, Scientific and Cultural Organization as the major IO for education – not all that much attention is paid to education, as might be expected of a general introductory book. However, mention is made of the creation of the separate Education Directorate in 2002 and the enhanced significance of PISA in the OECD's policy work, and of the significance of its other statistical and indicators work and the annual publication of *Education at a Glance*. The major contribution of the book for policy sociologists in education is the framework it offers for understanding the nature and impact of the OECD's education work.

Keeping up with Shanghai: lessons in running the global education race

Tucker's (2011) edited book, *Surpassing Shanghai*, constitutes a significant intervention into contemporary education reform debates in the US, at a time when US policy-makers are looking outwards for reform ideas. Drawing on research conducted by the OECD and the US National Centre on Education and the Economy, requested by US education secretary Arne Duncan following the publication of the PISA 2009 results, the book provides five case studies of top-performing education systems 'in the highest ranks in terms of quality, equity and productivity' (Tucker 2011, 172). These include Shanghai-China, Finland, Japan, Singapore and Canada (specifically Ontario; see also Martino and Rezai-Rashti 2013). The five case studies employ a methodology that combines analysis of PISA survey data with an industrial benchmarking approach.[1] The theoretical framework for the study is based on a model of the relationships between economic and educational development, with the goal for nations being the complementary development of high-skill, high-wage knowledge-based economies and professional, creative, mass education systems to serve them.

The book opens with a Foreword by Linda-Darling Hammond, who shows how current US education reform strategies contrast starkly with those undertaken by the top-performing systems examined here (which is also evident in Sahlberg's *Finnish Lessons*), and an Introduction by Tucker that emphasises the importance of international comparisons and benchmarking in the context of globalising labour markets and changing demands on education as nations and individuals compete in a new global 'war for talent' (Brown and Tannock 2009). Following the five case studies, a synthesis of key reform themes is provided, focusing on the areas of systemic quality, equity and productivity, as well as a brief and more programmatic concluding chapter that details a model reform plan for US education systems.

The title of the book, *Surpassing Shanghai*, reflects the widespread contemporary imagination of education as a global 'race' for economic competitiveness, which has been made possible by the rise of international comparative assessments of human capital such as PISA, and the International Association for the Evaluation of Educational Achievement's Trends in International Mathematics and Science Study and Progress in International Reading Literacy Study. The inefficiency of the US education system, which spends more on schooling than most other systems, but achieves only average results on PISA, provides an economic rationale for the type of international comparison and benchmarking undertaken here.

This economic and education policy orthodoxy (pushed by the OECD, we would add) frames the analyses and the key themes that are drawn out across the cases. It is not possible to provide a fulsome overview of each case study here, or each of the factors that is described as accounting for the educational success of particular systems. These include the use of international benchmarking, the alignment of instruction, specific approaches to curriculum and external examination, high standards and the provision of corresponding support for all students, including different levels of funding to support those in most need (Tucker 2011, 205). Instead, we focus on the conjunction of culture and context that appears to enable *coherent* system reform and the focus on *teacher quality*, that Tucker (2011) emphasises are common across all cases.

Notably, in three of the systems examined here – Shanghai, Finland and Singapore – recent and relatively rapid economic development has combined with a strong cultural emphasis on the importance of education. The insightful historical contextualisation illustrates the imperatives, in these three cases at least, to reform education systems through a coherent and comprehensive approach guided by clear goals and often strong, centralised planning and leadership. Indeed, Tucker (2011, 205) argues that 'coherence in the design of the overall system itself' is the most important factor in its success, along with teacher quality. The education systems of Finland and Singapore have both developed dramatically since the 1950s, while the present Shanghai system has emerged since the Chinese economic reforms and opening up in the late 1970s. The Japanese system, also examined here, has a longer history, but shares a strong cultural emphasis on education and has pursued comprehensive reforms based on international benchmarking since the latter half of the nineteenth century (see Takayama 2007). As a result, the systems of Finland, Shanghai and Singapore have been coherently re-designed at a time when educational competencies measured by PISA have become central in new knowledge-based economies. Indeed, Tucker (2011) suggests that 'the big story is really about the convergence of two major developments: the trajectory of global economic development and the workforce needed to teach our children in the current stage of global economic development' (171). The OECD has been involved in helping to specify the skills and competencies that give contemporary human capital its value and has become a prominent actor in education policy globally due to its measurement and comparison of skills within nations.

Each case in this book also emphasises the importance of high-quality teachers, defined here as those possessing 'a high level of general intelligence, a solid mastery of the subjects to be taught, and a demonstrated aptitude for engaging students and helping them understand what is being taught' (Tucker 2011, 178). The book makes a sustained case for policy settings in respect of teacher education, remuneration, standards and development that drive up the status of teaching as a profession in order to attract the academically strongest applicants to training institutions and to encourage collegial forms of accountability and research-driven improvement in schools and systems. A similar stance on teachers and teacher education is contained in Sahlberg's (2011) account of Finnish school system reforms dealt below. From the political strategy of the McGuinty government in Ontario, which pursued reforms that involved the buy-in and development of the present workforce, to efforts in Finland and Singapore to raise the status of teaching and academic standards of entrants into teacher education, the importance of recruiting the best prospective teachers and investing heavily in their development is a theme throughout. Importantly, increasing the professionalism of teachers can help in the establishment of high trust systems, where bottom-up professional accountability replaces more punitive external accountabilities, such as those which have been popular but unsuccessful in the US.

Surpassing Shanghai is a useful book that paints a picture of the contemporary global economy in which education has become central to future prospects of the nation and to individuals and families. In this context, the top-performing systems on PISA are those in which politicians, educators, students and families are all strongly motivated to achieve top educational outcomes. In such systems, pervasive reform is focused on the cultivation of the most highly sought after skills and dispositions for all students (the importance of science and mathematics knowledge is stressed throughout, as well as capacities for creativity and innovation), while simultaneously investing in teachers as highly skilled knowledge professionals themselves. However, as Sahlberg (2011) has demonstrated, such a focus needs to be complemented by relevant social policies that seek to mediate the impact of economic globalisation and the growth of inequality both between and within nations.

Finnish Lessons: the importance of context to progressive systemic reform

Sahlberg, the author of *Finnish Lessons* (2011), is well placed to provide a knowledgeable, informative and telling account of educational change in Finland, which has resulted in a schooling system that, according to its PISA results, is both equitable and of high quality. Sahlberg currently works in the Ministry of Education in Finland, has been a teacher there, a teacher educator, senior policy-maker and has worked for IOs such as the World Bank and European Commission. He thus knows the Finnish system intimately from the inside and knows other systems and policy developments well, enabling him to proffer a most telling international comparison of education policy reform. The result is an important book that makes a wonderful contribution to policy sociology in education and to comparative education.

Finnish Lessons is in the Teachers College Series, *School Reform*. This is a good thing in our view, as the US has tended to be quite insular in terms of school reform. Indeed, Luke (2011) has argued that this might be the moment when the US begins to look outwards again for models of reform, given the poor comparative performance of the US on international testing and the impressive performance of Shanghai on PISA 2009, in the context of the so-called Asian century. The US President has compared this education policy moment for the US with the education policy impact of Sputnik in 1957 (Sellar and Lingard 2013a).

The book has a Series Foreword by Anne Lieberman and a general foreword by Andy Hargreaves. Both provide excellent summative accounts of the main points made by Sahlberg. Lieberman stresses the significance in Sahlberg's account of research-based teacher education programmes and the centrality of teacher research and inquiry into teaching practices in Finland. She also notes, as is well known, that all Finnish teachers have a Masters degree and that the profession has high status, and the extent of teacher and school autonomy and lack of standardised tests, with reform and change emanating from teachers and school leaders in a bottom-up, professionally informed fashion. Hargreaves, *inter alia*, juxtaposes Sahlberg's granular account of Finnish school reforms with those in the US and in much of the rest of the world. He stresses that the Finns 'own' their school and systemic vision, rather than renting one from elsewhere, framed by the global educational policy discourse.

In our view, the strength of Sahlberg's account is its veracity, deriving from the author's experiences and research, and the emphasis given to the history and context of school reform and the necessity of longer term rather than short-term reform. In Finland, there appears to be more congruence between the temporalities of real school reform and political temporalities surrounding such reform, unlike most politically driven systemic reform in Anglo-American countries. On the signif-icance of history, Sahlberg quotes a former Director-General of Education who said:

'the Nordic welfare state was constructed using three political ideals: the legacy of liberated peasants, the spirit of capitalism, and the utopia of socialism' (24). Further, Sahlberg notes the need for social policies to support education policy and the multidimensionality of effective systemic school reform. He observes: 'there is no single reason why any educational system succeeds or fails. Instead, there is a network of interrelated factors – educational, political and cultural – that function differently in different situations (Sahlberg 2011, 6).

As well as multidimensionality and the need for complementary social policies, Sahlberg stresses the significance of the local, the specific, and the vernacular in effective school reform. Yet he does draw some lessons from successful systemic reform in Finland, which he argues 'appear to transcend culture' (6). The first, he suggests, is the inspiring vision of what a good public schooling system ought to be; central here has been the provision of nine years of basic schooling in common for all (*peruskoula*), which he refers to as the 'Finnish Dream'. The second lesson he articulates is that Finland has not been insular in respect of school reform – it has looked outwards to its neighbour nations and other parts of the world – but these ideas and lessons have always been rearticulated into the Finnish context. He calls this the 'Finnish Way': policy learning rather than policy borrowing. The third lesson, which he believes has cross-national salience, is the respect for teachers and schools in the Finnish system. He notes:

> Finland has built world-class teacher education programs. And Finland pays its teachers well. But the true Finnish difference is that teachers in Finland may exercise their professional judgment both widely and freely in the schools. They control curriculum, student assessment, school improvement, and community involvement. (Sahlberg 2011, 7)

In Sahlberg's terms, Finnish teachers are given the professional autonomy, based on their teacher education, to be the type of teacher that they envisaged when choosing the profession, unlike the situation in many other national systems.

Finnish Lessons has become very influential internationally in a short period of time. This is perhaps because of Sahlberg's encapsulation of what drives systemic school reform in the Anglo-American nations and elsewhere, in the clever and telling acronym, GERM (Global Education Reform Movement). This is the focus of Chapter 4, 'The Finnish Way: Competitive Welfare State', where he juxtaposes GERM with the Finnish Way (nicely encapsulated in Table 4.1). This Table is a wonderful tool for teaching comparative global education policy, for opening up discussions about systemic and school reform in this era of an emergent global education policy field.

Sahlberg contrasts GERM and the Finnish Way according to five criteria, namely, standardised teaching and learning; focus on literacy and numeracy; teaching prescribed curriculum; borrowing market-oriented reform ideas; and test-based accountability and control. Against these criteria, Sahlberg constructs a most informative set of binaries. He juxtaposes the prescription and uniformity imposed top-down in GERM with the greater flexibility, school and teacher autonomy in Finland, predicated upon trust and respect for highly qualified and professional teachers. He also contrasts the width of curriculum provision in Finland with the narrow focus on literacy and numeracy in GERM, driven by high-stakes standardised tests that are absent in Finland. He notes that resources in Finland are used efficiently and targeted on those who are in danger of falling behind early in their schooling careers. He also points out the market reforms and managerialism within GERM and the ways in which school reforms in Finland are based instead on good educational practices. In Sahlberg's (2011, 9) words, 'The Finnish experience shows that consistent focus on equity and cooperation – not choice and competition – can lead to an education system where all children learn well'. We would add the significance of all young people attending government schools, which limits between-school differences. Sahlberg also notes the significance of cross-school collaborative networks in percolating good reform ideas through schools and across the system. This is in stark contrast to most systems in the world, which under the sway of neoliberalism and market ideas manifest as GERM, put schools in isolated competition with each other and which fail to recognise the relationality between top and bottom performing schools.

What is also significant in Sahlberg's account is the synergy, a real and significant complementarity, across education and other social policies in Finland. It is important to recognise that Finland has a very low Gini Coefficient of inequality. This contextualising (and also historicising) of the Finnish school system is important. Condron (2011) has recently demonstrated that if the Gini Coefficient of inequality in the US was the same as in Finland, the US would do much better on PISA. Yet, school reform there decontextualises and focuses on schools and, increasingly in policy terms, only on teachers. We think in many ways that the OECD analyses of PISA performance also tend to decontextualise in similar fashion, emphasising policy effects over history and structural factors.

Of course, it is Finland's performance on PISA that has brought its schooling system to the attention of policy makers across the globe in this era of an emergent global education policy field. Sahlberg, author of the widely cited paper published in this journal, 'Education policies for raising student learning: the Finnish approach' (2007), demonstrates most ably the contextual and historical framing of school reform in Finland, noting particularly the economic and reform impact of the collapse of the Soviet Union on Finland, and the rise of Nokia, both of which were paralleled by a focused, holistic approach to schooling reform redolent of similar systemic approaches in other top performing systems on PISA. Simola (2005) has also written about the significance of earlier Finnish history to the creation of an inclusive government schooling system for all, while Rinne and his colleagues (2002) have shown how the global policy discourse of neoliberalism has affected politics and public policy-making in Finland, but its direct effects in schooling policy have been limited. In part, Sahlberg's argument would be that this is because of a public consensus, as well as consensus across conservative and progressive political parties, in support for egalitarian and inclusive schooling policy.

This is an important book that ought to be read widely by policy-makers, Ministers for Education, policy sociologists and educational researchers. It is an important book because it documents the 30-year reform and restructuring of Finnish schooling. Since the first PISA in 2000, Finland has achieved at the top of the performance ladder, demonstrating a schooling system that is both high quality and highly equitable. Finnish success has taken time and been underpinned by a consistent vernacular vision for schooling. This long time frame of reform contrasts starkly with the fast, top-down reform expected by most Ministers for Education in most countries. Sahlberg also shows how the Finnish system is highly efficient in terms of expenditure. While Finland, due to its stellar performance on PISA, has come to the attention of policy-makers around the world, and has thus become an important reference society for reform in other schooling systems, Sahlberg emphasises the necessity of policy learning, rather than simply policy borrowing. One of his lessons would be that context and history matter deeply and cannot be borrowed. This book is significant for showing how the multiple interrelated features of the Finnish system contribute collectively to its outstanding performance, complemented by specific social policies that ensure a quite equal society. This confirms Wilkinson and Pickett's (2009) insight that the extent of inequality and extent of the gap between top and bottom income earners are important factors in determining equitable or inequitable schooling outcomes. This is another important *Finnish Lesson*.

Analysis and conclusion: the OECD and global education governance

The four books reviewed here have taken us from a general account of the history, structure and function of the OECD to a detailed analysis of the Finnish education system, which owes its recognition as a world leader to the influential contemporary education work of the OECD. The organization and functions of the OECD have evolved substantially in response to significant global political and economic changes during its 50-year history; its education work has been an important part of this evolution in recent years. As both Carroll and Kellow (2011) and Woodward (2009) show, the OECD's intergovernmental structure has been its hallmark and a significant factor in its capacity to exert soft power in member countries and beyond.

Since the mid-1990s, the OECD has increased its agency as a policy actor in education globally and this has contributed to the revitalisation of its role since the end of the cold war. We argue, drawing on and extending from Woodward's (2009) typology of OECD governance modes, that this agency is exerted through *infrastructural* governance, a product of the international networks and systems it has established to collect and compare statistical data in education, and *epistemological* governance, which reflects its well-established capacity to shape the views of key actors in education across local, national and global scales (see Sellar and Lingard 2013b; Lingard and Sellar 2013b). We understand infrastructural governance as a subset of the palliative governance described by Woodward (2009) and in relation to Sassen's (2007) observation that globalisation involves the creation of global infrastructures. Epistemological governance cuts across the normative and cognitive governance modes of governance described by Woodward (2009). It describes the way in which common perspectives on education and economic policy support the education work of the OECD and this commonality is in turn strengthened by the OECD's education work and policy lessons drawn from systems that it has helped to identify as high performing.

The OECD has been particularly well placed to increase its influence in education during the 1990s and 2000s, a period when education and economic policy has reached a point of convergence. Through its influential work on knowledge-based economies, lifelong learning and skills, the OECD has helped to shape understandings of the education systems that national governments must create to increase productivity and sustain economic growth. At the same time, the OECD has developed and increasingly extended the reach of PISA and other assessments that measure the skills and competencies it has identified as being important in the new century. There is a self-perpetuating dynamic here, through which the OECD both prescribes education policy approaches and assesses the performance of national education systems in these terms. This dynamic is central to the OECD's strengthened epistemological governance role in education globally and we see this as connected to the way in which the education work of the OECD has shaped the assumptive worlds or policy habitus of the policy-makers who drive reforms within nations

Tucker (2011) and Sahlberg (2011) both demonstrate how the PISA programme, and the broader education work of the OECD, has helped to reconstitute reference societies in education (see Sellar and Lingard 2013a). Nations now look to Finland, and other top-performing systems such as Shanghai, as they imagine themselves competing in a global education race. What stands out in *Surpassing Shanghai* is that many of the education systems that perform very well on PISA have undergone carefully planned, centrally driven reforms during a period when human capital has increased in importance for national economies. We also note the vital importance of recognising the interrelation of local specificity and more universally valorised education and economic policy settings that underpins the success of many top-performing systems.

However, the influence of the OECD's education policy work depends, to a significant extent, on stressing the importance of policy factors over the effects of cultural and social context. Cultural and historical explanations for the success of education systems cannot be used to justify reforms in other nations, whereas pointing to specific policy settings as the cause of success can provide governments with leverage for internal reform agendas. While it is certainly important for policy learning purposes to distil the effects of policy from other factors, there is a risk here that the comparative analyses facilitated by the OECD's statistical work can pay insufficient attention to system specific factors. This is of particular concern in relation to the effects of structural inequality on educational success. While PISA does focus on the equity of schooling systems, we note how structural inequality in society beyond schooling is often elided as an explanation for poor quality and poor equity outcomes on PISA. Indeed, the necessity of confronting deep and abiding socio-economic inequality as a way towards more equitable and quality schooling provision is an important lesson that we take from the OECD's data work in global governance in education. However, national systems often fail to learn this lesson from international comparisons of performance. Rather, they use such data as ammunition for strengthening their own reform agendas, often deepening the features of GERM. We argue the need to learn from other systems and to recognise that schools and teachers can make a difference, but that schooling policy needs to be vernacularised and focused on building trust in teacher professionalism, complemented by appropriate social policies addressing economic inequalities.

Acknowledgements
This paper is based on research undertaken as part of an Australian Research Council (ARC) funded Discovery Project (DP1094850), Schooling the Nation in an Age of Globalisation: National Curriculum, Accountabilities and their Effects.

Note
1. Notably, the sample size and selection of informants varies considerably between cases. More than 20 interviews with teachers, school principals, academics, senior managers and other education stakeholders, as well as school visits, underpin the Shanghai case,

while in contrast, the Canadian case draws on nine interviews with academics and political leaders closely involved in the reform agenda that is examined.

References

Ball, S. 2012. *Global Education Inc.: New Policy Networks and the Neo-Liberal Imaginary.* London: Routledge.

Bourdieu, P. 2003. *Firing Back Against the Tyranny of the Market.* London: Verso.

Brown, P., and S. Tannock. 2009. "Education, Meritocracy and the Global War for Talent." *Journal of Education Policy* 24: 377–392.

Carroll, P., and A. Kellow. 2011. *The OECD: A Study of Organizational Adaptation.* Cheltenham: Edward Elgar.

Condron, D. 2011. "Egalitarianism and Educational Excellence: Compatible Goals for Affluent Societies?" *Educational Researcher* 40: 47–55.

Henry, M., B. Lingard, S. Taylor, and F. Rizvi. 2001. *The OECD, Globalisation and Education Policy.* Oxford: Pergamon.

Lingard, B. 2011. "Policy as Numbers: Ac/Counting for Educational Research." *Australian Educational Researcher* 38 (4): 355–382.

Lingard, B., and S. Rawolle. 2011. "New Scalar Politics: Implications for Education Policy." *Comparative Education* 47 (4): 489–502.

Lingard, B., S. Rawolle, and S. Taylor. 2005. "Globalizing Policy Sociology in Education: Working with Bourdieu." *Journal of Education Policy* 20 (6): 759–777.

Lingard, B., and S. Sellar. 2013a. "Globalization and Sociology of Education Policy: The Case of PISA." In *Contemporary Debates in the Sociology of Education*, edited by R. Brooks, M. Mccormack, and K. Bhopal. London: Palgrave.

Lingard, B., and S. Sellar. 2013b. "'Catalyst Data': Perverse Systemic Effects of Audit and Accountability in Australian Schooling." *Journal of Education Policy.* doi:10.1080/02680939.2012.758815.

Luke, A. 2011. "Generalising Across Borders: Policy and the Limits of Educational Science." *Educational Researcher* 40: 367–377.

Martino, W., and G. Rezai-Rashti. 2013. "Policy as Numbers, 'Gap Talk' and the Global Rescaling of Educational Accountability in Canada." *Journal of Education Policy.* doi:10.1080/02680939.2013.767074.

Novoa, A., and T. Yariv-Mashal. 2003. "Comparative Research in Education: A Mode of Governance or Historical Journey?" *Comparative Education* 39 (4): 423–438.

Ozga, J. 2009. "Governing Education Through Data in England: From Regulation to Self-Evaluation." *Journal of Education Policy* 24 (2): 149–162.

Rhodes, R. 1997. *Understanding Governance.* Buckingham: Open University Press.

Rinne, R., J. Kivirauma, and H. Simola. 2002. "Shoots of Revisionist Education Policy or Just Slow Readjustment?" *Journal of Education Policy* 17 (6): 643–659.

Rosenau, J.N. 2005. "Globalization and Governance: Bleak Prospects for Sustainability." In *Challenges for Globalization*, edited by A. Pfaller and M. Lerch, 201–216. Piscataway, NJ: Transaction.

Sahlberg, P. 2007. "Education Policies for Raising Student Learning: The Finnish Approach." *Journal of Education Policy* 22 (2): 147–171.

Sahlberg, P. 2011. *Finnish Lessons: What Can the World Learn from Educational Change in Finland?* New York, NY: Teachers College Press.

Sassen, S. 2007. *Sociology of Globalization.* New York, NY: W.W. Norton.

Sellar, S., and B. Lingard. 2013a. Looking East: Shanghai, PISA 2009 and the Reconstitution of Reference Societies in the Global Education Policy Field. Comparative Education.

Sellar, S., and B. Lingard. 2013b. "Expanding PISA and the Role of the OECD in Global Educational Governance." In *Who Succeeds at PISA and Why? The Role of International Benchmarking in Emerging Global Governance*, edited by H.-D. Meyer and A. Benavot. Oxford: Symposium Books.

Simola, H. 2005. "The Finnish Miracle of PISA: Historical and Sociological Remarks on Teaching and Teacher Education." *Comparative Education* 41 (4): 455–470.

Takayama, K. 2007. "A Nation at Risk Crosses the Pacific: Transnational Borrowing of the U.S. Crisis Discourse in the Debate on Education Reform in Japan." *Comparative Education Review* 51: 423–446.

Tucker, M., ed. 2011. *Surpassing Shanghai: An Agenda for American Education Built on the World's Leading Systems.* Cambridge: Harvard Education Press.

Wilkinson, R., and K. Pickett. 2009. *The Spirit Level: Why More Equal Societies Almost Always do Better.* London: Allen Lane.

Woodward, R. 2009. *The Organisation for Economic Co-operation and Development.* London: Routledge.

Index

Note: page numbers in **bold** type refer to Tables; page numbers followed by 'n' and another number refer to endnotes.

For Product Safety Concerns and Information please contact our EU
representative GPSR@taylorandfrancis.com Taylor & Francis Verlag GmbH,
Kaufingerstraße 24, 80331 München, Germany

Batch number: 08153807

Printed by Printforce, the Netherlands